CANADIANS IN WAR AND PEACEKEEPING

ALSO BY JOHN GARDAM

The National War Memorial
Seventy Years After 1914 – 1984
The Legacy
Fifty Years After
Korea Volunteer
The Canadian Peacekeeper
Ordinary Heroes
Commissionaires: An Organization with a Proud History
Ortona 1943–1998

Front cover photograph taken by Corporal Frank Hudec of the CF Photo Unit on June 16,1999 at the Perley and Rideau Veterans' Health Centre.

Back cover photograph: the author in front of The Canadian Peacekeeping Monument. Gov. Gen. Adrienne Clarkson, left, presenting The Canadian Peacekeeping Service Medal on September 6, 2000. Photo taken by Jeff Bassett, *Ottawa Sun*.

All profits received by the author from the sale of this book will be donated to the Foundation at the Perley and Rideau Veterans' Health Centre in Ottawa.

CANADIANS
in **WAR** *and*
PEACEKEEPING

by

JOHN GARDAM

Published by

 GENERAL STORE
GSPH PUBLISHING HOUSE

Box 28, 1694 Burnstown, Ontario, Canada K0J 1G0
Telephone (613) 432-7697 or 1-800-465-6072

ISBN 1-894263-28-6
Printed and bound in Canada

Copyright 2000

Layout and Design by Derek McEwen
Printing by Custom Printers of Renfrew Ltd.
General Store Publishing House
Burnstown, Ontario, Canada

Canadian Cataloguing in Publication Data

Gardam, John, 1931-
     Canadians in war and peacekeeping

Includes bibliographical references.
ISBN 1-894263-28-6

     1. Canada–History, Military–20th century. 2. Canada–
Armed Forces–Biography. 3. Peacekeeping forces–
Canada–Biography. I. Title.

U54.C2G37 2000   355'.00971'0904   C00-901334-2

I would like to dedicate this book to all those
veterans and peacekeepers
who gave me their stories and to those members
of the Canadian Forces who are still involved in
Canada's Defence Policy around the world.

I would also like to dedicate this book to our
nine grandchildren, Sarah, Jonathan, Kate, Erin,
Jacob, Kevin, Emilie, Annabelle and Olivia. May
they never know war, but always be aware of
what veterans have done for them and Canada.

CONTENTS

FOREWORD

I was very pleased and quite honoured when John Gardam asked me to write the foreword to his latest book. It was most fitting that the request came on the bridge of HMCS *Charlottetown* in Charlottetown harbour. David, the Gardams' third son, was the captain of the ship.

John is very well versed in recording oral history about our Canadian veterans. In *Canadians in War and Peacekeeping* he has expanded his scope to include a select group of veterans on the cover. I am pleased and privileged to say that I know or knew most of them personally. In that context quotes from forewords of two of John's earlier books seem particularly appropriate. In *Seventy Years After 1914-1984* (Gardam, 1993), a former deputy minister of Veterans' Affairs, Lieutenant General E.L.M. Burns, wrote: "Canadian veterans don't seek praise for what they did, don't expect much in the way of recognition." In *Korea Volunteer* (Gardam, 1994), Dr. Desmond Morton, director of the McGill Institute for the Study of Canada, wrote:

> The memories John Gardam has collected are seldom sad and never self-pitying . . . he has put human faces back into an episode (Korean War) Canadians should remember with some anguish and much pride.

Vice Admiral Murray (retired)

Readers of *Canadians in War and Peacekeeping* will also be left with "some anguish and much pride." In the fall of 1999, I was fortunate enough to participate in the Veterans' Affairs Canada's 55th Anniversary of the Liberation of Italy and Pilgrimage with over sixty veterans of that difficult campaign and to observe the unveiling of the beautiful and compelling Ortona Monument. In that delegation were Smokey Smith and Ted Griffiths, who are among the veterans whose gripping stories are told in this book.

The peacekeeping missions recounted here are also among my

personal memories of the recent past. Further, the chapters on the Cold War Warrior, the Peacekeeping Monument, the Veteran and the Unknown Soldier record previously little-known facts in these important areas.

John states in his Introduction, "The stories blend together as the military profession continues to perform in the post-cold-war era." Readers of this book will learn that Canada's military men and women have always done their professional utmost to succeed and continue to do so. Unfortunately sometimes-sensational media coverage of isolated events do not always do justice to the generally superb and frequently courageous efforts of the vast majority of the members of the Canadian Forces. This book should help set the record straight in a more balanced manner.

As the deputy minister of Veterans' Affairs and a very proud former member of the Royal Canadian Navy and the Canadian Forces it gives me great pleasure to highly recommend this book to all those who want to learn more about what Canadians in uniform have done and are doing to help make the world a better place in which to live and to enhance Canada's global reputation.

Reverting to the language of my former service, may I also say "Bravo Zulu" John, on another terrific effort.

Larry Murray
Deputy Minister
Veterans' Affairs Canada

INTRODUCTION

❝ It is also true that whenever our 'unmilitary people' have entered military service—in war and in peace— they have proven consistently to be among the very best soldiers [and sailors and airmen] there are. **❞**

> (From *We Stand on Guard*, by General A.J.G.D. de Chastelain, Chief of the Defence Staff. Foreword to the book, 1992.)

This book has been in my mind ever since my first published work, *The National War Memorial*, in 1982. The books and booklets that I have published since that time have all had the same theme: to inform and to record military historical events of the past. This book is unique in that it covers the deeds of Canadians in both war and peace. It will describe one person's view of just how the military is different from other professions in Canada. Not one person in this book carried out his duties to Canada to become rich and famous. There is unselfish dedication towards an honourable cause, be it hostile action or in maintaining peace in various countries of the world. The stories blend together as the military profession continues to perform in the post-cold-war era and keeping the peace becomes a "growth industry."

My work with Canada's Peacekeeping Monument and **Canada Remembers** in 1993–1995 has given me the golden opportunity to observe what Canadians have done in the name of their country. One could not help but be moved when a Hong Kong veteran, Roger Cyr, spoke in December 1995 in the Stanley Military Cemetery about his friends and relatives buried there. The Far East pilgrimage at the end of **Canada Remembers** had a small number of the original "cast" with their personal stories of war and imprisonment.

In 1994 and 1998 two important works were published which had a profound impact on me and renewed my interest in producing this book. In the first one, *A Nation Too Good to Lose*, the Right Honorable Joe Clark (1994) wrote of his feelings about Canada. The references to the military profession were many, but this quotation reinforces my contention that the importance of our sailors, soldiers and airmen— men and women in uniform—cannot be overemphasized. Joe Clark wrote:

> Internationally, what causes other nations to turn to
> Canada when there are tensions to defuse, or differences
> to bridge, is that we prove ourselves consistently even-
> handed and pragmatic, and often successful.

When the Peacekeeping Monument on Sussex Drive was unveiled, it was a very proud moment for me. I was the Department of National Defence project director for the monument, along with the project director for the National Capital Commission, and we produced a monument of national importance. We ensured that the monument would serve forever as a tribute to peacekeepers who had served or are still serving around the world being "consistently even-handed and pragmatic, and often successful." I have included a chapter on the monument, the first time the story has appeared in print.

A work of great influence on me was *Who Killed Canadian History?* by Jack Granatstein (1998). This book is of great significance to not only Canadians, but to all nations who fail to teach and explain the importance of the past—our history. Jack Granatstein wrote:

> Somehow, without Canadians really noticing it, the debt
> owed to those who fought and died to secure our future
> has been swept aside. The sense grows that once the vets
> have all finally died and their embarrassing presence is no
> more, Remembrance Day observances will be allowed to
> lapse.

In the year 2000, Canada honoured its very own UNKNOWN SOLDIER. The unidentified remains of a First World War soldier were brought to Ottawa, lay in state in the Parliament Buildings, and were buried in front of the National War Memorial. On the 28th of May, the significance of "sacrifice for country" came into focus for those who saw the final burial place of our Unknown Soldier. It represents all the sailors, soldiers and airmen who have done their duty for Canada. Wars have taken their toll with over 110,000 dead from the First and Second World Wars, over 500 from Korea and as of now over 100 peacekeepers.

The death toll is but part of the true significance of the cost in human lives; one has to add all those with wounds, amputations and problems of the mind. Our veterans are seldom seen in any numbers, and Remembrance Day is but one hour in the year. I am on various boards of the Perley and Rideau Veterans' Health Centre here in Ottawa and speak frequently to many of the 250 veterans who are permanent residents of that facility. It will be noted that this book has been dedicated to those very special men and women and their sacrifices. May their dedication and service to their country never be forgotten. Chapter twenty-five, "The Veteran," is a tribute to those men and women who are permanent residents of the Perley and Rideau Veterans' Health Centre.

A book that was of particular assistance to me was *We Stand on Guard: An Illustrated History of the Canadian Army*, published in 1992 by a friend and brother officer John Marteinson.

It will be seen that some of the stories in this book have been written by the individuals who were the actual participants in the events; I could not improve upon them. I asked friends to put their words down on paper so that those actions of which I was never a part would not be forgotten.

My sincere hope is that *Canadians in War and Peacekeeping* will be used by schools to educate, by veterans to recall the past, and by peacekeepers young and old; and that it will rekindle the flame of interest in Canada's military history.

PROLOGUE

THE COVER STORY

The cover of this book has a story and it sets the tone for the entire book. *Canadians in War and Peacekeeping* tells of events of ordinary Canadians who served their country in war and, in later years, in peacekeeping and peacemaking. The accounts that appear in this book are of my choosing: collectively they describe what service people do in the name of Canada. They did not perform their deeds for fame and fortune but for the love of their country. The five wartime veterans on the cover of this book all have one thing in common: they are permanent residents of the Perley and Rideau Veterans' Health Centre in Ottawa.

This facility, which opened in October 1995, is the permanent home of 450 people, 250 of whom are veterans. The original veteran residents came from the Rideau Veterans' Home in Ottawa, where they had been cared for by the Department of Veterans' Affairs until 1992, when the Perley Hospital became responsible for the administration of the Rideau Veterans' Home. In March 1996 veterans from the chronic care unit of the National Defence Medical Centre in Ottawa were also relocated to the Perley Rideau.

Lloyd Wickwire

The Perley and Rideau Veterans' Health Centre is funded by the Ontario Ministry of Health and Long-term Care and, for the next several years, the Department of Veterans' Affairs of the federal government.

The flags used in the cover photograph all have a special significance, for they were carried by the Canadian Forces **Canada Remembers** contingent in Sicily and Italy during May 1994, in England in May and June 1994, and then to parades in France, Belgium and Holland. In 1995 the flag party visited Belgium, Holland, France and Moscow; and finally, in

December 1995, there were parades in Burma, Singapore, Hong Kong and Japan. The flags were presented to the Perley Rideau Health Centre by Vice Admiral Larry Murray on behalf of the minister of National Defence and were placed in Lupton Hall and the Chapel at the Centre. The United Nations flag was presented later once a former peacekeeper, Lieutenant Colonel Barry Tackaberry, became a resident. In 1998 the Canadian flag was loaned to the Ortona veterans when they visited Italy in December of that year.

On June 15, 1999 the residents were chosen to pose with the flags, and the health centre staff chose sailors, soldiers and airmen to represent their former service. The author displayed the United Nations flag, as the chosen resident was too frail to take part in the event.

A gentleman of over 100 years of age and a veteran of the First World War displayed the Canadian flag. **Lloyd Wickwire** joined the army on March 10, 1916 in Truro, Nova Scotia, where he started his military training; he then moved to Aldershot Military Camp and began his training as a signaller. The 193 Battalion of the Canadian Expeditionary Force was made up of recruits from Nova Scotia.

The 193rd went over to England in 1917 to Witley Camp, where Lloyd continued his training as a signaller, coming out top of his class. In March 1918 he went to France where he became a member of the 85th Battalion Canadian Expeditionary Force as a signaller. The badge of the 85th was a maple leaf with the Nova Scotia Highlanders in part of the title. Lloyd was wounded in the Amiens offensive in August 1918.

After the war Lloyd returned to Halifax and was demobilized in April 1919. He graduated as an electrical engineer and qualified for and received his commission as a lieutenant in the reserves in the early 1920s. In 1939, Lloyd, while working for Noranda Mines, was hired by the Department of Veterans' Affairs as assistant district administrator in Montreal. His first job was to update the electrical plant for St. Anne de Bellevue Veterans' Hospital, which had been built twenty years earlier. He also worked at another World War One hospital, Camp Hill Hospital in Halifax, where he overhauled the mechanical services. After four years in Halifax he came to Ottawa, where he spent two years as an electrical engineer working for the Department of Veterans' Affairs. Lloyd's next position was with Indian Affairs, where he worked as chief of Engineering and Construction until he retired in 1964. Lloyd became a resident of the Perley and Rideau Veterans' Health Centre in May 1997. In 1999, he was awarded the Legion of Honour by the French government. Lloyd died on January 26, 2000.

John St. Louis

When **John St. Louis** enlisted in the army in Ottawa in 1940, he joined the Field Ambulance, Royal Canadian Army Medical Corps. He had been a corporal in the Machine Gun Corps in the Reserves. He became a member of the Royal Canadian Army Service Corps [RCASC] and served in a variety of positions including cook and ambulance driver; and in the ammunition supply column. He went to England in the 1940s, and because he was trained in first aid he was attached to the Canadian Army Medical Corps. John was married with two children when he joined, and the fact that they would be cared for if anything happened to him gave him a feeling of security. John's unit was sent to Italy and he has memories of the harbour at Bari being bombed, and of being 200 feet from Mount Vesuvius when it erupted on March 19, 1943.

At Ortona over Christmas 1943, John St. Louis was still with the RCASC and was employed in delivering ammunition and food and also in evacuating the walking wounded. He remembers driving into Ortona and finding many wounded and dead soldiers in a large barn. The medical units came up and took care of the wounded. As the war in Italy came to an end for the Canadians, John St. Louis went to Marseilles by tank landing craft and then drove to Holland. When the war came to an end John was in Nijmegan.

He was discharged in Ottawa in 1946 and went to work for National Health and Welfare and later worked for the National Printing Bureau, from where he retired in 1993. On August 17, 1998 John was a patient in the Ottawa General Hospital when he was told he had been accepted at the Perley and Rideau Veterans' Health Centre.

Lionel Lalonde from Hull, Quebec joined the Royal Canadian Air Force in August 1941 and began his pilot training at Stratford, Ontario. He was later sent to Lethbridge, Alberta to be trained as an observer (navigator). On April 13, 1943 Lionel had completed training and went overseas. He became a navigator/bombardier and was posted to 408 Squadron. He flew eighteen missions before he was medically removed from flying and was discharged in November 1945.

The Department of Health and Welfare (Department of Veterans' Affairs) hired Lionel and he remained with them until he retired in 1976. After his retirement, he spent his summers in Ottawa and his winters in Florida. In 1993 he developed circulatory problems and within a short time had several amputations of his legs. Lionel was admitted to the Rideau Veterans' Home in November 1993 and relocated to the new health centre in October 1995. He was a popular resident who served on various committees and was president of the Veteran Resident Council. Lionel died on the 14th of May 2000.

Lionel Lalonde

Don Mackenzie joined the Navy in 1940, and took his naval training in Montreal. When asked about his first ship, he chuckled and said, "It was my first and last ship—HMCS *Nabob*." This ship was special to the Royal Canadian Navy. "She was the largest ship operated by the Canadian Navy at that time [1994], with a displacement of 15,000 tons" (Schull, 1987). Don served in the *Nabob* during the fierce fighting of August 1944 when she was part of a large force that sailed for Norwegian waters to try and sink the German battleship *Tirpitz*. On the 24th of August, "without any advance warning, a torpedo from an undetected U-boat struck *Nabob* on the starboard side" (Schull, 1987).

The situation on board *Nabob* was serious, as all electrical power had failed. The hole in her side was fifty feet long and forty feet deep. The crew worked non-stop to keep her from sinking. Four hours later the crew managed to get power to the main engines. *Nabob* and her

Don Mackenzie

crew had 1,100 miles to sail to the naval base at Scapa Flow in Northern Scotland. On making it back to port it was decided to scuttle the ship, since it would be too difficult and expensive to effect the repairs needed to make her seaworthy again.

By a quirk of fate, Don was not on the ship when she was torpedoed. He was responsible for scheduling the crew's shore leave and had allocated leave to himself just prior to *Nabob's* departure on its final mission. Photographs of the mammoth hole made by the torpedo indicate that it hit the ship just where Don's cabin would have been.

Don was discharged in 1946. After the war he worked for a short while as a clerk at St. Anne de Bellevue Military Hospital in Montreal. He moved to Ottawa in 1955 where he worked as a cataloguer with the Museums of Canada, retiring in 1969. An amateur geologist and an avid collector for many years, Don had collected a number of fossils and

John Gardam

Indian artifacts, mainly arrowheads, in his many excavations. He amassed a collection of over 20,000 bottles of various shapes and sizes, at the time the largest collection ever put together in Ontario. He became a resident at the Perley Rideau in 1997.

John Gardam is in the cover photo because the one peacekeeping veteran was too ill to be photographed. John served in the Middle East as a peacekeeper with the Fort Garry Horse Reconnaissance Squadron in 1959. He is a member of the Canadian Association of Veterans in United Nations Peacekeeping. He serves on three committees at the Perley Rideau Veterans' Health Centre in Ottawa.

Bob Dawson was working in the aircraft industry when war broke out. When he tried to enlist he was told he could not join because of his civilian job at Vickers Industry in Montreal. When he again attempted to join the Royal Canadian Navy and was asked where he worked, Bob said that he was unemployed—and he was then accepted into the DEMS (Defensively Equipped Merchant Ship) section of the Navy. People such as Bob spent "their war" sailing the seas and manning the guns aboard merchant ships. Bob joined the navy in October 1939 and took his gunnery training in Halifax.

Bob Dawson had the distinction of having survived three sinkings by German U-boats. The first two occasions were in the Atlantic and the third was in the St. Lawrence River. According to Naval records, U-69 was based in Western France, whence it sailed on its fifth mission on August 16, 1942 and returned on November 5th. Its mission during these three months was to lay mines off the U.S. coast, and it was then sent to the Gulf of St. Lawrence. While

Bob Dawson

there, "U-69 was able to creep up the St. Lawrence River within 300 kms of Quebec City. There, off Metis Beach, it sank the Canadian freighter SS *Carolus*, taking eleven lives" (Hadley, 1985). As with his other two sinking experiences, Petty Officer Bob Dawson saved himself by jumping off the deck of the sinking ship.

Bob was in Montreal when the war ended. He returned to the aircraft industry. He became a resident of the health centre in November 1997.

PART I   WAR

**Private Jack Bernard of the British Columbia Regiment says
farewell to his young son. New Westminster, 1940.**

CHAPTER 1

BATTLE OF MOREUIL WOOD—
A STRATHCONA REMEMBERS

FRANK RICHMOND

IN THE SPRING OF 1996 while visiting British Columbia, my mother gave me a newspaper clipping from *The Times Colonist* entitled, "The Last Survivor," by Patrick Murphy. It was a story about Frank Richmond, aged ninety-nine, giving his recollections of the Battle of Moreuil Wood, which was fought at the end of March 1918. This particular battle was known to me, because I had served in peacetime in all three regiments of the Canadian Cavalry Brigade—Royal Canadian Dragoons, Lord Strathcona's Horse and the Fort Garry Horse. So what made this battle so important that I should include it as the only First World War chapter?

In *We Stand On Guard*, John Marteinson (1992) writes that as 1918 began and Russia left the war and Italy suffered major defeats, the German army was now able to go on the offensive. The Germans had the strategic advantage at the time but they knew the American army was about to enter the field of battle. On the Canadian front, Prime Minister Borden had won the November 1917 election on the promise to do something about conscription. It would be late summer 1918 before these reluctant conscripts would be in France. As written in *We Stand On Guard*:

> ... at 1430 on 21 March 1918 ... the fire of 6,000 guns [German] drenched the southernmost sixty-five kilometres of the British line. ... [It was] the most ferocious thus far experienced during the whole of the war. ... German storm troopers swarmed forward ... whole companies [of British] had been wiped out, positions were bypassed and surrounded. Thirty-seven German infantry divisions penetrated to the rear. The German drive toward Amiens carried on for nine days

1

before it was halted. . . . By 29 March German troops
were exhausted . . . but Amiens was in sight . . . a gap
existed at the junction of the French and British armies.
It was at this point that the Canadian Cavalry Brigade
was called upon to play out its most significant role of the
whole war.

The Germans were about to fight their way into Amiens and on
the 30th of March they were in control of Moreuil Ridge. Brigadier
Seely, commander of the Canadian Cavalry, ordered his three regiments
to Castel on the Avre River (see map). The battle to clear the Germans
from Moreuil Wood was about to begin. As can be seen from the map,
all three regiments were involved even though the original plan had the
Fort Garry Horse in reserve. Charging into woods filled with German
machine-gunners is in no textbook on how to employ cavalry, but the
Germans had to be stopped, and at any cost.

Seely's plan called for the RCD to occupy the southern and eastern
corners of the wood. One Strathcona squadron was to go around the
northeast corner [C Sqn], and the other Strathcona squadrons were to
advance on foot through the wood from the west. The plan did not
work out as envisaged, for right at the start "C" Squadron RCD was met
by a hail of machine-gun bullets. "C" Squadron Strathconas met
hundreds of German infantry. The Straths charged them but over
seventy percent of "C" Squadron fell. Despite this the Straths routed
the Germans. Two squadrons of the FGH were also put into the fray.
By noon the Canadians had cleared all but the southern end of the
wood. The German advance had been stopped; "the effort to split the
British and French armies had failed."

It was a close and costly battle for the Canadians. In *Always a
Strathcona*, W.B. Fraser (1976) writes, "The cost had been heavy: killed
in action 37, wounded 120 out of 350 engaged." In *The Gate*,
Marteinson and Service (1971) do not give the Garry losses but state
that there were "488 from the Canadian Cavalry Brigade." In *Dragoon*,
Breneton Greenhous (1982) does not give regimental casualties of the
RCD, but states that out of the 488 casualties "three officers and 72
other ranks were killed." Simple arithmetic thus shows that almost half
of the losses were Strathconas. Lieutenant Flowerdew, wounded four
times, was awarded a posthumous Victoria Cross.

The stage has been set for the "big picture." Here is the first-
hand account of Frank Richmond, a soldier whose efforts and
memories give some understanding of the battle in late March 1918
and its importance.

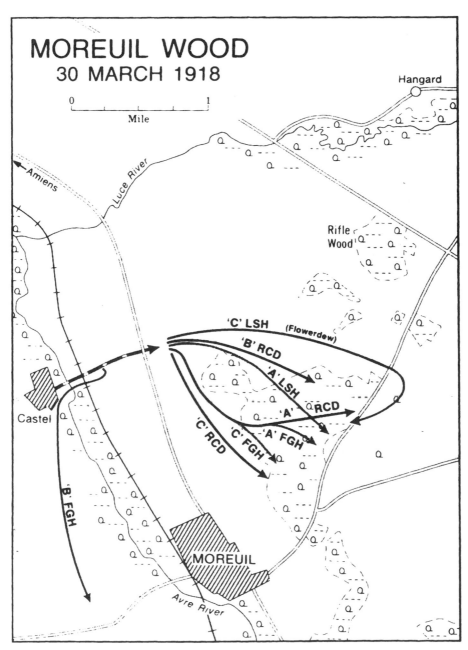

MOREUIL WOOD
30 MARCH 1918

0 _____ 1
Mile

Hangard

Amiens

Luce River

Rifle
Wood

'C' LSH (Flowerdew)
'B' RCD
'A' LSH
'A' RCD
'A'
'C' RCD
'C' FGH
'A' FGH

Castel

'B' FGH

MOREUIL

Avre River

The Battle of 30 March 1918

Frank Richmond in 1996:
100 years old

In the interview held in March 1996 Frank was just about to celebrate his 100th birthday! Although very hard of hearing and almost blind, Frank spoke clearly and proudly of that battle for Moreuil Wood.

Frank's story begins with his enrolment in the army in Winnipeg on 15 April 1916 at the age of seventeen. He went overseas at once with a cavalry reinforcement draft. With little or no training, after a short stay in England he went to France. Frank had a brother in Lord Strathcona's Horse and he wanted to join him. One day Frank took a walk to where the Strathconas were, and he found his brother speaking to the commanding officer. The CO said, "Is this a new Strathcona?" When he learned there was a problem for Frank to get transferred from the Remount Depot he said, "We will have to shake things up a bit." In no time Frank was a Strathcona.

The cavalry spent a long time waiting to be committed to battle. Time was spent in the trenches, taking supplies forward with pack animals and just waiting. Frank's time had come however, when his regiment and the rest of the brigade were ordered to stem the German advance at Moreuil Ridge at the end of March 1918. Frank was a trooper in "A" Squadron and ended up in the attack into the centre of Moreuil Wood. When the squadron arrived at the wood they were still mounted, but in Frank's words, "We moved forward mounted. I did not dismount. We reached the eastern side of the

Frank as a Strathcona

wood and made contact with the remnants of 'C' Squadron." (This is the same account that is in *Always a Strathcona* [Fraser, 1976].) To understand the severe losses to "C" Squadron, this line from *Always a Strathcona* tells the way it was: "One section of the Fort Garry Horse went to support the Strathconas, 'C' Squadron was now reduced to fourteen effective." When a cavalryman's horse is cut down, the rider may still be able to fight, but he is no longer an effective part of the mounted force. The battle was over and the Germans had been stopped, for the moment. The Strathcona history states that:

> The German push of March 30 had been stopped cold at
> Moreuil Wood, and the single contributing factor may
> well have been the success of the three squadrons of Lord
> Strathcona's Horse. . . . For his action at Moreuil Wood,
> Flowerdew was awarded the Victoria Cross,
> posthumously. [The Citation read as follows:] There can
> be no doubt that this officer's great valour was a prime
> factor in the capture of the position.

A freak accident caused Frank to be wounded as he was moving away from the wood. He was shot in the shoulder. Jack, his cavalry charge, was also shot, and the gallant pair did not see action again. Frank woke up as he was being evacuated by ambulance to a hospital. He says:

> For me the war was over. After awhile I was told I was to
> go to a convalescent camp in France. The nurse then said
> I was off to Blighty [England]. As I sailed on a hospital
> ship I could look out of the porthole and see the French
> countryside at La Havre. That night I was in England at
> Basingstoke. In no time I was on my way to
> Southhampton, getting ready to go home. We sailed for
> Halifax on a ship in which there were a lot of wounded.
> In Halifax we were met by a most efficient staff who
> loaded us onto a train that took me to Winnipeg where a
> family friend met me. He put me on another train for
> Mather in southern Manitoba.

Frank reflected when I asked him for anything special he remembered from his time in the cavalry. His words, clearly spoken, were:

> About my horse. I was in "A" Squadron and all the
> horses were supposed to have names beginning with an
> "A." I called my horse "Jack."

Frank and the horse he rode at Moreuil Wood, 30 March 1918

When he reflected upon his horse and the war, he continued with what he considered was important—the law of the cavalry trooper that had been taught to all reinforcements in the Remount Depot:

> In order of priority came your horse, your weapon, your comrades, and finally yourself.

A rare book in my library, *Adventure*, by the Right Honourable J.E.B. Seely (1930), contains the author's own account of what he saw and did at the Battle of Moreuil Wood. Seely's words add credence to this story:

> I saw at once that the position was desperate, if not fatal.
> If the enemy captured the ridge [Moreuil] which I had

just left, the main [defensive] line from Amiens to Paris
would be definitely broken . . . the French and the British
would be compelled to retire. . . . All our sea power, even
the great host of determined soldiers now crossing from
the United States would not avail to save the Allied
Cause. All we had fought for, and bled for, for nearly four
years would be lost.

Much has been made of Gordon Flowerdew's Victoria Cross and
there is no doubt that it is praise properly placed. This former NCO
was now in command of his squadron as a lieutenant, and was riding
alongside the brigade commander. When told that this squadron of
Strathconas had the most "adventurous task of all," Flowerdew smiled
and said, "I know, sir, I know, it is a splendid moment. I will try not to
fail you." This act of leadership in the face of possible death is what
makes a good leader a great one. It is that style of leadership that
makes legends. In Flowerdew's citation for the Victoria Cross, it
mentions:

> Although the squadron had then lost about 70 per cent of
> its members, killed and wounded from rifle and machine
> gun fire . . . the enemy broke and retired [retreated]. . . .
> Flowerdew was dangerously wounded through both
> thighs during the operation, but continued to cheer on
> his men.

Flowerdew's last words when he received two bullet wounds in the
chest, as his horse crashed to the ground, were, "Carry on, boys. We
have won."

One can look back on this battle fought over eighty-two years ago
and say, "Why is so little known or remembered by Canadians today?"
It is sad that the deeds of our heroes from wartime have passed into
obscurity.

Frank left the Army in 1918 and found work in Winnipeg. In 1924
he saw a military display consisting of a Strathcona Horse musical ride,
artillery gun team and the PPCLI doing a display of foot and weapons
drill. Someone beside Frank said, "Would you go back in the army?"
"Tomorrow," was Frank's reply, and he went to the Strathcona's area the
next day and saw the commanding officer, whose retort was a brief
"Yes." This resulted in Lieutenant Colonel C.E. Connolly (who was the
RSM in 1915) saying, "Swear him in." Frank was back with his wartime
friends.

Frank was serving in the regiment when the Second World War began. He saw service in Camp Borden, Ontario as a major at the Armoured Fighting Vehicle Centre responsible for gunnery training until the war ended.

In 1947 Frank retired from the army to Barrie, Ontario. He later moved to Victoria, B.C., where he built his own home. Frank's wife of fifty years died in 1979. Frank passed away just after his 100th birthday. He had two children, two grandchildren and two great-grandchildren.

CHAPTER 2

A PROUD "ROYAL"
WHO SERVED HIS COUNTRY VERY WELL

PAT BOGERT

IN THE YEARS 1994 and 1995 during the Fiftieth Anniversary of the Second World War, I met a retired Canadian Army major general, Pat Bogert, and his wife Trudy. As we visited war cemeteries in Sicily and Italy he recounted events of long ago. I decided he would be one of the good choices for the Second World War portion of this book.

Pat Bogert was born in Toronto in 1908 and after being educated in Montreal and Ottawa he became a cadet at the Royal Military College in Kingston in 1926. He graduated in 1930 and was commissioned in the Royal Canadian Regiment (RCR), serving in London with "C" Company, in Toronto with "B" Company, and finally in the Army-RCAF Intelligence section of the Army Headquarters in Ottawa.

In 1939 he was about to leave for India to undergo Staff College training when the Second World War began. As a lieutenant, with six years' service, he was appointed to the headquarters of the 1st Canadian Division and was in England before Christmas. Advancement courses and promotions came fast and furious. Pat attended the War Staff Course in 1940 and upon graduation was the brigade major of 3 Canadian Infantry Brigade. He returned to the RCR as a company commander for six months prior to promotion to LCol, when he was

Cadet Bogert, RMC, 1926-1930

sent to the Middle East as an observer. It was here that he got to see troops in action for the first time and to learn of the vast administrative support required to sustain operations in battle.

In *West Novas*, a history of the West Nova Scotia Regiment, Thomas H. Raddall (1947) recounts the next event in Pat Bogert's career:

> On July 22nd [1942] Lt. Col. M. "Pat" Bogert took over command of the West Novas and spent the day in an inspection of the regiment and in personal talks with the officers and NCOs. A Canadian veteran of the fighting in Libya, he quickly won the esteem and confidence of every officer and man, and was destined to lead them into battle on fields very far away from any they had contemplated.

This command was to be one of the finest in the true meaning of "respect and affection." It is a story that continues to this very day as the West Novas' veterans parade in dwindling numbers so long after the Second World War. Various veterans wrote of their recollections of this fine man. Honourary Lieutenant Colonel Ross Guy, MC wrote in his February 1995 letter:

> Like other regiments we had our problems from a command point of view. Prior to sailing for the Mediterranean we had serious difficulties. We, the officers of the regiment, asked that Lieutenant Colonel Bogert come back from his staff duties [at 2nd Canadian Corps HQ]. At the very last minute he came on board— never did you see such a happy group. . . . He was always very patient with the junior officers and taught us a great deal . . .

Bill Thexton of Wolfville, Nova Scotia spoke of Pat Bogert in his September 1994 letter as follows:

> He always seemed to rise to the occasion when the going got tough, and set a wonderful example. He was an extremely brave man, and was invariably to be found somewhere up forward, personally leading the battalion, however stiff the climb or hard the marching. When he gave an order one always felt that his reasoning was sound and that he would not knowingly send you into an untenable position. [Later on he wrote of this incident.]

After the capture of the village of Libertina we were subjected to a lot of shellfire. . . . I shall never forget the sight of Lt Col Bogert sitting upright in his slit trench eating sardines on hardtack biscuits. A shell landed nearby and the blast blew the sardines off. He erupted into gales of laughter, which did wonders for our morale.

Later, in September 1944, the West Novas captured San Lorenzo after three days of fierce fighting. Lt Col Bogert [who was acting brigade commander at the time] walked up the hill into our positions. Shells were landing, dust and dirt, blown-down buildings, bodies and knocked-out tanks all around us. It was typical of this fine man to come forward and share the dangers of his front-line soldiers.

In a more philosophical vein Harry Eisenhauer, at the West Novas' reunion held on September 3, 1989, takes these words from an address:

There remains the question: "Why did we go?" Well, each of us has a different answer to that question also. We were still in the throes of a depression and maybe some of us went because we had no other job to turn to. But, in spite of the harshness of the Depression years, our generation was above all a sentimental one, and a loyal one. We sang patriotic songs like the *Maple Leaf Forever* and *Rule Britannia*—and love songs like *Blueberry Hill* and *I'll Never Smile Again*. And we went to war because this was our country and no darn squarehead was going to take it away from us if we could prevent it. And it didn't matter that three-fourths of the people in Lunenburg Co., including myself, were squareheads anyway. And then there were those two little princesses over there—Elizabeth and Margaret Rose—and we weren't about to let them be taken over by the Hun, either!

It is, I hope, to our credit that we have never lost that sentimentality in an age which is sometimes very cynical and often morally depressing. Indeed, it is the lasting quality of that sentimentality that brings us back to a reunion with old comrades year after year. We relive and retell the stories of our battles and escapades and we remember those of our comrades who did not return from overseas or who have since been taken by the passage of

time. We live—and we should die—in a bond of
companionship that nothing can ever take away from us.

It is my view that the above words spell out what makes wartime
military men so unique, so different from those who have not fought in
a war. To a lesser degree those who have gone overseas as peacekeepers
in the post-war years also treasure those memories when, away from
home and family, a bond is forged that lasts forever.

In 1989 Harry Eisenhauer went back to Italy with his wife and they
went to visit the War Graves Cemetery at Ravenna where there are over
600 Canadians buried. Harry's story continues:

> However, in my own sentimental way, both beforehand
> and after I visited the cemetery, I imagined myself
> standing before my friend's grave. What should I, in my
> remembrance, say to him? What would he seem to be
> saying to me? Eventually, these thoughts, although I am
> not a poet, expressed themselves in verse. Perhaps they
> are similar to thoughts some of you may have had as you
> stood before the grave of a dear friend. I would be the
> first to disclaim any literary merit for these verses, but
> with them I close and thank you again for having me as
> your guest speaker today.

> **VISIT FROM AN OLD FRIEND**
> So, you've come at last, old friend!
> To where they laid my bones,
> You read the name beneath my cross,
> "Major James Harvey Jones."
> Yes, this is where they buried me
> When I had died,
> That day you cried for me.
>
> 'Tis true they say I died as heroes go,
> I scorned to bow for shot and shell,
> But boldly led on against the foe
> And thus I fell.
> Death comes swiftly for the brave.
> This brush with glory
> Meant the grave for me.
> Oh, that I had lived like you,
> To see the victory won
> And gained fair Scotia's shore anew,

When all the fight was done.
To have claimed a loved one for my bride
Or hushed a baby when it cried.
These hopes all died with me.

Nay! Turn not in anguish from this place,
Or harbour any guilt that for God's grace
You might lie here with me.
But go with head held high,
I cannot truly die,
While still you cry for me.

On his return to Canada, Harry Eisenhauer graduated from Dalhousie Law School and now is retired in Calgary, Alberta. His letter of December 1994 gives a first-hand account of Pat Bogert, for Harry was the unit intelligence officer (IO). As the IO he attended the Brigade Commander's Orders when a forthcoming battle would be outlined for the fighting soldiers and he was with the colonel during the battle. Harry's letter of December 1994 says:

> I was the IO during all of Lt Col Bogert's period of command. It was my job to accompany him to all orders groups and to see to it that his maps were updated. I had the opportunity to have close contact with him over a long period of time. He was one of those COs who stayed up front where the action was. He was well forward with the company in contact with the enemy. This had advantages and disadvantages once battle was joined. He could see what was happening, but as our radios were so poor he often lost contact with the other companies and the brigade.
>
> At Catenanuova in Sicily we were less than 100 yards behind one of our platoons making a counterattack against the enemy. "C" Company routed the enemy with a bayonet charge. It was at that time that he took time to assist Lt Ross Guy in bringing down our artillery fire upon the enemy. This meant that Ross's platoon was able to defeat the enemy counterattack.
>
> When circumstances permitted, we travelled in the CO's open Jeep, driven by "Snake Eyes" Gates, one of the unit characters. On one occasion a German 88 [anti-tank gun] took "pot shots" at us as we drove out of Catenanuova.

In the bleak days of the fall of 1943 the CO worked non-stop to preserve his men in battle and to provide some comfort in the areas out of direct contact with the enemy. It was at the battle for "The Gully" that fierce fighting took place and later at Vino Ridge we had heavy losses. The colonel was shot in the leg and had to be evacuated, never to return to his beloved West Novas as CO.

Harry closes by stating the obvious: "I'm sure no other commanding officer is held with such affection by the West Novas' Veterans."

As each account came before me, all mentioned "Bo Force" where Pat Bogert and the West Novas distinguished themselves. A former captain, Donald Rice, now a doctor in Willowdale, summarizes the battle in his August 1994 letter:

> During the brief 3-1/2 months, during which time I served under Col. Bogert, the experience that I best remember was the special, mobile "Bo Force"—named after Col. Bogert and composed of the West Nova Scotia regiment, a squadron of tanks and supporting forces of engineers, signallers, and artillery.
>
> The objective of this special force was to capture the important rail and road junction of Potenza, situated in the centre of the toe of Italy, approximately 120 miles north of the coastal town of Catanzaro, and about midway between the town of Bari on the Adriatic coast and Salerno on the west coast—south of Naples. The larger objective was to relieve the pressure on General Clark's US 5th Army, which had landed at Salerno on 9 September 1943, and was meeting serious resistance from German forces determined to destroy the hard-won beachheads established by the Americans.
>
> Bo Force began its mission on 16 September 1943, at Catanzaro Marina, and ended with the capture of Potenza on 20 September 1943. The exercise was characterized by several dashes along the coast in landing craft infantry (LCIs), and repeated short skirmishes with German demolition units, as we pushed inland along mountain roads, with their frequent bridges and ravines. The challenge to Bo Force was to maintain sufficient speed in our advance, and to create a constant pressure

on the enemy that would prevent or hinder the placing of effective demolition that would impede our advance.

The exercise was completely successful, and far exceeded the expectations of the most optimistic planning at Divisional Headquarters.

It was an exciting and rewarding experience to be a part of Bo Force. The unit was at full strength; morale was at the highest level; we were engaged in a special mission; and while the regiment had already experienced the taste of real warfare in Sicily, there was still an attitude of eagerness on the part of all ranks to do battle with the enemy—an attitude that had not yet been marred by the mental and physical fatigue that is a natural sequel to prolonged action by an infantry soldier.

The success of Bo Force is testimony to the leadership qualities of its commander—Col. Pat Bogert. Through this and subsequent actions, members of the West Nova Scotia Regiment reflected the confidence placed in Col. Bogert—a confidence built on mutual respect that was a credit to the entire regiment. I consider myself fortunate to have shared in this experience.

The official account is to be found in *The Canadians in Italy*, by LCol G.W.L. Nicholson (1957) of the Directorate of History. A well-written account is in *Canadian Military History* by Lee A. Windsor (1995), who had an 11 September 1993 interview with Pat Bogert to add credence. The item follows:

General Simonds proposed that a heavily motorized group from 3rd Brigade [Penhale] would advance from Villapiana on 17 September. Penhale assigned the task to Lt. Col M.P. Bogert of the West Novas with a squadron of the Calgary Tanks, a field battery from 1RCHA, a troop of anti-tank and one of anti-aircraft artillery, a platoon of MMGs of the Saskatoon Light Infantry, a platoon of engineers from 1 Field Company and, finally, a company of 9 Field Ambulance RCAMC. The advance began at noon. "Bo Force" was on its way!

In the first two days Pat Bogert pushed his soldiers along Highway 92. The retreating enemy had blown bridges and culverts but the engineers prepared detours

and the advance continued. The infantry rode on the
Sherman tanks of the Calgaries and marched in the same
punishing way they had trained in England and fought in
Sicily. The West Novas moved so quickly that they drove
off a party of German engineers before they could blow a
bridge. Pat Bogert produced a plan of attack from maps
at two a.m. on 20 September and finally entered Potenza
to the "wild ovation of the Italian inhabitants."

Pat Bogert was not awarded a decoration for his skill in
commanding Bo Force; however, later on 9 October 1943 while leading
his unit at Gildone his bravery was rewarded. The citation for the
Distinguished Service Order reads as follows:

DISTINGUISHED SERVICE ORDER
Lt-Col Mortimer Patrick BOGERT

On 9 Oct 43, Lieutenant-Colonel BOGERT,
leading his battalion by night during its advance to
GILDONE came under heavy machine-gun fire while
crossing the river to the south of JELSI. In the face of
sustained fire, Lieutenant-Colonel BOGERT coolly and
skilfully directed a flanking movement which dislodged
the enemy from their positions.

When the enemy withdrew to the hills beyond the
river line and occupied prepared positions on
commanding ridges, Lieutenant-Colonel BOGERT, by a
quick, accurate appreciation and cool, forceful leadership
retained the initiative. Driving the enemy from their new
positions and inflicting many casualties, he led his
regiment through a pouring rain to its final objective,
over ground which, owing to deep mud, rendered
movement under fire difficult and hazardous.

Lieutenant-Colonel BOGERT's leadership and skill,
his determination and courage, were responsible for the
complete success of an operation which enabled flanking
Battalions to maintain a rapid advance.

Signed by: T.G. Gibson, Brig. Comd. 3 Cdn Inf Bde
             C. Vokes, Maj-Gen. GOC 1 Cdn Div
             M. Winfrey, Lt. Gen. Comd 13 Corps
             B.L. Montgomery, Gen. GOC Eighth Army
             H .R. Alexander, Gen. GOC-inC 15 Army Gp

**Pat Bogert and LCol Reed Smith at Brookwood
Cemetery, England, May 1994**

As I spoke to Pat Bogert in Northern Italy about Bo Force, I could
not help but wonder: if more of the wartime leaders had had that same
adrenaline rush in action that makes the soldiers want to follow their
CO anywhere, then maybe some of the other battles would have had
better results. It was a proven fact in action that great leaders could
accomplish greater things by their very presence. It was that example of
wartime leadership that showed up again in Korea and, to a much lesser
scale, in peacekeeping missions.

After being wounded on 12 December 1943, Pat Bogert finally was
released from the Convalescent Hospital in Sorento to learn that he had
been promoted to colonel and posted to Canadian Military
Headquarters in London, England. In April he returned to Italy to 1st
Canadian Division, reverting to his previous rank. The rank of colonel
was used for staff positions and in some training establishments. The
wartime practise of promoting from LCol to Brigadier in operational
formations was used in the British Commonwealth Armies. On 5
September 1944, as recorded in *The Canadians in Italy* (Nicholson,
1957), "The 3rd Canadian Brigade was temporarily under the command
of Lt-Col. M.P. Bogert, who had taken over when Brigadier Beratchez
was hurt in a flying accident." He was to remain in command of his
former brigade until the next month when "he took command of 2nd
Brigade on 7 October." He was to remain in command until 4 June
1945.

To some it may seem strange that a temporary commander would
step in, in the heat of battle, and commence active battlefield leadership.

The brigade staff were highly skilled in the operational control of the fighting arms and administrative support. Standing Operating Procedures (SOPs) had been refined within the division so that not too much was left to chance. At the unit level NCOs had moved into officer positions, company commanders were now COs, and so on. The Canadians in Italy were a highly trained and aggressive fighting force and had won respect from the Germans they had fought against along the whole length of Italy. They also had gained an international reputation within the Allied Forces.

In northwest Europe, Pat Bogert's brigade is written up in *The Victory Campaign*, by Colonel C.P. Stacey (1960), of the Directorate of History. He writes these words concerning 14 April 1945:

> Brigadier M.P. Bogert was instructed to eliminate all
> enemy from the west bank of the Ijssel as far south as
> Dieren, where his brigade would establish contact with
> the 49th [British] Division. The boundary between the
> two divisions in this area was now to be the Apeldoorn
> Canal.

The war was coming to an end, and a radio operator at Divisional Headquarters was contacted by a German counterpart. It became obvious that surrender was imminent. Brigadier Pat Bogert, his IO, who spoke German, and a soldier carrying a white flag went to the prearranged place. Pat Bogert recalled these memories in a tape recording he made in April 1995:

> There was this German general with a huge nose and red
> face. I told him he had to come with us and be
> blindfolded. He objected but gave in and got into my
> Jeep and we drove to a rendezvous. Everyone of
> importance was there including the Queen of Holland's
> husband. I was then told I could repeat the process the
> next day. The prisoner turned out to be the senior
> German general in all of Holland.

The war ended in Holland and Germany; peace at last. Pat Bogert became the commander of 18 Canadian Infantry Brigade in the Army of Occupation. He returned home after six-and-one-half years overseas, only to revert to the rank of colonel as the commander of the Military District in Kingston, Ontario. Three years later he was promoted to brigadier and moved to Vancouver, British Columbia to command British Columbia Area. In 1951 he was a student at the National

Defence College for a year and then he became the Director, General Military Training at Army Headquarters in Ottawa in 1952. It was at this time in history when Canada had a full fighting brigade in Korea and another one with NATO in Germany. Pat was then notified he was to replace Brigadier John Rockingham as commander of the 25th Canadian Brigade in Korea. The reference for this period of service is in *Strange Battleground*, by LCol H.F. Wood (1966) of the Directorate of History. A synopsis of his career for that year is as follows:

Command of the Brigade Group passed from John Rockingham to Brigadier Pat Bogert who arrived at Brigade Headquarters on the night of 20-21 April 1952. The next day the two brigadiers visited the forward trenches and they were "marked by the burst of an enemy 120-mm shell close enough to put Bogert out of action." Luckily there was no injury but the next day Bogert awoke to find he had the mumps. [As an aside I learned in 1994 that Rockingham was none too gracious about the mumps. Bogert was moved to a draughty tent to get over the mumps whilst Rockingham continued to live in the comfort of his vehicle.]

On 27 April Rockingham was free to leave Korea and Pat Bogert was back to commanding a Brigade in action, a job he had done for many months in both Italy and North West Europe. So what was the situation once the rotation had been completed? The individual units were all based upon the permanent force units trained in their Defence of Canada role. They were not based on units enlisted for eighteen months. There was cohesion and unit morale was high. The strategic plan called for a solid defence with a well-orchestrated withdrawal if one was required. This resulted in the fact that "they spent twenty-two of their thirty months of fighting in defensive positions."

In June, Pat Bogert, following Divisional direction, "issued a directive permitting units to discontinue fighting patrols however this did not have the desired effect of lowering the casualty rate." Shelling, mines and probing patrols by the Chinese/North Koreans exacted their toll. In late June for some "unexplained" reason raids were reinstituted with heavy Canadian losses and no captured prisoners. One of the more publicised and unpopular duties was the role of guarding prisoners of war on Koje Island. It was well handled by the RCR.

Pat Bogert's next challenge had nothing to do with the day operations of the Canadians and their conduct of the war;it was to integrate South Korean soldiers, 100 per infantry unit, right into the platoons. [See *Korea Volunteer*, by the author.] With some success the "Katcom" plan was implemented. Rotation 1953 was now a fact and on 21 April Brigadier Jean Allard, an officer with Italian and NW Europe experience, assumed command.

Pat served in Army Headquarters, Ottawa for the next five years in the Adjutant Generals Branch and then for four years at Fort Frontenac, Kingston, Ontario, where this renowned soldier was to command the Canadian Army Staff College. His demand for quality staff work was felt by the hundreds of students who took this critical career course. The final promotion to major general and appointment as General Officer Commanding Eastern Command was his final act as a soldier. One of the many units under his command was the West Novas—his link with his past had come full circle. When I was in Apeldoorn, Holland in June 1995 with **Canada Remembers**, I saw the West Novas with their wartime commander. The pride and affection was there for all to see. Pat Bogert never let them down in war or in peace. He continues to serve his country well.

Major General Pat Bogert recently celebrated his eighty-eighth birthday (1996). He and his wife Trudy then lived in England. In August 1996, Pat Bogert and his wife visited Nova Scotia and New Brunswick. While at CFB Gagetown he went to the rifle range and fired five shots out of six into the centre of the target.

Pat Bogert passed away in England before the publication of this book, a great man who will be sorely missed.

Firing on the rifle range, CFB Gagetown, NB, 1996

CHAPTER 3

"SMOKEY" SMITH, VICTORIA CROSS

ERNEST A. SMITH

In 1954 I was employed as a Canadian Army recruiting officer in Vancouver, British Columbia. The New Westminster recruiting office sergeant was Smokey Smith, Victoria Cross. Early each Monday he would come to my office to receive his weekly quota of recruits and I would stand to attention and salute his Victoria Cross. The next time we met was forty years later when the Veterans' Affairs pilgrimage, **Canada Remembers,** was en route to Sicily and Italy, and Smokey and his wife Esther were on the tour. As we went from one Commonwealth War Grave cemetery to another, Smokey would explain to me and others just who these soldiers were from the Seaforth Highlanders of Canada. At one such grave he softly spoke, saying, "If I had died and this fellow had lived, he would have won the VC." The Smiths travelled with the pilgrimages for all of 1994 and 1995. In the Far East in December 1995 I asked him if I could write his story for this book. He agreed and this is Smokey's story.

I am indebted to Neil Robinson, a lawyer from Veterans' Affairs Canada, who conducted a long videotaped interview in the Smiths' home in the autumn of 1996. Smokey's story is there for all to see and hear. Excerpts from that tape follow:

> Ernest A. Smith was born in New Westminster, BC in
> 1914. He was the eldest of three sons and they all served
> in the Canadian Army in the Second World War. As was
> the wartime army's habit, K52880 Private Smith was
> given a nickname: "Smokey." It is by that name that he is
> known by all, from the Queen Mother, to governor
> generals, prime ministers, and the rest of his friends.
>   Smokey joined the Seaforth Highlanders of Canada
> in April 1940; this was not his local regiment from New

Westminster, for many of his former schoolteachers were in that unit and he decided to serve elsewhere. After a few weeks' basic training in Toronto, at the Exhibition Grounds, he sailed for England on the *Monarch of Bermuda* as a reinforcement to join his unit, which had been in England since before Christmas 1939. Smokey had learned to maintain and fire the Lewis machine gun, so he was put on anti-aircraft duty for the fourteen-day voyage.

The Seaforth reinforcements travelled in style on the mixed military and civilian passenger list—"three to a stateroom," recalled Smokey. The reinforcement draft went to Borden Army Camp, where the German Air Force bombed Smith and his friends [among other things]. The Seaforths trained, marched, dug and suffered through the English weather.

In June of 1943 the First Canadian Division was "embarked for an unknown destination"; in due time they were told that the forthcoming action was the invasion of Sicily. On 10 July, Smokey Smith waded ashore at Pachino. Resistance was light, as the Italian defenders did not put up much of a fight; there were two killed and a few wounded in the Seaforths. Soon thereafter the German defenders, masters of the withdrawal, introduced the Canadians to the 88mm anti-aircraft gun being used in the ground role against tanks, infantry and wheeled vehicles. In a battle near the volcano Mount Etna, Smokey was wounded in the chest by a rifle grenade and was flown to North Africa for treatment. [When the **Canada Remembers** contingent paraded at the Agira War Cemetery, Smokey and Esther tried to view the fifty-seven Seaforth graves. The grim realities of the 1943 battles were there for all the veterans to see on that tour.]

Two months later, Smokey rejoined the Seaforths in Italy, still bandaged from his wounds. The war against the Germans, the Italian mud and the rains produced a stoic outlook on life for the infantry private: dig in at all times, never run short of ammunition, all battles are the same and realize that the German soldier was a formidable foe with his weapons, mines and superior tanks. With this wonderful attitude about battles it is no wonder that the

Battle of the Moro River is remembered as "that is where I lost my lighter." The Battle for Ortona was described as "the place where we found a use for the projector infantry anti-tank (PIAT)"—mouseholing, it was called, punching holes in walls and not getting shot at in the streets. Chris Volkes, the division commander, said that before Ortona "everything was a nursery rhyme."

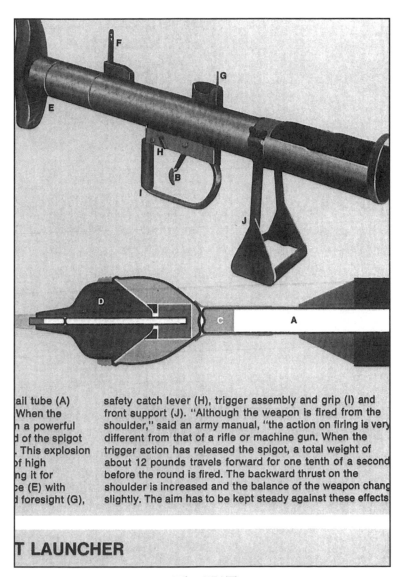

ail tube (A) ... When the ... n a powerful ... d of the spigot ... . This explosion ... f high ... ng it for ... e (E) with ... d foresight (G),

safety catch lever (H), trigger assembly and grip (I) and front support (J). "Although the weapon is fired from the shoulder," said an army manual, "the action on firing is very different from that of a rifle or machine gun. When the trigger action has released the spigot, a total weight of about 12 pounds travels forward for one tenth of a second before the round is fired. The backward thrust on the shoulder is increased and the balance of the weapon chang slightly. The aim has to be kept steady against these effects

T LAUNCHER

The PIAT

On the day before Christmas 1943, the Seaforths had a
roast pork dinner in an abandoned church. Smokey did
not leave the safety of his position, where he was firing
the 6-pounder anti-tank gun, to walk down the shell-
strafed streets. He dined on "a roasted chicken donated
by the Italians." The one thing Smith did miss out on
was the "one bottle of Canadian beer."

Ortona may well have been "the Stalingrad of the
West." Smokey remembers that he spent most of that
battle "burying my friends and foe just to the rear of the
battle." Padre Durnford of the Seaforths kept telling
Smokey and the rest of the detail to "place them facing
the enemy"; all the burial party wanted to do was to place
them in their final resting place and get out of there!

The reinforcement situation was now desperate in Italy, as D-Day
(June 6, 1944) was taking the reinforcements that had been slated for
Italy. Smokey recalled, "We had two kinds of reinforcements, former
wounded and the youngsters direct from Canada." The training had
been abbreviated to such a point that "we had to train them just prior to
a battle, how to fight and how to stay alive." In the fall of 1944 the rains
came and the small creeks became rivers. Bill McAndrew's new (1996)
book *Canadians and the Italian Campaign 1943-1945* explains what
happened in late October:

> Lieutenant Colonel M.P. Bogert, now commanding
> 2nd Brigade, ordered the PPCLI to establish a
> bridgehead over the Savio, which, at the time, was "waist
> high, the current swift and the water gap 15-20 yards."
> Sappers would then erect a bridge and the Seaforths
> would go through to their objective on the main Cesena-
> Ravenna road 1500 metres beyond. The Patricias had a
> bad start. Major E.W. Cutbill, commanding "A"
> Company, reported: "We had very short notice and time
> only to make a quick recce from the windows of "C"
> Company HQ. Owing to the short notice the company
> was 15 minutes late in crossing the start line, and so lost
> all benefit of the [friendly] artillery concentrations, and
> had instead a thoroughly awakened enemy who was
> expecting us because of the supporting artillery fire."

The German reaction to the river crossing was swift and violent.
The PPCLI had to be reinforced, so it became the Seaforths' turn.

The Seaforths decided to cross several hundred metres downstream. "B" and "D" companies waded across in a driving rain, and went through the German positions along the bank to take intermediate objectives 500 metres beyond. "A" and "C" companies followed and went straight on to the Cesena-Ravenna road. The tank-hunting platoon joined "C" Company on the right, in the village church of Pieve Sestina.

Smokey had joined the "tank hunters" armed with PIATS, Tommy guns and, when possible, 6-pounder anti-tank guns. In *The Seaforth Highlanders of Canada 1919-1965*, Reg Roy (1969) explains what happened to the Seaforths as they crossed the river:

Smokey Smith in Italy

Although each position was occupied by the Germans in some strength, we achieved almost complete surprise. [Smokey doubts the word surprised.] This, plus the filthy weather and the artillery fire, kept the enemy's heads down long enough for us to take our objectives without undue difficulty. No. 14 Platoon took out a machine-gun position and knocked out an enemy truck, taking 9 or 10 prisoners. No. 15 Platoon, after a short, sharp exchange of fire, took another dozen prisoners, and No. 13 Platoon, with no real opposition, took the church and its occupants, perhaps 10 or 12. Unfortunately Lieutenant Sid Dickinson was wounded [he lost an arm] in this action . . .

Including the tank hunters the total company strength was only about 50 all ranks, so 13 and 14 Platoons were merged, and a hurried defensive position was established in the vicinity of the road junction, based on the church.

Smokey's account in the video is terse but graphic. "We tank hunters were supporting the lead company. It was at night, raining, but we got to our assigned position at the crossroad." The river had risen six feet, there was no bridge in, no support weapons had gotten across, and, as Smokey put it, "We couldn't advance, couldn't get back, we were short of ammunition; my friend Jimmy Tennant was wounded and I helped him later [at the church] to cover and medical aid. I was now all alone." The Germans did not know how many Canadians were against them; in fact, it was a "one-man army": Private Smith. McAndrew's words tell it the way it was, as the German tanks, self-propelled guns and infantry put in a counterattack:

At a range of thirty feet and having to expose himself to the full view of the enemy, Private Smith fired the PIAT and hit the tank, putting it out of action. Ten German infantry [Smokey said it seemed many more] immediately jumped off the back of the tank and charged him [Smith] with Schmeissers and grenades. Without hesitation, Private Smith moved out on the road and, with his Tommy gun and at point-blank range, killed four Germans and drove the remainder back. Almost immediately another tank opened fire and more enemy infantry closed in on Smith's position. Obtaining some abandoned Tommy gun magazines from a ditch, he steadfastly held his position, protecting his comrade [Jimmy] and fighting the enemy with his Tommy gun until they finally gave up and withdrew in disorder.

One tank and both self-propelled guns had been destroyed by this time, but yet another tank swept the area with fire from a longer range.

No further immediate attack developed [Smokey then picked Jimmy Tennant out of the ditch and carried him to the church for medical aid]. As a result of all this the battalion was able to consolidate the bridgehead position so vital to the success of the whole operation, which led to the eventual capture of San Giorgio Di Cesena and a further advance to the Ronco River.

Thus, by the dogged determination, outstanding devotion to duty and superb gallantry of this private soldier, his comrades were so inspired that the bridgehead was held firm against all enemy attacks, pending the arrival of tanks and anti-tank guns some hours later.

Smokey Smith came out of the line and was told by Lieutenant Colonel Bell Irving, the commander of the Seaforths, that he would not be going back in. For a week the "top brass investigated what I had done," said Smokey. The 8th Army commander awarded Sergeant K.P. Thompson, the tank-hunting platoon commander, the Distinguished Conduct Medal. Smokey had been recommended for the Common-wealth's highest award for bravery, the Victoria Cross. Smokey's life was to change in a big way from that moment on.

When I interviewed Smokey in Ottawa on 4 April 1997, many corrections were made to the story I had written. Smokey did not agree with the historical research I had done, and here is his story, in his own words:

The battlefield after Pte Smith was finished with it

I was sent to the rear and told to drive the CO's Caravan [a room built on the back of a truck]. One day I drove it forward to where the CO wanted it. The CO saw me and said he did not want me within German artillery range. Bell Irving said, "Get this damn Smoke out of here, if anything happens to him I'm in deep trouble." Moose Molson and I had been invited to an Italian's home for a spaghetti dinner, with lots of wine. A dispatch rider arrived and said, "You have to come back to B Echelon right away." So that is where we went after we finished our meal. [At this point Smokey had not been told he had won the Victoria Cross.] Major Esson had this photo taken and then he said, "You'll need a kilt for Buckingham Palace." I questioned him about such a statement and the Pipe Major said, "You'll find out when you get there." I took the kilt off of Doc Galloway, a side drummer, and I gave him my battledress trousers [he still has the kilt].

Smokey went to Naples, where he was locked in the army's post office overnight, ensuring that he would be available to fly to London, England in the morning. He met Lieutenant General Price Montague, who was the chief of staff at Canadian Military Headquarters in London.

Outside Buckingham Palace, showing his VC to a Canadian Jeep driver

He asked Smokey "if he knew why he was in London," and Smokey said "that he knew Buckingham Palace and a medal was a possibility."

Later that night, King George the Sixth handed him the Victoria Cross in a private ceremony in his apartment at Buckingham Palace. Smokey was the only person being invested. King George did not pin the Victoria Cross on Smokey, but told him, "You are a very brave private; I have a present for you." The palace staff told him to put the medal in his battledress pocket. The concern was that Canadian newsmen would not get their stories back to Canada before the news broke in London. Price Montague said to Smokey, "For the rest of your life people will be after you and they will lionize you; you are now very important. Do you think you can handle that?" Smokey's reply was, "I think I can." Montague then said, "Forty reporters now want to see you downstairs; if you don't know the answers to their questions, just say 'No comment!'" Smokey went and faced the press and used "no comment" right at the start! He said, "The general told me to say that!"

Later Smokey took a very cold flight in a Liberator bomber from Scotland to Quebec and then a Trans Canada Airlines flight to Vancouver. Smokey said, "In forty-eight hours I had gone from London to home."

The other Victoria Cross winner from British Columbia was Major John Mahoney of the Westminster Regiment, and he had won his decoration at the Melfa River in May 1944. Smokey was accorded all the honours and then sent on tour to sell War Bonds. He commented with a smile, "I was getting eighty-six dollars a month, the civilians got three hundred a week!"

Smokey was then placed in the Kent Regiment, which was made up of "Zombies" (men who would not volunteer to serve overseas). "I was told that I could not go back into action for I had paid my debts." What a sad way to end the war. When the Seaforths came home to Vancouver to march up Grenville Street, there were "only eighteen originals" in the parade.

Smokey rejoined the army in 1951; he wanted to go to Korea but was denied. In 1964 he retired from the army and worked with his wife Esther in the photography business. His summary of the past was given with a great deal of pride:

> Canada had a big army and it was a good one. I liked the
> army and was proud to serve in it. We were like brothers
> in the Seaforths, depending on each other. Canada has
> looked after its veterans very well. I am a Canadian
> through and through—a real Canadian and proud of it.

Smokey was at the Canadian National War Memorial on November 11, 1996. Esther was not with him; she had been admitted to hospital in British Columbia that very day. Smokey's lifelong partner Esther Smith died on December 4th, just before Christmas. Smokey would have been married fifty years on March 26, 1997.

Smokey Smith was awarded the Order of Canada in 1996, one of four in the world to have earned the honour to wear both the Victoria Cross and the Order of Canada. Smokey Smith lives with his daughter, Norma Jean, in Vancouver, British Columbia. With the death of Lt. Col. Cecil Ingersoll Merrit at the age of ninety-one, Smokey is now the last remaining Victoria Cross recipient in Canada.

John Gardam, Esther and Smokey, France, 1994

CHAPTER 4

FOUR HUNDRED YARDS—AND INTO THE "COURTYARD OF HELL"

TED GRIFFITHS

Duration MY TIME in the army and the Canadian Forces I met a great number of people. One such veteran was Ted Griffiths, formally of the Three Rivers Regiment. Ted served as a corporal during the Second World War and had a long career in the Canadian Forces. We became good friends because of our similar interests in the military, writing and other pursuits.

In 1998 Ted discussed a plan he had conceived to organize and conduct a pilgrimage to Ortona, Italy to have a reconciliation dinner with his wartime comrades and his former wartime enemies. I was appointed by the Department of Veterans' Affairs as the planner and conducting officer for the group. This event was called the "Reconciliation Dinner" and it took place in Ortona, Christmas 1998. I was fascinated with Ted's knowledge of the battle and asked him to tell his story in this book. Here is "The Battle of Ortona, Christmas 1943," as written by Ted (from *The Canadians in Italy* by Nicholson [1957]):

The weather couldn't have been worse. Cold, drizzling rain, the occasional drop in temperature when it turned to snow, gray overhanging cloud that added to the dismal, funeral scene, all combined to make life extremely miserable. To magnify our problem, the low-lying cloud also denied us air support from the Spitfire Squadrons of the Desert Air Force. And the mud! The slimy mud with a consistency akin to quick-drying cement clung to everything, impeding the movement of men, vehicles and mules. To the soggy, disheveled infantryman it turned every step into one of agony and frustration. Wheeled vehicles often were quickly mired down, and passengers were forced to dismount and push. Tanks, too, were no exception, as the mud built up to the point where it threw the track, immobilizing the vehicle. Even the struggling mules, loaded with ammunition, all too frequently surrendered to the cloying mud.

31

Sometimes they gave up the ghost and died standing in their tracks, propped up by deep mud.

The enemy, the battle-hardened veterans of Rotterdam, Leningrad, Crete, Greece, the Corinth Canal and North Africa, were doing their best to make our lives as short as possible. The 1st Parachute Division, cream of German Forces in Italy, bolstered by the 90th Panzer Grenadier Division, and aided by terrain that strongly favoured the defence, were making the 1st Canadian Infantry Division and the 1st Canadian Armoured Brigade pay in blood for every inch of ground. Fighting through olive groves and vineyard country—and the mud—restricted easy movement, and more than one Canadian body hung on the wire strung between the vines. The official Canadian Army history notes the determined resistance of the German defender, curtly remarking that, "paratroop snipers lurked in every fold of the ground."

"A" Squadron of the Three Rivers Regiment was tasked to support the Royal Canadian Regiment (RCR) in Operation "Morning Glory," which involved securing a crossroads on a high crest of ground outside Ortona that had been assigned the code name "Cider" [to give some secrecy to the actual battle]. The 1st Canadian Division had been attempting for nearly two weeks to secure "Cider," but determined—almost fanatical—resistance by the paratroops and grenadiers defeated attack after attack.

"A" Squadron moved up during the night to link up with the RCR before first light. The move was made even more difficult by the heavy mud, which gave birth to much swearing and cursing whenever a track was thrown. Fortunately, the going became a little easier as we gained the high ground leading into Ortona, and we were able to make contact with the RCR in time for necessary liaison with our infantry counterparts before "H Hour" [the code for the actual time of a military event, in this case the start of the battle].

The distance from the start line to the objective at "Cider" was all of 400 yards, but little did we know how many were to die before we got there. In moving into the forming-up area, I was pleased to learn that I would be supporting "C" Company of the RCR, which was the company I had joined in London, Ontario, when I enlisted in September 1939. Captain Chuck Lithgow commanded the company, and many of my old public and high school friends were still in it. I had but a moment to have a word with a few of them before the curtain rose on "Morning Glory" [code name for the actual battle].

Shortly before "H Hour" I found I had a problem within the troop. Our troop sergeant was not present and I cannot recall whether he had been wounded, was sick, or what. However, acting in his place I was beginning to worry about our troop leader, who was growing increasingly nervous and unsure of himself. With "H Hour" rapidly approaching, I couldn't get him out of the slit trench, no matter how much I talked. In the end, I jumped into the trench with him, and placing my revolver under his chin I told him that if he didn't get out of the trench I would blow his damned head off. Not even this threat penetrated. He was completely out of it, and fortunately Major Ted Smith, our squadron commander, came by in time to witness the scene. He told me to get in my tank and command the troop. The troop leader disappeared, never to be seen again in the regiment.

Great care had been taken in preparing the fire support plan. All gunner regiments in 5th Corps—three medium and nine field regiments, plus one battery of heavy anti-aircraft artillery, all in all over 500 guns—were dedicated in support of our attack. At "H Hour" all hell broke loose as the 500 guns literally chewed the ground ahead to pieces. Then "C" Company began to move forward slowly, with our tanks slightly behind to provide covering fire. As so often happens in war, the attack did not go according to plan. The gunners had made their fire plan based on maps superimposed on Italian maps, which were notoriously inaccurate. Shortly, a battalion off to our right flank began to report that "friendly fire" was falling on their position, causing casualties. Up to this point "C" Company had been following in close to our artillery barrage, killing the enemy before he realized the barrage had passed. Because of the shells dropping on the troops on our flank, the gunners suddenly raised their fire another 400 yards in advance, and cut out all protective fire on the right flank. The paratroops took immediate advantage of the change, and the course of the battle changed in an instant. The official Canadian Army history sums up the situation quite succinctly: "the modification of the fire plan had also given the enemy unexpected freedom of action, [and] a murderous cross-fire laced into the Canadians. Men dropped like flies. The two leading companies were smashed to pieces, all officers becoming casualties."

Ted in front of Mount Etna, Sicily, July 1943

I damned them at the time, but I have to acknowledge the military efficiency of the German snipers. This day we were cursed with them. As usual, though, the infantry took the brunt of the sniper threat in this real-life shooting gallery. A sniper also wounded Major Bill Mathers, the acting commanding officer of the RCR, which added to the overall confusion caused by alteration of the artillery fire support plan. It seemed that whenever a tank crew commander stuck his head above the cupola, he was shot. My long-time friend, John Gallagher, troop sergeant in No. 3 Troop, got hit just after we crossed the start line, taking off part of his face; he was to spend years in reconstructive surgery. Ever the wit, John has said:

> The infantry were moving along with us and, as I glanced to my left to see an infantry soldier who was wounded and waving for help, I took a bullet just below my right ear. I fell to the floor of the tank. . . . Luckily the medics were close by and I was evacuated to the first aid station. On the way there we were under mortar fire, but having been given a shot of morphine I could have cared less what was going on. Great stuff, that morphine!

The RCR kept trying to advance, making slow, often costly, movement towards "Cider." All our tanks kept up a steady fire at one German machine-gun position after another. The enemy persisted in small, local forays and men were often locked in hand-to-hand combat. Just ahead, I noticed Skinny, an old boyhood pal I went to school with, and with whom I had spoken only an hour before. He had banged the side of my tank as he went by, and now he was hunkered behind a small wall surrounding a well. As he raised to take a shot, a sniper got him in the forehead. He was flung back by the force of the shot, with his helmet flying off in another direction. I'm unable to describe the anger I felt, but before the day was over I made the enemy pay many times over for his death.

Shortly, the enemy launched another local counterattack and to this day I will never forget the almost robotic manner in which they kept charging directly into our fire. It seemed that regardless how many you hit, they kept on coming. Up ahead my old comrade from "Boys Town" at Wolseley Barracks, "Red" Forrest, was fighting like a fiend, and in the day's action he was to earn himself the Distinguished Conduct Medal. Chuck Lithgow was wounded and all officers and senior NCOs became casualties within a short time. Our squadron leader, Ted Smith, and headquarters troop of three tanks, on the right, managed to get up close to "Cider," but when the infantry couldn't get up to support them he was forced to withdraw. Moving back his tank struck a mine, and when Ross Houston, the second in command, came alongside to take off his crew he, too, hit another mine. Thank goodness I was over on the left, and in an ideal position to give them covering fire, for the German paras had launched yet another attack, and were right on their tail.

The battle came to its dismal end with both sides licking their wounds. The RCR had suffered dreadfully. Both "C" and "D" Companies had only a handful of men left —"C" with fifteen, and "D" with fourteen. The battalion of 850 by nightfall was reduced to eighteen officers and 159 men. And we had only gained 100 yards when darkness descended. The RCR war diary notes that mortar, machine gun and shellfire were so intense that "the attack was completely broken up . . . and casualties were very heavy, and although the tanks gave every possible assistance the infantry could make no headway against the many hidden machine guns." Our losses in "A" Squadron for the day were a total of six tanks, as the Germans set on fire the two that had struck mines earlier. Of more importance, we lost a goodly number of crew commanders to enemy snipers, so in many cases troopers commanded tanks in the absence of an officer or NCO.

As I wandered through our lines I learned that, besides Skinny, many of my school and playground friends also died that day. The men who survived were heavy-hearted as they looked around at how few were left. To give aid and comfort, up came Captain "Rusty" Wilkes, the RCR chaplain—one of the finer figures serving in the Chaplain Corps in Italy. His personality, presence, words of wisdom and comfort did much to strengthen the inner resolve of those who were, once again, to be thrown into the crucible of death in the morning.

We spent the night with the RCR, and stuck close to our tanks, as the Germans had numerous fighting patrols out, while we didn't have enough men left to counter them. My crew started up the Primus stove inside the turret, and soon we had a warm meal of stew and bully beef. The smell of our cooking was noticed outside, and shortly a hungry infanteer banged on the turret to ask if we had anything to spare. The familiar voice was my boyhood friend, Freddie Edwards from Thorndale, who lived next door to my grandparents. I am grateful that Freddie survived the war, and many years later he treated me to an excellent meal as thanks for the stew and bully beef.

During the night the RCR dragged forward every man who could be spared from Headquarters and Support Companies to reinforce the rifle companies, and the battalion was reorganized on a basis of three companies of sixty-five men each to get ready for another attack in the morning.

All our tanks were running low, or were out of ammunition, so a frantic call was made for replenishment, and a demand for gas, too. Although we had covered very few miles during the day, the engines had been running non-stop for the better part of twenty-four hours.

Next morning, December 19th, the attack began with an intense artillery barrage, which—this time—did not alter from the plan. The advance was almost anti-climactic, compared to the carnage of the day before. With little enemy resistance, and the RCR suffering only three casualties, we stood astride the crossroads know as "Cider." But at what a dreadful cost. Today, the Canadian Moro River Cemetery, where 1,375 of our comrades remain at rest, is mute testimony to the absolute futility of war, and the ages on the headstones are silent reminders of a lost generation.

As we stood at the crossroads, little did we know that our efforts had brought us only to the outskirts of a place Matthew Halton of the CBC [father of David] would later describe as "The Courtyard of Hell." Ortona lay ahead! A name that would become seared in my mind for the rest of my days.

Captain Frank Johnson, commanding "C" Squadron, joined up with a company of the Loyal Edmonton Regiment commanded by Major Jim Stone, and began to move slowly forward towards the town. Trouble was not long in calling. Lieutenant Tommy Melvin commanded the point troop, and as he moved about 200 yards beyond "Cider" crossroads, he passed over a culvert that the enemy had filled with an explosive charge. A *Fallschirmjägerpionier* [front line engineers] party in a nearby barn detonated the charge as Melvin moved over the culvert. The tank was shattered beyond recognition with a five-ton turret being thrown over 150 yards. The crew of five was killed instantly. The German party then came out with their hands up, to be taken prisoner by the Edmontons.

The ground on the left being unsatisfactory for deployment, Frank Johnson moved his remaining tanks into a field on the right of the road. The Germans, naturally, had liberally sown the entire field with mines, and soon three more tanks were disabled. However, the Edmontons moved on, supported by the remaining "C" Squadron tanks, and by last light were in Ortona itself.

Frank Johnson, who, with Jim Stone, was given verbal orders by Lieutenant Colonel Jefferson, commanding the Edmontons, said the colonel at the time thought the Germans would likely withdraw, and that Ortona could be taken by one infantry company supported by a squadron of tanks. Little did Colonel Jefferson, or anyone else on the Allied side, know that Hitler had ordered Ortona would be held—and the paras were determined to obey.

Meanwhile, the Seaforth Highlanders of Canada, from Vancouver, repeated a feat from a previous battle in Sicily, by scaling the cliffs south of the town during the night, and joining up with the Edmontons. Also, during the night anti-tank guns and medium machine guns from the Saskatchewan Light Infantry (MG) managed to get up to strengthen the day's gain. Even with their support the situation remained extremely dicey, as the Germans were actively aggressive. The next few days were to teach us just how much more proficient, and offensive, the 1st Parachute Division was, compared to other divisions of the German army we had encountered to date.

With "C" Squadron continuing in support of the Eddies, "A" Squadron came in to support the Seaforths in the north half of the town. The official history describes Ortona as a leftover from the medieval days of Venetian dominance in the Adriatic, and says, "the Old Town with its tall, narrow houses and dark, cramped streets, merged into the more modern section that had grown up on the flat tableland to the south."

As we slowly moved into town we quickly became aware that the Germans had systematically blown up houses, creating obstacles that would force us on to routes they had selected as "killing grounds."

Many of the civilians had fled to the countryside, and were hiding in caves or huddled in the railway tunnel below the town. There were some, though, who remained in their basements as the fighting raged around and above them. The fighting became so bitter, and the damage so extensive as the town was slowly reduced to piles of rubble, that civilian casualties grew higher day by day. There was an old woman who ventured out her front door, only to be shot by a German sniper. Her body fell back against the house and slowly sunk to the ground. With her legs extended into the street there was no room to manoeuvre past her as we went by. Gradually her legs were ground into the cobbled street, and by the second day only her torso was left. There she remained like a silent sentinel as we wound our way past her for the next few days. But with death, there also came life. In a nearby house, already partially damaged, a woman was ready to give birth, and two or three infanteers had to stop hunting Germans to aid in the delivery. One, a medical orderly, had a tin of sulfa powder and I understand the lady's private parts, and the newborn, were liberally sprinkled with it.

As we cautiously made our way through the enclosed, narrow streets we had no idea how strenuously the 1st Para and 90th Grenadiers would defend the town. Some of us, especially those in from the beginning at the beaches in Sicily, had grown hardened, or callous, and the sight of death was almost a daily occurrence. But nothing we had encountered before readied us for what was to come in the next few days. Nor did we appreciate that we were entering a battle for which no instructional manual had been written. Therefore, we were forced to devise tactics for the scene—and the scene changed street by street and house by house. The Germans, on the other hand, had the terrible experience of Stalingrad to draw upon, and their tactics throughout the battle reflected it.

The poor "taken-for-granted" infanteer was again to bear the brunt of this battle. Death was at every door, whether it be from Germans inside, or because the door was booby-trapped. We, in tanks, were slightly better off, for the armour shielded us from bullets and shrapnel. However, it offered no protection from anti-tank guns, mines and other surprise weapons the enemy introduced during the battle. We soon learned that street fighting, going from house to house, consumed prodigious amounts of ammunition. As a result, our supply vehicles were constantly shuttling from ammunition dumps [in the rear] to an ammunition point [on the very edge of the battle] on the outskirts of the town. Also the barrels of our .30 calibre machine guns began to wear out rather quickly due to the excessive amount of firing. These were but two of many lessons we were to learn in the next few days—and the Germans had more surprises up their sleeve that we would soon encounter.

From early morning of the 21st, "A" Squadron moved in support of the Seaforths, who were responsible for the area north and west of the main street, Corso Vittorio Emanuele, and both they and we knew we were in for a determined fight. Once again many of the narrow streets were blocked by rubble from houses the enemy had detonated, in order to drive us into their selected "killing ground." Any and all movement by the infantry, or us, was met with immediate anti-tank and machine-gun fire. Right at the outset the Seaforths had a hard fight to clear the paras from the Church of Santa Maria di Constantinopoli, and their regimental war diary reports:

> "C" Company engaging enemy, with the support of tanks
> in the vicinity of the church. . . . Reports many enemy
> machine-gun posts in the church firing on them. The
> company's casualties being seven killed and many
> wounded during the attack on the church.

This was just the beginning—seven killed in trying to take a church! I must confess that the German paras fought with great skill and determination, exacting a deadly toll for every house or building. An early tactic we encountered was when they had set up prepared demolition charges in a house; then, by opening fire on the Seaforths as they advanced, would drive them into the house selected for demolition, before blowing the charge, burying everyone.

With the intensity of the fighting growing daily, we slowly inched our way through the narrow streets of the town, and we also moved into the history books. The unbridled savagery of the fighting—street by street, house by house, and frequently floor by floor—would lead the press to describe the scene as "The Stalingrad of the West." As history now records, Ortona was the only battle in World War II in which any army of the Western allied powers, British, American, French or Canadian, fought a sustained battle day after day, in a built-up area.

Throughout the 22nd and 23rd we continued in support of the Seaforths, all the while under sustained mortar, machine-gun and anti-tank fire. The Seaforth anti-tank platoon truck was destroyed in one mortar "stonk" [point where a group of mortar shells landed together], and the NCO in charge of our squadron ammunition point reported that the Germans were feeling around his area and that we must shortly move it, or it would be destroyed as well.

The 24th, the day before Christmas, was like the others, as we slowly ground our way forward through dust and smoke in the narrow, confined streets. With absolute ferocity the Germans held on to each house, making us pay dearly before withdrawing into the next house. By now our troops had developed a technique called "mouseholing"— where a hole was blown in the wall of one house allowing for entry into the next. This meant that troops did not have to venture out on the street, where their presence always brought sustained fire from the paras. Blowing through the wall, troops would clear the ground floor and work their way upstairs. When the upper floor was cleared they would blow through to the next house, enter it and then clear the house this time from top to bottom. A note in the Seaforth's war diary notes, "at times [we] were in the strange position of being in the same building as the enemy . . ."

The stench of death was everywhere. It permeated your clothing, and it clung to the hairs in your nostrils, so you were never free of it. Enemy sniping was so accurate that the more we "mouseholed" the better, as it kept the troops from having to venture outside. The proficiency of the enemy snipers made life on the street rather short for anyone who sallied forth. In fact, they were so accurate, and persistent, that tank commanders were forced to "button up" by closing the turret hatch. This cut down one's range of vision, and created an almost claustrophobic atmosphere inside.

The smell of three unwashed bodies, added to the smoke and smell from the main tank cannon, the turret and co-drivers' machine guns, made life less than pleasant when the hatch was closed. Added to the snipers, the Germans began the nasty habit of dropping grenades or magnetic beehive explosive charges into the turret from upper-storey windows. This meant we kept closed up a lot of the time.

The 24th was not a particularly good day. At one point, a Seaforth was trying to pass information to me on the location of an enemy machine gun that was holding up the company's advance. A sniper shot him, killing him instantly. Even though death was all around us, the shock of his dying before my eyes filled me with a terrible rage, and I gave my gunner an order to destroy everything in sight on both sides of the street. And he did—without question—by placing one or more rounds of 75mm high-explosive shot, on delay, into each house ahead of us, thereby killing or flushing out anyone who may have been in them. Those flushed out were quickly dispatched by the Seaforths.

A lesson we learned early on in Sicily was how effective our 75mm explosive rounds were if we used the delayed-action fuse. By turning a screw on the shell casing, the explosion was delayed for .05 seconds, long enough to penetrate an outer wall before exploding inside. We used this technique extensively throughout the Ortona battle, and later I went into a couple of houses to see how effective this method was. I emerged with no doubt in my mind—arms, legs, a headless torso, and bodies were strewn about like an obscene depiction of Dante's *Inferno*.

Also, on the 24th, a mortar round exploded within the confines of a narrow street, wounding Ted Smith, our squadron commander (who subsequently died of his wounds), killing two others, wounding Lou Maraskas, the battle captain, and a number of others. Ross Houston assumed temporary command of the squadron at this point. We lacked junior officers at this time, and some troops, my own included, were commanded by NCOs, for troop leaders (lieutenants) were in short supply.

Late in the afternoon of the 24th we were running out of ammunition, and when I called back to Ross Houston he told me to hold on until another troop came up to relieve me. As my tanks began to move back, a sniper in the tower of the Church of Santa Maria delle Grazie opened up on the Seaforths, who were now in what we called Dead Horse Square (a dead horse was lying in the square during the fighting). The lead tank of the incoming troop quickly disposed of the sniper with one well-aimed round.

After restocking with ammunition and gas, we were ordered to get washed and move over to the Church of Santa Maria di Constantinopoli where, together with a platoon of the Seaforths, we had a Christmas dinner. It was a pleasant break, even if only for a few minutes. A Seaforth officer, Lieutenant Wilf Gildersleeve, played the organ and we all sang a carol before returning to the business of the day. (Little did I dream that fifty-five years hence I would sit in the same church, with Wilf Gildersleeve again at the organ. The difference this time, though, would be that sitting beside us would be veterans of the 1st German Parachute division, with whom we would join in a Dinner of Reconciliation.)

Had I known what the next hour would bring, I might have been tempted to remain in the church and ask for a second helping. When we finished eating, Ross Houston told me to get up and see the Seaforth company and platoon commanders I would be supporting in the morning.

Making my way through the narrow, pitch-black streets I grew increasingly nervous, for I didn't encounter a soul, nor could I detect the presence of any infanteers. It was as quiet as a tomb, something quite unusual instead of the normal crash of gunfire. Uncertain, I stopped near a corner, where I tried to orient myself. Suddenly, in the silence, I became aware of approaching footsteps. Not knowing who it was, and unsure of where I was, I didn't want to make any noise by using my pistol if I were forced to, so I quickly removed a commando knife I carried in the sleeve of my tunic. The faint glimmer of a silvery belt buckle as the person turned the corner told me he was German. Lunging forward, I drove the knife in deeply just above the belt buckle, then swiftly drew it upwards, effectively gutting him before he could utter a word. Realizing I was in German territory I hastily turned to retrace my steps, and eventually made contact with the Seaforths without further incident.

Over the next day or so I saw the German body of Christmas Eve still slumped against the wall, and one day I stopped to go through his pockets where I found his service book; only to discover he hadn't reached his seventeenth birthday. Given the brutality of the day I thought nothing more of the incident but, with the passage of time, it has increasingly haunted me—and continues to do so to this day. Time has taught me how easy it is to kill, but how hard to forget.

I cannot let the 24th pass by without comment from the enemy perspective. In 1998 I came into possession of a portion of a daily diary kept by Obergefreiter Karl Bayerlein, a *Fallschirmjägerpionier* in the 1st Parachute Combat

Engineer Battalion. An entry for the 23rd clearly shows that our pressure was beginning to wear the enemy down. Bayerlein had written:

Heavy enemy shellfire falling on the town, the enemy continues to advance with tanks and infantry. We are tired from continuously standing to [being alert, ready for action]. Anyone who comes back throws himself on straw in the cellar and sleeps like the dead. Again we blow up houses and lay mines; the enemy is supposed to be channeled in a certain direction, into the market square. I was on an upper floor when Canadian infantry burst in down below. I quickly throw two hand grenades down below, and quickly withdraw into the house next door. Behind our backs along side streets that could not all be kept under surveillance or defended, enemy tanks push ahead across Corso Umberto and in the direction of the castle. Now only the largest buildings resist the continuous shellfire; there is destruction and rubble everywhere.

Christmas Day, 1943, is a day I will always remember. Over the years this day has been impossible for me to forget; notwithstanding, in later years, the joys of family and grandchildren. Even as I write, I become very tearful as I recall how the day began. Returning to Dead Horse Square I found the Seaforths had lost a number of men after they took a school on the south side of the square. The paras had blown it up after the Seaforths occupied the building, and now with machine-gun and mortar fire were impeding the Seaforths as they tried to rescue their comrades.

Much of the fire was coming from the Church of Santa Maria delle Grazie where, yesterday afternoon, one "A" Squadron tank had taken out a sniper in the tower on the church. The huge church doors were open, giving the German gunners an unrestricted field of fire, so I ordered my gunner to open fire. Within seconds we destroyed the front of the church, which had stood for hundreds of years, then the infantry moved in to complete the nasty work of taking out any Germans left alive. If this weren't enough, the enemy was barricaded in the hospital next door to the church and, when the Seaforths moved in, the Germans opened with a withering crossfire of machine guns from the ground floor of the hospital, and from some buildings on the south side of the square. I was then forced to destroy the hospital, before the infantry could go in with the bayonet to take the paras out. This terrible day finally drew to its conclusion with a welcome sight when from the bowels of the hospital came a host of civilians headed by a priest. Years later, after having the honour to unveil a memorial to those killed in the battle, I met the seven-year-old boy who was immediately behind the priest—now a man of sixty-two. I was mightily embarrassed when, with tears in his eyes, he threw his arms around me and roundly kissed my cheek.

I am forced to confess that Christmas has never regained allure and solemnity for me since December 1943; every Christmas morning I still see Seaforth bodies scattered across that damned square. Even today I find it difficult to fully describe all the actions of this dreadful day, and many of the events are never far from my mind. I never thought for one moment that fifty years hence I would sit in this same church, with my grandson, and finally break down and let a half-century's worth of tears burst forth.

The Seaforth CO, on the 26th, reported that our tanks were being used to advantage, and his companies were advancing steadily house to house. Their regimental war diary records, "Our supporting tanks were firing point blank at the houses neutralizing enemy fire." Then, "A" Company reported that a small, flat trajectory weapon from the upstairs window of a house had fired upon one of the tanks supporting them. The "Beehive," a magnetic, hollow-shaped charge, was the first surprise weapon the Germans introduced in this battle. Now, the flat trajectory weapon was our introduction to the German bazooka—the *Panzerschreck*, or tank terror. On the south side of town, opposite the Eddies, they also brought in flame-throwers, but this weapon must have been in short supply for we never encountered it in the Seaforth area.

This mad dance of death finally drew to its conclusion on the morning of the 28th when patrols reported that the enemy had withdrawn from the town. Years later, in 1998, Feldwebel Fritz Illi, who had commanded a platoon in the 2nd Battalion of the 3rd Regiment in the 1st Parachute Division, told me that when he received the order to withdraw, his men simply picked up their weapons and moved out—without any Canadian infantry detecting their movement.

The battle over, we were left with the battered, empty shell of a centuries-old medieval town, and the increasingly pungent odor of death. Bodies sprawled in grotesque shapes cluttered the doorways and rooms of many houses, while others had begun to rot under the rubble. Destroyed or booby-trapped houses and heavily mined streets hindered burial parties frantically digging for bodies. The primeval violence of the battle was recognized by the Eddies, whose war diary on the 28th said, "As a rule, the foe either removes his dead, or buries them on the spot. Ortona has been the exception; approximately 100 dead have been left lying [where they died] due to his hasty withdrawal."

The grey, leaden sky that periodically spewed forth a drizzling, bone-chilling rain did little to raise our morale, as troops dug frantically to uncover those who might be still alive in the rubble. One of the few lucky ones was Lance Corporal Roy Boyd of the Loyal Edmonton Regiment, who was buried for three-and-a-half days before being found. Added to the problem of falling masonry, and the lack of heavy recovery equipment, was the danger from hundreds of mines sown all over the town by retreating German forces.

The visual evidence of the ferocity of the fighting that lay bare for all to see brings to mind—for a reason I cannot explain—the prescient words of Winston Churchill, written in 1897 during the Malakand Campaign in India, when he said, "The keener the competition, the greater the honour of success. In sport, in courage, and in the sight of heaven, all men meet on equal terms." Looking back, years later, I am obliged to admit the German soldier fought with the utmost courage and determination. Although he was my enemy, I willingly salute his ability. This praise, however, in no way detracts from my admiration and respect for the Canadian soldier, especially the over-exposed, under-appreciated infantryman who withstood the brunt of battle with fortitude, self-assurance and gallantry.

In a broadcast to the people back in Canada, Matthew Halton of the CBC said, in part:

> Nothing in this war or in any other has there been
> anything more bitter and intense. The Canadians beat
> two of the finest divisions that ever marched in a long
> fury of fire and death ending in the appalling week of
> Ortona.

Our infantry casualties were horrendous and, sadly, there are 1,375 graves in the Commonwealth War Graves Moro River Cemetery outside of Ortona. Our regimental casualties were light compared to the infantry, but recorded were fourteen killed, twenty-one wounded, five tanks destroyed, and more than a dozen damaged. The 1st Canadian Infantry Division was almost a skeleton, and the 1st Canadian Armoured Brigade was not much better. Troops were totally exhausted and badly in need of rest and reinforcement; equipment was in short supply, and what we had was badly in need of repair and maintenance. Despite the shape we were in, all units gave up many of their remaining battle-experienced officers and NCOs so they could return to England to strengthen Canadian units preparing for the forthcoming Normandy invasion. A few days' respite allowed us the opportunity to look after our equipment, which badly needed maintenance, and to absorb new reinforcements into tank crews, all the while ensuring they were adequately trained to perform their job.

It would be unworthy of me at this point if I did not acknowledge, as always happens in war, that civilians bear a crushing burden when fighting takes place around them, and Ortona was no exception. As I mentioned before, many civilians fled to the countryside, or were hiding in caves or tunnels. Even so, there were over 278 citizens killed in the town during the course of the battle, and many more were to die in the months ahead when unexploded German mines and demolitions took their toll.

But to return to the nastiness of daily life, as we entered 1944 we were not surprised to find that the year appeared to offer nothing but a repetition of what we had already experienced. Any hope the war would end in 1944 was quickly dashed when we looked at the map to see the number of ravines, rivers, gullies and mountains still ahead. The German army remained intact; it was well led and was conducting a magnificent defensive campaign—and it was determined to make us pay for every inch of ground we gained.

In mid-January we moved up to support the 11th Infantry Brigade in their attack at the Arielli River, but little did I realize that this was to be my last battle with the regiment. After the battle, the regiment moved back to the Laciano area for the winter because operations were gradually running down. Weather conditions had become so bad that movement was next to impossible and living required something better than a slit trench.

Ted in London, Ontario, 1945

Some time earlier, my squadron commander at the time, Ted Smith, asked if I were interested in a commission. After some thought, I had replied in the affirmative and thought nothing more about it. Shortly after arriving in the Lanciano area, I was surprised one day to be told to get myself down to brigade headquarters, where I underwent a series of tests to determine my suitability as an officer. Evidently I made the grade and soon I was off to Avellino for more tests—this time before a high-priced board of officers brought out from England.

Meanwhile, at the unit, the regimental newspaper, *The Turret* (accidentally misspelled by the original editor—and it remains the same today, but is now published by our successor regiment, 12e Regiment blinde du Canada), had a short item:

> SSM E.L. Wells and Cpl. E.R. Griffiths, both of "A" Squadron, last week left to face a selection board at a base town. Word has been received that they were successful and will proceed to an OCTU, on their first step toward receiving the king's commission.

Leaving the regiment was a heart-rending experience, and I think that had we been in a line, I would have declined to go. One does not live, play, drink, fight and chase women with a group over a long time, without developing a serious attachment to them—and so it was with the regiment, especially "A" Squadron. With tears in my eyes, and a monstrous hangover, I began the slow trek back to England.

Back in dear old Blighty I met more selection boards, but in the end I arrived at the Royal Military College at Sandhurst, where I found myself in a troop of young gentlemen from the best schools of England, all of them destined for the Brigade of Guards. Many of them had yet to have their first shave, and I soon found myself cast in the role of an old soldier. After many escapades, I finally graduated and quickly disappeared into the intelligence world, where the problem of the day was preparing to counter German plans to undermine and obstruct the forthcoming occupation of Germany.

And so ended my first war—Korea was still five years away.

Ted and John Gardam, Christmas Day, 1998 at the German cemetery, Cassino, Italy

CHAPTER 5

THE PILOT OF
"PISTOL PACKIN' MAMMA"

GORDON WEBB

As a TEENAGER growing up in Hamilton, Ontario, Gordon Webb said he was like so many of his age when he "developed a keen interest in aeroplanes." He wrote to me in early 1997 and said, "I used to marvel at what fun it must be to frolic about in the sunshine and warm blue sky chasing those soft fleecy clouds."

After the outbreak of war in 1939, Mr. and Mrs. Webb knew that some or all of their four sons would join up and fight for Canada. Join they did, with John in the army, Norm in the Royal Canadian Navy, Maurice later at age sixteen joining the Merchant Navy, and Gordon becoming a pilot in the Royal Canadian Air Force. The Webb boys had a great example to follow in that their father had served in the First War in the 48th Highlanders of Canada, and was wounded three times, the last time at Vimy Ridge in April 1917, where he received an almost fatal head wound.

Gordon enlisted in September 1941 and learned to fly at Goderich and Centralia, Ontario. Soon after receiving his wings, Gordon was sent to the RCAF Manning Depot in Bournemouth, England, where there were hundreds of aircrew waiting to be sent to squadrons. Much to Gordon's surprise, his name was called out after just five days and he was told to report to a unit to fly the Oxford. He then went on to fly the Whitley. Gordon recalls that:

> The Whitley was arguably the worst bomber aircraft in the allied inventory. It can best be described as an assemblage of aircraft parts flying along in loose formation. It was underpowered and difficult to manoeuvre. On a good night and with great patience it might be coaxed up to 13,000 feet. It did, however, have one redeeming feature: it somewhat resembled the

47

The three Webbs: Norman, John and Gordon

German Dornier aircraft. This resemblance took on great importance one night just north of Paris when our crew became frighteningly aware that two 190s were near to us, one on either side. I ordered "no gunfire" and told the wireless operator to be ready to fire the colours of the day to make the 190 pilots think we were one of theirs. The 190s disappeared into the dark. They either hadn't seen us or indeed mistook us as friendly. (All crews were given the colours of the day just prior to takeoff. How this information got into the Allies' hands one can only guess, but it was one of those things crews were pleased to have.)

With absolutely no feeling of regret nor sadness, Gordon said goodbye to the Whitley, and along with his crew converted to the Handley Page Halifax, and then on to 432 Heavy Bomber Squadron at Eastmore in Yorkshire. The crew was assigned to Halifax "M for Mother," which quickly became "Pistol Packin' Mamma," after a popular song of the day.

Gordon explained that the gathering together of a crew was more based upon friendships than evidence of previous qualifications. The crew grew very close. They tended to stick together off duty and became like family. Gordon recalls going to the home of George Hutchinson, his Royal Air Force mid-upper gunner. Mrs. Hutchinson was quite worried about the safety of George, their only child. Gordon said, "She asked me to look out for him." Gordon felt his responsibility keenly; his skill as a pilot was one of the keys to the safety of all of the crew. Two weeks later George was badly injured, and later died of his injuries. This loss is one of many that haunt Gordon to this day.

The Halifax at maximum takeoff weighed 65,000 pounds. It carried about 13,000 pounds of bombs at a cruising speed of 225 mph. For its day it was a fine aircraft, but compared to today's aircraft, its instrumentation and cockpit lighting were truly primitive.

The sole *raison d'être* for Bomber Command's existence was the bombing of selected targets in occupied Europe. Obviously penetrating and dealing with the well-trained and highly capable German defences carried considerable risk. Gordon goes on to say:

> For example, during one raid on Nuremberg in March
> 1944, more allied aircrew were lost than during the
> entire Battle of Britain. Not so obvious, however, were
> the risks associated with flying heavy bombers on and off
> British wartime airfields, usually in the dark and in poor
> weather conditions.

As an experienced and well-qualified pilot of a bomber, Gordon says, "Too little has been written on the first takeoff with a full bomb

"Pistol Packin' Mamma"—the fifth Halifax to carry the name

RCAF crew prior to the Pathfinder.
Back row: **Johnnie, Ed, Al, George**; *front row*: **Cy, Gordon, Vic**

load." He described how he felt the very first time he took off with a bomb load of up to 13,000 pounds, a crew of seven, dark poor runway lighting and awful weather conditions. The aircraft had to be operating perfectly because a faulty engine on takeoff could spell disaster. Considering the standard of instruments and navigational aids available, pilots with as few as 250-300 hours' total flying time faced quite a challenge. Similarly, many a bomber pilot, nursing his aircraft home, felt his heart sink when he received word, usually over the North Sea or English Channel, that his base was fogged in as were all other bases that his fuel would allow him to reach. The aircraft must still be landed in spite of conditions that would test any pilot, even with today's sophisticated instrumentation and bad weather approach facilities. Gordon describes a raid over Wilhelmshaven, Germany that captures the spirit of the pilot and his crew in an unusual situation:

> It was a daylight raid, unusual for us, and we were to arrive over the target at three p.m. It must have been a

Saturday because I recall thinking that I hoped that children would not be in the movie houses. One of our squadron aircraft was flying off our port wing and to the rear, undoubtedly taking some comfort from having us nearby. There was a lot of flak; I looked back again and saw the aircraft vanish in a burst of black smoke. He had "bought it." Back at base during debriefing I told the debriefing officer that the plane had been shot down and that I had not seen any survivors, nor was it possible that anyone could have survived. Years later in Toronto after the war, whom did I see in front of the Royal York Hotel, but the pilot of that aircraft. He had been the only survivor, blown clear out of the cockpit. In a one in ten million chance his parachute, by some miracle, opened and lowered him unconscious to the ground. After months in hospital he spent the rest of the war as a prisoner of war. That day in Toronto was like seeing a ghost!

Another action that has to be judged as fate was an event during an operation to Frankfurt, Germany. It was a very dark night, and everything seemed just fine. About thirty minutes from the target, I mentioned to the crew that I didn't like it, it seemed a little too quiet for me. I felt very uneasy. I decided to go with a little higher altitude. I climbed 500 feet and no sooner had I leveled off than there was a very loud WUMP! The whole aeroplane shook. The German anti-aircraft gunners obviously had been tracking us on radar and my change of altitude at that moment must have fouled up their programming. Some "second sense" had caused me to move and thus we avoided a direct hit!

After twenty-six operations Gordon and his crew finished flying with the main force and were selected to go to Pathfinder Training School to convert to the Lancaster Bomber for a tour of operations with the Pathfinder's Force. This elite group had been formed to accurately mark the target so that the main force could be more effective. Forty-six operations later, Gordon was sent home to Canada on leave. His war was about to come to an end. Reporting to Hagersville after his leave, Gordon was all set to return to England to fly Dakotas for Transport Command. He was shocked to hear he was to remain in Canada to give appearances and sell War Bonds. Gordon said "NO" and was told he would do it or be released. His curt "call me mister" had a rather unexpected effect and he left the RCAF in February 1945, just four months before the war ended.

This story should end here, but Gordon Webb's career changed within the year to see him back in uniform after receiving a letter from RCAF Headquarters requesting that he return to active duty. Gordon's stint as a student at McMaster University came to an abrupt halt. The flying career of Gordon Webb took on international significance when he was selected to fly with United States Strategic Air Command (SAC) in 1946. Following this tour he joined 426 Thunderbird Squadron, which among other things was involved in the Korean Airlift that operated out of McCord Airbase in Washington state to Japan. His next move was to San Antonio, Texas where as C97 Aircraft Commander he flew on international flights with a break to join a C119 Tactical Squadron operating in Korea.

Gordon and his USAF crew, 1947

In 1955 Gordon was transferred to Ottawa to fly with 412 VIP Squadron. One of the most memorable trips was during a flight to London, England with Prime Minister John Diefenbaker and General George Pearkes VC, MND. Gordon recalls:

> The prime minister was attending his first Common-
> wealth Conference. Ramp time in London was 1000
> hours local, which we had to meet within thirty seconds.
> The weather was as bad as it gets. To add to our
> problems, the prime minister asked if we would mind if
> he stood behind my seat during the approach and
> landing. We fitted him with earphones. We landed with
> no sign of the runway until just before touchdown. As he
> was preparing to meet all the dignitaries awaiting his
> arrival, he touched me on the shoulder, and with that
> famous shake of the head said, "Now that is what I call
> something else." He was a great passenger.

When Gordon was with the Directorate Transport and Reconnaissance Operations in National Defence Headquarters, AVM Hugh Campbell, who was retiring, came to his office to say goodbye and asked him, "Where would you like to go?" Military Air Transport Service was the instant answer and once again Gordon was flying for the Americans out of McGuire Air Force Base in New Jersey.

A story of interest came about when Gordon was flying a C-118 from the United States to Madrid, Spain. The itinerary called for a brief stop at the United Sates Naval Base at Rota in the south of Spain. Unknown to the crew, on the day prior to their arrival the Spanish had extracted a very firm commitment from the American Naval Base Commander that no, repeat no, third nationals were to be allowed on the base without prior authorization from the Spanish area commander. Gordon was seen walking from the aircraft to the Operations Centre. This caused a rather excited American base commander to rush down to the Operations Centre, where he explained the touchy situation vis-à-vis the Spanish, and said that Gordon would have to remain on the base until the matter was cleared up. Gordon explained that he couldn't do that unless, of course, the base could accommodate the hundred or so passengers and crew. The base commander was somewhat puzzled until he realized that Gordon was the pilot and the aircraft just wasn't going anywhere without him. The base commander threw his hands up in the air and departed without so much as a goodbye. Gordon and aircraft departed. Gordon's crew, all United States Air Force, smiled all the way to Madrid.

Later Canada agreed to provide air support to Zambia during its separation from South Rhodesia. Gordon was put in charge of the operation. Before leaving Canada, Gordon was told to report to Ottawa for a briefing. A general met him at Uplands Airport and said that since he had no solid information about what was going on out there, his only advice was to do whatever needed to be done. Gordon offered that that was possibly the best briefing he had ever received!

Gordon and his team set up headquarters at Kinsasha in the Congo and the ensuing airlift to Zambia was quite remarkable. It is of concern to the author that no formal recognition of this mission has been included in the Canadian Forces history.

This former pilot of "Pistol Packin' Mamma" received both the Distinguished Flying Cross in 1943 and a "bar" to the DFC in 1944. Both the RCAF and the USAF recognized Gordon's long post-war career as a pilot and he is the only non-American to wear the USAF Diamond award for exemplary flying.

Gordon's career spanned both wartime and peacekeeping missions, and this is what makes him such an excellent choice to be in this book. He was married in 1950 and he and his wife Audrey had two sons. Audrey died ten years ago. Gordon now lives in Nepean, Ontario.

CHAPTER 6

DOWN TO THE SEA IN SHIPS—
DEFENSIVELY EQUIPPED
MERCHANT SHIPS

FRANK PEARSON

O<small>NE OF THE</small> pleasures of writing oral history of the wartime years is that the author gets to choose which story will be published. I have always been interested in those Royal Canadian Navy sailors who served aboard merchant ships as part of the ship's protective system. In *DEMS at War*, by Max Reid, this passage sets the stage for the story of Frank Pearson of Victoria, British Columbia:

> Month after month of boring gun watches on some remote sea, with one ship in seven lost, was not the exotic life at sea envisaged by some 2,000 young Canadian naval reservists. These men served as gunners, signalmen and telegraphists in Allied merchant ships during World War II. This branch of the wartime navy was called DEMS, Defensively Equipped Merchant Ships. To some of its younger members, it was translated as "Don't Ever Mention Ships."

To understand the scope of DEMS as it applied to Canada's Merchant Navy, one has to realize that in 1939 Canada had "forty-one deep sea ships over 1000 tons and ended the war with 173." These figures may not seem too impressive until one realizes that "159 ships were built, ten acquired and thirty-seven ships were lost to the enemy or disposed of." This accomplishment from a nation also heavily involved in building naval warships of all types, plus aircraft, weapons and vehicles for the war effort, was magnificent.

Canada was also involved in building ships for Britain. Their merchant ships were named after Canadian forts. (The Canadian merchant ships were named after Canadian parks.) Shipyards from as far west as Victoria Machinery Depot Company in Victoria, British

Columbia to Foundation Maritime Ltd., Pictou, Nova Scotia, with twelve other yards in between, attests to the total involvement of Canadian industry. (From a family point of view, my uncle, Clive Gardam, died on the job in VMD in Victoria during the war.)

The planners for the building of merchant ships did not forget their aim, which was to "move war materials." These ships would not always travel in convoy escorted by naval ships and had to take a hand in protecting themselves from enemy sub-surface and surface ships, as well as aircraft. The Canadian park ship was "more heavily armed than a naval frigate."

When I interviewed Frank Pearson in Victoria, British Columbia on 15 March 1996, a new world unfolded before me.

Frank's story of how he became a gunner began in December 1942 when he joined the Royal Canadian Navy (RCN), taking his basic training aboard HMCS *Naden*, Victoria. The next stop was HMCS *Chippawa*, Winnipeg for more basic training; advanced basic was at Cornwallis, Nova Scotia for four more months. It was "off to sea" at this point aboard HMCS *Stonetown*, which was on the triangle run Halifax-Newfoundland-Boston. It was here that all the classroom lessons were put to practical use.

By this stage of the war the RCN's demand for manpower was expanding at a very high rate. Sailors were wanted for new ships, new weapons, an expanding naval air force, security of shore-based facilities and, above all else, to replace casualties at sea. Frank was asked to volunteer for one of three jobs, combined operations: commandos, shore guard duty in Newfoundland or DEMS. Frank chose DEMS and headed back to Cornwallis for the DEMS course. This was the second course conducted by the RCN. Frank said he was trained on "fifteen different types of weapons." As Max Reid outlines in his book, a typical Canadian park ship would have:

> 4 inch HA/LA gun (aft)
> 12 pounder (3 inch) (forward)
> 6 x 20 mm Oerlikons
> 2 x Twin 50 calibre machine guns
> 20 Rail Pillar Box Anti-aircraft Rocket Projector
> 6 x parachute and cable devices
> anti-torpedo nets
> degaussing
> 8 x smoke floats
> small arms

A small DEMS detachment of up to fifteen junior ratings would have to be fully skilled in the use of all the above. Not just firing the weapons, carrying out maintenance, stowing ammunition, and training Merchant Navy members in gun crew duties, but advising the Merchant Navy "master" in how to "fight" the ship as well. DEMS crewmen were a most versatile group where personal initiative was essential. All of this seamanship and skill with weapons followed three basic rules:

> Don't open fire too early/waste ammunition/lead the
> target. Don't lag (it's hard to catch up).
> Watch the nose of the aircraft (not the tracer).

The whole business of making weapons in a country where there was no armament industry was indeed a national achievement. Such firms as Canadian National Railways, Massey-Harris, Canadian Pacific, General Motors Canada, John Inglis and Beatty Washing Machine Companies, and Bata Shoes all built weapons of various calibres.

Just where on a merchant ship each of the weapons would be mounted was worked out according to the ship's configuration. In each case the ship designers had to protect against enemy aircraft, submarines on the surface or submerged, mines (contact or electrical) and surface raiders. In every case the arc of fire had to be established and limits set to avoid firing on the ship's funnel or deck cargo. Every ship had a different installation and when a DEMS gunner was assigned to a new merchant ship he had to become acquainted with the layout, and fast!

Frank explained the firing methods for the various weapons aboard ship. He said that he had heard of "one Australian DEMS who got so excited that he fired at a formation of seven Japanese planes. He fired all the rockets at once and in so doing shot down five of them!" (Max Reid noted that if this story was a fact then the "burst range of 1500 yards with a spread of 15 degrees" made the story a miracle.) Fire control of the weapons was done by the senior gun layer, who could be an able seaman, or, in a few cases, a chief or petty officer. The Trade Division, Naval Service Headquarters in Ottawa had the overall control over the DEMS network as well as the control of the ships.

The manning of merchant ships was done differently than in the navy. Crews "signed on" for a voyage. The officers either remained with the same ship or were reassigned by the owners to a different ship. DEMS sailors were controlled by the DEMS Manning Depots on both coasts; Montreal sailors were "landed" at the end of a voyage, given leave and additional training, then reassigned to another ship. Any spare time was filled with naval tasks such as deammunitioning and ammunitioning merchant ships going into refit or docking. Fisheries ships were used for this task, for they had both the boom for transferring cargo, plus a hold to store the ammunition. These were part of the Royal Canadian Navy Fisherman's Reserve, which had been established prior to September 1939.

Frank Pearson, RCN

Frank describes his first trip as follows:

> My first ship left in December 1943 with a load of Port Albernie lumber. It was the SS *Beaton Park* [she had been commissioned in October 1943 at the Burrard Drydock Company, North Vancouver, BC]. We went alone to the Panama Canal and joined a convoy in Balboa, then on to Trinidad, and finally docked at Cape Town. As I recall a convoy was just 300 miles east of Buenos Aires when it was attacked by U-boats and lost five ships from the convoy, including a tanker, which burned for five days. As was the practise, no ship could stop to see if there were any survivors. Convoys could not get involved in the attack.
>
> The SS *Beaton Park* sailed unescorted to Montevideo, Uruguay, where the coal was unloaded and a cargo of hides from Buenos Aires was put in the newly swept-out holds. We got to see the famous *Graf Spee* sunk just outside the harbour.

After rounding Cape Horn the voyage took them back to New Westminster. Frank was then landed at the Manning Depot until his name came "to the top of the roster"; then he was assigned to SS *Windermere Park* (1944). She was one of the most heavily armed park ships and there were fourteen DEMS gunners aboard. The convoy departed from Puget Sound in company with SS *Coronation Park*, which had only been commissioned in November 1944. The cargo was ammunition for the United States forces fighting in the Pacific War. After a brief pause offshore from San Francisco, a large convoy escorted by the US Navy sailed for Hawaii for fuel and then on to Leyte for the invasion of Manila in the Philippines. These were the only two Canadian ships to be so deployed.

After many false starts the Canadians finally sailed for their destination behind the invasion forces. Frank said, "You could see the battle group being followed by miles and miles of landing craft." The *Windermere* was assigned to an anchor position off Blue Beach, surrounded by sunken merchant ships that had gone down during an earlier battle with the Japanese aircraft.

Some days later it was the *Windermere's* turn to be unloaded by the port battalions of US military. There were three weeks of air raids while being unloaded, but *Windermere* was not hit. Once the duties in the Pacific were over, the ship headed back to Canada in ballast for thirty-three days in a very rough sea. En route back to US waters a Japanese submarine attacked them. Frank says:

> The torpedo was coming towards us. The CPO/DEMS Paddy Sims was on the bridge with the "master." Paddy said, "turn starboard," and the torpedo missed the merchant ship by fifty feet. It must have been the U-boat's last one because he never fired again. Next day there was a surface battle between the U-boat and an American ship.

Frank's next ship was rather different: the SS *Princess Charlotte*, a passenger ferry sailing between Victoria, Seattle and Vancouver. The

Frank at work

DEMS gunners kept their hand in firing at targets and smoke pots dropped overboard. This caused great interest from the passengers when the 12-pounder was fired out to sea. After three months and just one "shoot," Frank was assigned to SS *Dorval Park*. The war had ended in Europe, but full wartime precautions were still enforced at sea, as Japan had not surrendered.

The voyage was south to Cape Horn, having spent two nights in Punta Arenas. When the ship headed towards the Atlantic there was a bad blizzard, speed was reduced and land was sighted too late. The *Dorval Park* was aground! The tide was going out. In time two Chilean tugs pulled the ship off and took her back into Punta Arenas. After a quick fix the ship sailed for Cape Town. Reduced speed and leaks into the hold did not make for a pleasant voyage. Frank explained that good news was coming:

> Four days on the way to Cape Town the radio message was received that the war was over! Then the message came to throw all ammunition overboard. There were eight DEMS aboard and the message came that six of them were to return by the "fastest possible means." It turned out that the *Dorval Park* was the "fastest possible" and so it was sent to Baltimore with the DEMS working on preserving the guns in heavy grease. Once in the USA, a train was taken to Halifax, Nova Scotia and then home to Victoria just before Christmas 1945. On December 28th the war was over.

After the war Frank Pearson joined the Merchant Navy in 1946 and "sailed the seven seas." He married a girl from Scotland and settled down in Victoria, British Columbia. He went to work in the dockyards, where he worked for over thirty years. At the same time he was to become a reservist on HMCS *Malahat* in July 1976. He had thirty-five years in the civil service when he left in 1985. Frank and his wife live in Victoria, where Frank is a very active member of the Chiefs and Petty Officers Association.

CHAPTER 7

POW NUMBER 354 SURVIVES HONG KONG AND JAPAN

RENE CHARRON

For the first time in my career as a writer of oral history, I found the ultimate gift—a 100-page diary written just after a soldier was freed from almost four years as a prisoner of war. Rene Charron, a clerk from "C" Force Headquarters in Hong Kong, had access to pencil and paper, kept his notes, and transcribed them right after returning to Canada. This permanent record reads as if the events took place just yesterday.

In 1981, Carl Vincent, an archivist in Ottawa, wrote *No Reason Why: The Canadian Hong Kong Tragedy*, a book based on primary sources dealing with Canadian involvement in Hong Kong in 1941. With these two resources in hand I interviewed eighty-one-year-old Rene Charron in January 1995, fifty-four years after the event. His story is one of suffering, deprivation and courage. A small man of five feet, three inches, Rene feels that maybe his size was an asset, as his captors never regarded him a menace. Small in size, yes, but this was a man who devoted his time to younger, stronger men who needed a friend to support them when the Japanese treatment became more and more brutal and demanding, causing some to break under the strain. Rene Charron was a stranger to me until January 25, 1995, the date of our interview, and yet I felt immediately that I had met a man of great strength and wisdom who has always made the best of all circumstances.

This story begins in 1939 in Montreal, Quebec. Rene Charron joined the Canadian Grenadier Guards in 1939 for one reason: his brother was already serving in the regiment. Rene was twenty-seven years old and a personal secretary with Champlain Oil in Montreal. Guardsmen are supposed to be at least five feet, ten inches; Rene was not! When he went for his medical and they laughed at his size, he told them, "I am joining the Guards from the neck up!"

After a short interval he decided to join the active army for, now married to Mary, a Scottish lass, he would receive an additional fifty cents a day. Fully qualified clerks were hard to find and Rene was warned for service in London, England. As a member of the Corps of Military Staff Clerks, his destination was changed in Ottawa. "I was told I was to go to Hong Kong, but I could tell no one—it was a secret," said Rene. Secrets were made to be kept in those days and when Rene phoned Mary to say goodbye he said, "You will not be hearing from me for a while because I am going far away." Mary knew it was not to be England but she had no idea that her husband was leaving for the Far East. On Thursday, October 24, 1941, Rene left Ottawa by train for Vancouver.

When the soldiers arrived at Vancouver they were moved quickly to dockside. Quoting from Rene's 100-page diary,

Cpl. Charron, Montreal, 1940

these words give an indication of the urgency of the move:

> As we paraded from the train to the ship [the *Awatea*], we were greeted by many. . . . It was a pity these boys were not given time to speak to their people. I heard one of them say, "I'm sure that is my mother standing there with my sister—gee, I wish I could speak to them."

The quarters in the hold for the privates and corporals were awful, and as Rene saw the skyline of Vancouver disappearing he felt "very lonely."

The next day Corporal Charron saw Colonel Hennessy for the first time. Rene described him as "a fine officer, nice to his men, but stubborn at times." He promoted Rene to sergeant, which meant he no longer had to live in the hold. Colonel Pat Hennessy was the senior administrative officer of "C" Force and he would be Rene's superior in Hong Kong.

The first stop en route was Honolulu and everything was normal and peaceful. Rene recalled:

> What a place for a honeymoon. . . . It struck me with a kind of pain that, when the world could be so lovely a place as this, how could so much mutilating the face of nature, wrecking its beauty, destroying men, take place.

Rene's fears would soon become a reality when he became a player in the war.

With "C" Force sailing to Hong Kong and battle a certainty, it is appropriate to ask the question, why were Canadians sent to Hong Kong? Within government circles and in some places in the Canadian Army there was a feeling that although the nation had been at war since 1939 and the air force and the navy had been in action, the army had not "fired a shot in anger." In Carl Vincent's book, the finger points at two people: Major General A.E. Grasett, who was the commander in Hong Kong until July 1941, and Major General Harry Crerar, chief of the general staff in Ottawa. Grasett passed through Canada en route home to England and he briefed his friend from RMC days, Harry Crerar, on the Hong Kong situation. Carl Vincent (1981) writes in *No Reason Why:*

> It would have been strange for Grasett to suggest to his superiors the probable willingness of Canada to supply troops for Hong Kong [which he did] without at least a tacit commitment from the Canadian chief of staff. The virtual rubber-stamp endorsement given by Crerar to the subsequent British request gives some indication that it came as no surprise to him.

The British had no reason to doubt Canadian sincerity, for a note sent from the senior British General (Sir John Dill) for submission to Prime Minister Churchill said in part:

> . . . Grasett suggests the Canadian government might be agreeable to provide [infantry reinforcements] . . . relief might be possible and such reinforcement might well prolong resistance for a further considerable period. [Reinforcement] would provide a strong psychological stimulus to the garrison and to the colony.

Churchill accepted the proposal but added the proviso that "a further decision should be made before the battalions actually sailed." When the Canadian government got the request for "one or two Canadian battalions to be provided," the die was cast. At the Cabinet

War Committee held on September 23, 1941, "agreement in principle was reached." Mackenzie King, the prime minister of Canada, insisted on gaining the assent of Ralston, the minister of National Defence, who was in Los Angeles at that time. With almost indecent haste, Ralson was rushed for a decision. In a phone call to Crerar, Ralston was reassured with the CGS's words, "The Canadian Army should take this on." All that was left was to decide which two battalions would go.

The Canadian Army's method of listing units by their level of training was well established: Class A were well advanced and ready for overseas soon; Class B had their intermediate training complete and were ready for coastal defence; and Class C were "those units which, due to either recent employment or insufficient training, are not recommended for operations training at the present time." It will be hard for the reader to fathom why two units from Class C were chosen, but that was the case. The two units chosen were The Royal Rifles of Canada from Quebec City and the Winnipeg Grenadiers from Manitoba. The Royal Rifles had been on guard duty in Newfoundland, the Winnipeg Grenadiers were doing the same in Jamaica.

To be fair to the generals of the time, both units had been mobilized since 1939 and 1940 and, according to C.P. Stacey, "were of proven efficiency. . . . It seems doubtful whether units more efficient could have been obtained." The Class C listing was assigned more because the units had been back in Canada for only a short while. The Winnipeg Grenadiers were on leave when ordered to join "C" Force. The overall commander was J.K. Lawson, a Permanent Force officer promoted to brigadier from colonel. Rene recalls that "the brigadier was concerned over the number of untrained re-enforcements they [the battalions] had received immediately prior to embarkation." Stacey mentions that "of 448 new volunteers transferred [in] . . . 120 had received less than sixteen weeks' training . . . the minimum before being sent overseas."

Apart from some rifle training, firing of machine guns, and, for Rene, an introduction to the Thompson sub-machine gun, there was not much that could be done to correct shortfalls. On Monday, November 10, 1941, word was passed to all aboard that the final destination was Hong Kong, which was reached six days later. Nowhere in Rene's diary or in the history books is it mentioned that Churchill's direction, "A decision should be made before the battalions actually sail" was ever actioned. Canadians were in a theatre of war and they became involved very quickly.

"C" Force disembarked at Kowloon, the southernmost tip of the New Territories. It was here that the soldiers sorted out their kits, were given lectures on the local situation and started to appreciate the strange sights and sounds of the orient. The headquarters and living accommodations were set up in the Jubilee Building. Rene wrote, "Labour being cheap, we hired a Chinese boy to shine our buttons and shoes." This luxury was not to last long, for on November 22 there was a move to "China Command on the Island of Hong Kong." December 7th dawned and everyone was told that the Japanese had attacked at Pearl Harbour; the war had begun. The very next day the Japanese bombed Kai Tak Airport and destroyed all five Royal Air Force planes. Colonel Hennessy gave the order to his staff to move to a house on the Peak along with the Pay Corps and Postal groups.

What has to be made clear is that the administrative group was not close to the fighting nor to brigade headquarters, so Rene did not see the actual fighting. This was all to change on Friday, December 12 when "the Indian Artillery set up two 3.6 inch guns not fifty feet from the headquarters." The next day Hennessy and Captain Davies, the paymaster, went to Wong Nei Chong, brigade headquarters. The Indian guns were located by the Japanese aircraft and soon Japanese artillery started to pound the area around the house. Rene recalled, "Shell after shell came pouring into our little area high on the Peak." The two guns were destroyed, plus sections of the house. Colonel Hennessy returned, surprised that all in his group had survived the shelling—he had seen the bombardment from the hills.

On Sunday, December 14, the siege began; the Japanese navy shelled the island from all sides, and nowhere was safe. Three days later Rene came under shellfire and a fellow soldier landed on top of him in his rush to safety. Rene's words, "You had better find yourself another hole, I don't want to share mine with you" reminds one of the sense of humour one sometimes has when under severe stress.

The headquarters house was in bad shape but the Canadians were still working there. Friday, December 19 saw both officers ambushed by the Japanese but they both managed to escape. Colonel Hennessy knew the situation was grave—he gave everyone a drink, saying, "Cheers, if they [the Japanese] come our way, we'll give them a good reception." The reception would be the very next day, as the shelling grew more intense. The clerks went to the basement and the colonel was supposed to follow shortly. Twenty minutes later, after heavy shelling, they found the colonel badly wounded and Captain Davies dead. Hennessy's legs had been torn to shreds; he was conscious but bleeding profusely. Rene says:

> We applied first aid as best we could; we laid him on a
> door . . . and carried him out of the vestibule. [Later] I

got my water bottle and [the colonel's] bottle of whisky, rinsed out his mouth and gave him a good gulp. He would ask me in that low tired voice, "lift my legs," and when I would pretend to lift them a little, he would sigh and feel so relieved.

Clarke, one of the Canadian clerks, went for help and returned with a British medical officer and some Chinese coolies. The doctor removed the tourniquet with Rene's help. Rene writes:

My hands were a crimson red. We placed Colonel Hennessy's stumps in splints and bandaged them tightly and then placed him on a stretcher. Just 200 yards up the road en route to a hospital, we stopped; the Colonel sighed, motioned to be put down, and he died.

The Canadian clerks were now leaderless; they reported to the British headquarters but in no time rejoined Captain Bush at the Victoria Barracks. While getting supplies together, the two cars being used were subjected to a bombing. Rene recalls:

I lay there stunned, my whole body aching. Brunet came over to me and said, "What happened to your face, you're bleeding?" . . . I noticed that blood was running down my sleeve . . . I couldn't walk. He picked me up and carried me into the . . . War Memorial Hospital. I was taken to the operating room, where Major Crawford removed shrapnel from cheek, thigh, right arm and eye socket. He called me a very lucky lad.

The nurses tended the wounded and Rene says this of them:

One is amazed at the energy, courage and effort required of a nursing sister, whose duties never slacken or cease. Going from one bed to the other, lending a tender hand, a cheerful word no matter how tired she may be, one cannot help but admire them. After supper was over, the little nurse came to my bedside before going off duty to wish me a Merry Christmas.

The next day a Canadian officer moved Rene to the Hong Kong Hotel. They were shelled en route, taking cover where possible, but were covered by earth as a shell hit nearby. It was not a Merry Christmas, for Rene soon learned "That our Forces had surrendered the Island of Hong Kong in the afternoon of December the 25th."

The war was over for "C" Force and their allies. What followed were years of incarceration under the most inhumane conditions of the Second World War. Rene's diary has infinite detail of certain events. There are notes of despair when each week became blurred into a series of months. Rene was in hospital when the surrender came. He recalls one awful story about a Canadian officer who was convalescing from a gunshot wound and was subsequently killed with a hand grenade when he tried to stop a Japanese soldier from raping a woman. Rene says:

> There were many other instances where law governing
> warfare was ignored—wounded Canadians beheaded,
> others tied with wires, their shoes removed and then
> made to walk at the point of a bayonet. Those who could
> not were killed. We had been told that the Japanese
> would not take prisoners while in combat, their code
> being, "the winner wins, the loser dies."

The Canadians were rounded up and moved to North Point Camp on the Island of Hong Kong. The place was a shambles, huts falling apart, wooden beds, and toilet facilities consisting of poles along the sea wall upon which the prisoners had to balance, with the strong winds making it impossible to relax for a moment. Rene records, "Each hut 200 x 20 feet housed 180 men, twelve inches between each set of bunks." It was here that the number "354" was sewn onto all Rene's clothing; he had become a number—a number he will never forget.

**Number 354,
one year after capture**

Garbage and human waste attracted millions of flies and in no time dysentery ravaged the camp. Rene spent six days in the hospital with "total abstinence of food of any kind . . . and on my discharge I was seven pounds lighter." The quality and quantity of food got worse and worse. Rene ceased smoking because those who could would trade part of their meagre ration for a smoke. In March 1942, an event happened that deepened the rift between the officers and men, as "the officers drew their first money." A lieutenant got thirty yen, a captain sixty-five, and a major 120 yen per month. "The officers could now buy extra food and cigarettes." The men would get a small allowance later when they were forced to work outside of the camp. The only attempted escape, by four Canadians from North Point Camp, happened just after the rainy season. Rene recalls:

> They had timed the guard on his rounds and found that
> at eleven p.m. there was no guard covering the area near
> the hospital. They had made arrangements with a
> Chinese sampan operator they had met on a work party
> to get them to the mainland. At the appointed hour they
> made a clean getaway over the perimeter fence. Next day
> the escape was discovered, and they were beheaded by the
> Japanese without any trial or explanation. At the camp the
> prisoners were formed up on the square for hours in the
> rain. Finally everyone was ordered to sign a pledge not to
> escape. All did but one. He was so mistreated that he
> returned after six days, a broken man, crying and out of
> his mind. His stubbornness did not pay off, poor lad.

Work parties began in a big way. Very heavy tasks, little food and long hours. One task was to "enlarge the Kai Tak Airport on the Mainland." For this the POWs received "fifteen cents per day for a NCO and ten cents for a private." A tin of sardines cost $3.25, thus it took over a month's work to purchase one. At the end of June 1942 there was no longer meat in the ration. Beriberi then struck the prisoners. In Rene's words:

> It was like a continuous electrical pain going up and
> down the leg muscles. At times a numbness of the legs, as
> if they were freezing, then so hot. Some ran water over
> their feet to stop the pain, but this stopped the
> circulation, the foot turned black, toes rotted and this
> necessitated amputation.

On September 26 all POWs were moved to Shamshuipo Camp on the Chinese mainland; this was for all nationalities captured at Hong Kong. The conditions were beyond description. Rene continues:

> There were no beds, just a platform three feet off the
> ground. Each man had a three-foot space, alongside
> another. The platform was oozing with bedbugs and

fleas. Only when totally exhausted could a man sleep.
When we tried to sleep outside on the ground the
Japanese stopped the practise.

It will come as no surprise that these conditions would cause
another epidemic—this time it was diphtheria. "The death rate
mounted quickly, soon to reach a daily average of five." It was only after
eighty-nine POWs had died from diphtheria that the Japanese High
Command finally did something. Rene remembers that "A doctor Saito
visited and he put the blame on the Prisoner Medical Officers; he got so
mad he hit them in the face with a piece of hose." The senior Canadian,
Dr. Crawford, stood up to Saito and said, "If the Japanese are so
concerned over the great number of deaths in camp, why did they not
send serum?" After a few more days serum did arrive and the doctors
finally got the disease under control.

As if all the foregone events were not enough, a Japanese sergeant
came to the camp. He had spent time in British Columbia before
returning to Japan. The POWs called him the "Kamloops Kid" and his
first words were, "You are to obey all commands; if you disobey you will
be punished." Rene writes in his diary, "The brutality perpetrated by
this Japanese madman continued until we left for Japan on January 19,
1943." (When the war was over the War Crimes Court tried and
sentenced this particular sergeant to be hanged.)

An official of the Red Cross came to inspect. Food was trucked in,
Red Cross parcels were promised and, in general, a totally false picture
shown. No one was allowed to approach the official. The next day, when
the visit was over, the trucks came and took all the food and amenities away.

In December, Rene developed a very bad pain in his eyes. The
doctor ordered him to take his bedding and move to the hospital area.
After seventeen days of thinking, "Am I going blind?" he asked to go
back to his hut. His eyes got no worse and a pair of borrowed dark
glasses seemed to help.

Rene and some 800 Canadians were then loaded aboard the *Tatuta
Maru* and taken to Japan. They sailed for three days under the most
appalling conditions with no chance to visit the lavatory. The ship
docked at Nagasaki. With over 100 men in each rail car, the POWs
were taken to Kobe where 300 got off. The remainder, including Rene,
went on to Yokahama, where they were to work in the shipyards. The
work was hot and dirty and required very heavy lifting. By April Rene
had a serious problem with haemorrhoids. In no time the British
doctor in the camp was told to operate. When the Japanese were told
there was no anaesthetic the reply in Japanese was, "It's all right, this is

a small operation, it will not hurt." This event gained Rene a week off work. He will never forget the British doctor's words: "Well, son, I'll make it fast!"

The strain of imprisonment was getting to all of them and Rene wrote, "I was very discouraged. I had a young lad next to me—he was crying—the strain had been too much for him. I thought, will this never be over?" Rene's diary reflects his feelings in two sentences:

> February, March, April and May always the same, work-work.
> June, July and August, those miserable months—that suffocating heat and those damn flies.

Food got scarce and Rene said, "I was so hungry that I couldn't lift the sledge hammer to work on the pipes. I was down to ninety-eight pounds." The civilian workers tried to help the prisoners when they could. At long last a parcel from Canada came, the first and the last! Christmas 1943 came and went; one Red Cross parcel per man was issued. In January 1944 Rene was elated when eight letters arrived from home, dated 1942 and 1943 and complete with snapshots of family. The POWs who received no mail got to read their friends' mail, which helped to raise their spirits. Things were looking up, and in June the Japanese workmen told them that France had been invaded. The next exciting event occurred when Allied aircraft bombed Japan. In February they watched US B29s bombing and saw five shot down. The skies over Tokyo were all in flames. Rene wrote, "The most exciting night of our internment had come to an end."

In the first week of May the prisoners were told "to pack up and be ready to move to the northern part of Japan." The Canadians were to work in the coal mines. These are Rene's graphic words about his first time underground:

> We entered the tunnel and boarded a little train, which was lowered down the slope by a steel cable. This tunnel was the outlet for the hot air coming from the coalface; the heat was over 100 degrees. My clothes were wet with thick steam. I felt tightness in my heart. It seemed that we were leaving behind everything that was alive. My only comfort—I was not alone.

The descent went on right up to the coal face. Very soon the manual labour took its toll with blistered hands, feet burning hot, sulphurous water pouring out of the rock with the dreadful smell of rotten eggs. All of this was too much and one day Rene fainted. Work did not improve for the 5'3" soldier; he could not get the drill to the roof of the rock face so he was sent to work on the coal pile.

Air raids, rumours and stories from the Japanese made it obvious that the war was coming to an end. Then it happened. In the words of Rene Charron:

> August 17th—We're back on the job again filling those coal cars, but we can sense a feeling in the air. Something is up. They [the guards] are not acting as usual. They are listening to the radio in the shack next to the coal pile. The telephone rings. The Japanese answers, "*Mooshee, Mooshee, Hai . . . Wakaru* (Hello, Hello, Yes . . . I understand / literal translation)." He came up to us and said "*Shegoto Shemai* (stop working)." When we marched into camp the officers told us, "The war is over." My friend Brunet cried out with tears in his eyes, "We made it—we came a long way, but it's over now." What a feeling to be free at last!

It may seem as if the rest of the story would be an anti-climax, but not so. Next came the period of adjustment. The first change was not freedom, but food. The men searched the countryside for food, trading blankets and clothing taken from the Japanese soldiers. One lad was cooking over a small fire and when asked what was in the pot he said, "I've got chicken, onions, potatoes and carrots and I'm going to eat the whole damn thing, even if I roll over and die of a bellyache." The Americans parachuted food and cigarettes from fighters and on August 28th a B29 bomber dropped a note saying that soon a squadron of bombers would drop supplies. The note read:

> To the guys below
> I am in Saipan and will soon fly for 16 hours to your location. Hope we find you all right.
> Don't know how soon you will be out of that hole but we are going to drop supplies and say hello in one form or another.
> If some of you are in the States soon, I would appreciate a card. My address is:
> Lt. Reeves Byrd
> 1713 Greenleaf Drive
> Royal Oaks, Mich, USA.

(Eventually Rene did write and heard from the pilot's father. His son survived the war.)

Along with the food that was dropped came complete US uniforms. On September 9th they left the camp, were checked by doctors and then went aboard the USS *Iowa*. Rene says, "We could see the dockyards where we had worked. The American sailors gave us their bunks and treated us with such kindness." Next day a doctor said that Rene was fit to fly home by way of Guam, 1,550 miles away, island-hopping across the Pacific to Oakland, California, where the ex-POWs were greeted by a Canadian officer with funds for the rest of the way home. The sixty Canadians went by train to Vancouver, where Canadian uniforms were issued. Rene wrote in his diary, "29 September. We are on our last mile of our long journey. We'll be in Montreal at noon. I'm so excited I can't sit still." The two Montreal men, Rene and his friend Brunet, were met by a major general; they walked down the platform of Windsor station and there "was my mother, she broke through the crowd and held me so tight I could hardly breathe. I learned my dad had died a few months before my release." What of Mary? Rene says, "She was overseas with the Montreal (Eaton) Masquers Concert Party, playing the bagpipes for the troops."

Lt. Mary Charron, piper with the Montreal (Eaton) Masquers Concert Party, 1945

Mary was rushed home by ship to Halifax and by plane to Dorval. Rene closes his diary with the following:

> Mary arrived at Dorval and when I saw that silvery plane in the sky I felt such happiness and gratitude. At last, this moment for which we had been waiting and longing had come. We were together again.

When I asked Rene what sustained him through all those weeks, months and years, he said:

> I was a section leader; some nights I would hear one of
> the younger men crying on the sleeping platform.
> I would go and talk to him. While I was doing that for
> him I was doing it for myself. This had a great effect on
> me. It was that incentive to help my men that helped me.

All these years later Rene can speak of Hong Kong and Japan, the brutal treatment, lack of food, sickness and above all the endless days in captivity. He remembers the cruel guards: the "Frog," the "Black Prince" and the "Kamloops Kid." He also remembers the doctors who did their best to stop people from dying of their wounds and infectious diseases. He will never forget friendships forged in the fire of war.

As the POWs came home, the terrible losses from the battlefield, prisons and forced hard labour camps became public knowledge. The siege of Hong Kong lasted but days and the Canadian infantry from the Royal Rifles of Canada and Winnipeg Grenadiers were in some of the fiercest of battles. The total battle casualties from the Quebec City Regiment were seven officers and 253 other ranks. The Manitoba Regiment lost fifteen officers and 253 other ranks. There were four killed by the Japanese after capture, another nine died of wounds at time of capture. The figures go on and on, with sixty-seven officers and 1,349 other ranks returning, most in very poor health. The fatality rate for Hong Kong POWs was higher than those imprisoned by the Germans. At Hong Kong in the Commonwealth War Graves Cemetery at Sai Wan Bay there are 283 Canadians and at Stanley there are another twenty buried. In Japan at Yokohama there are the cremains (ashes) of 137 Canadians. At the ceremony at Sai Wan Bay in Hong Kong on November 11, 1994, Prime Minister Chretien said of the Canadians at Hong Kong:

> They went into battle against veteran enemy troops.
> They did so without hesitation—with confidence—with
> audacity. They carried the fight to the enemy,
> counterattacking even in the final hours. No troops ever
> fought more bravely or with greater skill against more
> hopeless odds. . . . Today we enjoy the legacy for which
> they paid. Let the generation remember today how that
> peace was won.

Roger Cyr, current president of the Hong Kong Veterans' Association, said on television recently, "There are some 465 to 470 of our friends left alive." The story of Hong Kong and Japan comes to a close with court cases demanding financial benefits for the veterans of "C" Force being presented at the United Nations. The case is not closed.

Rene was released from the Canadian Army in 1946, in Montreal, with the rank of warrant officer second class. In 1948, Rene and Mary moved to Valleyfield, Quebec, where Rene took on a senior secretarial position with Montreal Cottons (now Dominion Textile) at a salary of $50.00 a week. Mary died of cancer in 1951, leaving Rene with a three-year-old daughter, Patricia. Rene then married Madeleine in 1952, and they have two children, Jocelyne and Daniel. In 1990, Rene and Madeleine moved to Vanier to be close to their children and three grandchildren. Their son Daniel, a former major in the Armoured Corps, brought this story to me in January 1995. Rene is also a long-time member of the Valleyfield Branch of the Royal Canadian Legion.

Although the many years of suffering at the hands of the Japanese have taken their toll on Rene's body and soul, his wife and children are the first to say that he has always maintained a positive outlook on life. Indeed, surviving an experience such as this has made Rene, as well as his family, appreciate every moment of freedom life has to offer.

On 24 December 1995, Daniel phoned me to say his dad had died on 20 December, almost fifty-four years after he had been captured in Hong Kong.

The Charron family in Vanier, Ontario, June 1994

CHAPTER **8**

THE MERCHANT NAVY

BUD DOWNING

The Second World War segment of this book would not be complete without a Merchant Navy veteran's story. In November of 1999 I met such a veteran at the Bells Corners Legion: Bud Downing, whom I interviewed in late March of the following year.

The story of Bud Downing follows the path of many of the Canadians who served in the Merchant Navy in the Second World War. Bud's account follows:

> In early 1945 I was on the train heading for Halifax from Prescott, Ontario to join my first ship, *Hillcrest Park*. I signed aboard on March 6, 1945. The ship was alongside being loaded and I was assigned to the "black gang," shovelling coal. It was typical of the times, for my training in Prescott had been for oil, not coal fire engine rooms.
>
> The convoy formed up in Bedford Basin, about two hundred ships. Afterwards an American convoy joined us and it was said at that time that there were about a thousand ships. The escort consisted of an aircraft carrier, cruisers and many small escorts. On that trip we lost one ship to enemy action. We could make about nine knots and it took us over two weeks to cross the Atlantic. Thank goodness the *Hillcrest Park* was not assigned to "dead man's corner"—the rear left of the convoy. This was the ideal place for German U-boats to pick off stragglers.
>
> The ship went up the Thames River and docked just outside of London to empty the general cargo of lumber, food and other stores. The ship was then turned around

A "Park" ship

and came home empty in ballast. The return trip was
stormy, with three crewmembers receiving broken bones.
When we returned to Halifax, I "signed off ship." The
crew was asked if they wanted to sign on again, but as I
had trained as an oil-fired engineer I said NO and went
back to the Manning Depot in Montreal, where I was
given a week off.

I did not get an "oil-fired" ship as I had hoped. In
June 1954, I was signed on to the *Bloomfield Park*; it was
4,700 tons—almost half the size of my previous ship. She
was loaded with lumber with one-quarter of the cargo
being whiskey. We sailed for Greenland as a single ship
with no escort; it took two weeks' sailing to reach our
destination. I remember well that we never got into the
hold carrying the whiskey!

The ship went from port to port along the coastline,
where the fog and ice were hazards to navigation. There
were lookouts everywhere, but still we managed to hit an
iceberg! We got ready to abandon ship. The iceberg was
over nine storeys high, and we received a dent in the hull.
In the morning all we could see was icebergs everywhere.
We were loaded with Greenland cryolite [consisting
mainly of sodium-aluminum fluoride], so ballast was not
needed on our journey home.

When the war ended on VE Day, Bud was at sea and to celebrate
everyone was given just one shot of rum. Bud's ship continued on to

Boston and was in Port Alfred, Quebec, when VJ Day was celebrated. This time the crew got no rum at all!

In October 1945, Bud left the Merchant Navy. It was not long before he decided to leave home again and in 1951 he joined the RCAF, hoping to work on jet engines, but he never did. Bud's trade was electronics and he served for over twenty-six years, retiring as a flight sergeant. After taking off his light blue uniform, he worked for another twelve years as a civil servant in the field of electronics.

Bud's service in the Royal Canadian Legion began in 1945 and he still is a member of Branch 593 in Bells Corners, where he is past president and a life member. Bud and Shirley were married in 1952 in Germany where they were both serving at the time. To close Bud's story I have included this poem written by him.

TOO YOUNG

Too young to fight in Army brown
A laughing boy from a small town
Or gaunt farm lad both tried and true
Too young to fly in Air force blue

Yet old enough to sail through hell
To steer the ship through flack and shell
Deliver needed guns and stores
To far and distant shores

No shiny braid, no medals bright
When on his watch on cold black nights
No uniform or shiny crest
Where wind and waves did crest

He always saw the jobs were met
To work in cold on wind-swept deck
In wind and rain or driving snow
Or stir the fires of hell below

At seventeen, a man of steel
Who shovelled coal or took the wheel
He would not wait another year
To do his bit, he showed no fear

Oh he was young, too young to fight
But not too young to die some night
In bitter flame he's paid the cost
In waters cold, alone and lost

They came from every town and farm
To join the fight, keep friends from harm
And many died beneath the sea
Remembered by a few like me

No uniform was in their kit
In dungarees they sailed the ship
No dress of white or brown or blue
To take the cargo through

Too young to fight, too old to stay
Our brave young men were made that way
With courage, pride from deep inside
They did the job to stem the tide

So when you think of wars gone by
Of soldiers, sailors, airmen, try
To think of your brave merchant team
The old, old men of seventeen.

Bud Downing

Bud Downing

CHAPTER 9

ALMOST A CANADIAN VICTORIA CROSS FOR GREAT VALOUR IN KOREA

ERNEST POOLE

WHEN THE TIME CAME for a Korean War story, I recalled all those whom I had not been able to include in my 1994 book *Korea Volunteer*. Les Peate, the national secretary of the Korea Veterans' Association, came up with the citations concerning a Canadian Medical Corps corporal who was recommended for a Victoria Cross, the highest award for bravery in the British Commonwealth.

It took many months of research to locate Ernest Poole DCM, now retired in Bolton, Ontario. Lieutenant Colonel H. Wood wrote up Corporal Poole in *Strange Battleground* (1966). The Commonwealth Division commencing on 3 October 1951 conducted the action; all infantry battalions were involved plus artillery support. The operation had the code name COMMANDO. Here follows the story of Corporal Ernest Poole. The paragraph from Chapter IX reads:

> Corporal E.W. Poole, the NCO in charge of the "B" Company [2RCR] stretcher-bearers, was awarded the Distinguished Conduct Medal for the courage he displayed while evacuating the wounded. The first casualties, in particular, were struck down among thick underbrush on steep slopes. Poole searched them out under heavy fire; his disregard for his own safety enabled him to save the lives of at least five men.

The actual statements made to the commanding officer, Bob Keane, gives a much clearer picture from the eyewitnesses. Here are the words from the 4 platoon commander, "B" Company 2 RCR written on 5 October 1951, by Lieutenant Eric Devlin:

> On 4 Oct 51, during the United Nations' autumn offensive, "B" Company was committed in a leading role.

During the first phase of the attack my platoon was
leading and we reached our objective successfully. In the
second phase my platoon was in reserve.

While in reserve, at approximately 1745 hrs, I
learned that Lt W.D. Smallman, commanding 6 platoon,
had been wounded and his platoon had suffered a good
many casualties. I was ordered forward with my platoon
to take over the assault. We proceeded through the area
occupied by 6 platoon, and encountered intense enemy
small arms and shellfire. My platoon lost two wounded at
this time, and the remainder succeeded in reaching a
ridge two hundred yards to the front.

As I passed through 6 platoon, I observed Cpl Poole
tending the wounded. There was intense fire all around
him, yet he dodged his way from one man to the next,
with complete disregard for his own safety. When my
men were wounded he went to them immediately and
told me to go on, that he would see they had good care.
He threw himself down beside them and proceeded to
apply tourniquets, despite machine-gun fire in heavy
volume.

Early in the evening Cpl Poole came forward to me
and asked for men to be a stretcher party. I gave him
what men I could spare, and he continued to other
platoons to seek more men. He also managed to get
some Koreans to act as bearers and with them he started
out for the RAP [Regimental Aid Post] in darkness. A
section leader from 6 PL was detailed to lead the
stretcher party but he was wounded before they had gone
more than a few yards. Cpl Poole then assumed
leadership of the party and led it back to the RAP. He
returned at 0400 and went forward with us when we
completed our assault in the early morning.

During all the time that I saw Cpl Poole tending the
wounded, he was cheerful and devoted to the work he
was doing and at no time did he appear to give thought
to his own safety. His confident manner and his coolness
under fire gave great encouragement to all my platoon.

Private Roach was the "B" Company radio operator and his
viewpoint was from company headquarters. His story follows:

I am the 88 set wireless operator with Coy Head-quarters, "B" Company, 2nd Battalion RCR. On 4 Oct 51, "B" Company was leading in the battalion's part of the offensive of the United Nations. At approximately 1730 hrs we came under heavy enemy fire and L/Cpl Turgeon, the 300 set operator, was wounded in the stomach by machine-gun bullets. Cpl Poole, the company medical assistant, rushed forward to give him aid. There was severe enemy fire coming at us, and in a few minutes, Pte Riddler, the Artillery signaller, was mortally wounded, and Captain O'Brennan [actually a lieutenant], the forward observation officer, was also wounded.

In spite of the casualties, and in spite of the heavy volume of fire, Cpl Poole went from one to the other of these wounded and administered first aid, applying tourniquets and giving morphine. Cpl Poole carried each of the wounded back below the crest of the hill, out of the line of direct fire. Each time he returned for one of the men, he submitted himself to extreme danger, yet he was calm and cheerful throughout. I called to him to keep his head down, that he was going to get killed, and he answered, "I can't help it, I have a job to do and I'm going to do it."

Cpl Poole's courage and devotion to duty was beyond anything I have ever seen and his example gave all of us great encouragement.

Later that evening I saw Cpl Poole improvising stretchers from blankets and branches of trees, and lashing the wounded, who now numbered ten, onto the stretchers by using heavy vine as rope. He organized a carrying party from the platoons and Korean labourers, and started back with them to the RAP, which was about 3000 yards away, across extremely difficult country. All but one of the wounded were stretcher cases.

As Cpl Poole's party started out toward the RAP, they came under machine-gun fire from a tank on the right flank. Cpl Poole changed his route, and escaped from the fire, then proceeded back over unfamiliar ground, in darkness, to the RAP. During all this time the entire area was under heavy machine-gun and shellfire.

The regimental doctor with 2 RCR was Captain H.C. Stevenson, and his task was to treat all of the wounded at the Regimental Aid Post. His statement contains the opinion of the unit doctor. His praise follows:

> On 4 Oct 51, during "B" Company's offensive, L 800192 Corporal Poole E.W., RCAMC, gave outstanding service, showing the greatest bravery. His prompt and skilful treatment of the wounded undoubtedly saved the lives of at least one officer and three soldiers, as well as preventing the probable capture of two others.
>
> "B" Company first encountered stiff opposition at about 1100 hrs, losing two men wounded and one killed. Cpl Poole gave first aid, and then went forward with the advancing company.
>
> At about 1730 hrs "B" Company came under heavy fire from small arms, medium machine-gun and mortar fire. Two officers and seven other ranks were wounded, and one OR killed. Cpl Poole went forward under very heavy fire, with complete disregard for his own life, and treated these men on the spot. He then organized stretcher-bearing parties and led them back to Company HQ. He and his party were under heavy crossfire the whole time.
>
> If Cpl Poole had not evacuated these men as promptly as he did, at least two of the wounded would have fallen into Chinese hands because the positions were being overrun.
>
> After arriving back at Company HQ, Cpl Poole was faced with the task of evacuating two officers and seven ORs more than 3000 yards, over very rough ground, in the darkness and with every possibility his party might be surprised by Chinese patrols, which were becoming active. Cpl Poole carried out this task with determination and courage, and brought the wounded to the RAP.
>
> On examining the casualties, I found they had been exceptionally well attended. Splints, stretchers and tourniquets had been improvised in a remarkably skilful manner under extremely difficult circumstances, and the wounded were all comfortable and in good spirits.
>
> Due to the high degree of initiative, ability and complete disregard for his own life on the day of 4 Oct

51, the lives of one officer, ZB 4069 Lt W.D. Smallman, and three ORs, D 800228 L/Cpl Turgeon R.P., B 800210 L/Cpl Souliere E.R., and G 850154 Pte Davies A.J., were saved. His reassuring manner and high moral fibre inspired confidence and alleviated the anxiety and suffering of the casualties.

Cpl Poole's actions cannot be too highly honoured. I have never known a man with more courage, initiative, and disregard of personal safety, with such sense of duty and such a high standard of morals and personality.

Cpl Poole's work has been highly praised by his company commander on several occasions. He has been faithful and consistent in the performance of his duties, and has earned a reputation in his company and in the battalion that few men could equal.

Colonel Bob Keane had this citation written on 21 Oct 1951, concerning Cpl Ernest William Poole, and recommended him for the Victoria Cross:

CITATION

On 3 Oct 51 the 2nd Battalion, The Royal Canadian Regiment, was moving forward against enemy opposition as part of a general attack launched by our own forces.

"B" Company was ordered forward from the NAECHON feature, an intermediate objective, to the final object on the right flank of the battalion, the feature NABU'RI.

At 1745 hours No 6 Platoon came under very heavy and accurate Enemy small arms and mortar fire from the left flank and intense machine gun fire from the right flank. Within a few minutes, a dozen casualties had been suffered by the platoon, some of them critical. Because of the steep slopes and thick underbrush it was not possible to determine precisely the nature and location of all the casualties, and there was a real danger that some of them would be lost to the enemy where they fell.

L 800192 Corporal Poole, W.E., RCAMC was the NCO in charge of stretcher bearers with "B" Company during this operation; his actions in dealing with the casualties suffered gave evidence of courage of the highest order under enemy fire and contributed very markedly to the ultimate success of the operation.

Corporal Poole proceeded forwards through intense enemy mortar and shellfire to render first aid and arrange for the evacuation of the wounded. He was warned that he could be killed but he insisted, "I have a job to do and I am going to do it." He searched meticulously the whole area and did not stop until satisfied that all casualties had been accounted for. Enemy artillery and mortars were harassing the area, and enemy snipers and machine gunners made any movement hazardous; but nothing could deter him in his search for the wounded. Two of the casualties were again hit while he was tending them but he continued with unruffled calm to render aid.

While still under fire Corporal Poole improvised stretchers from rifles and branches of trees; he bound the casualties securely by using thick vines. He moved from man to man with complete disregard for his own safety; his steady hand and quiet courage brought relief to all the wounded.

No. 5 Platoon was ordered to pass through No. 6 Platoon in order to maintain the momentum of the attack. They too, came under heavy fire and suffered serious casualties. Corporal Poole was on hand at once and urged the platoon commander, "Go on, I will see that your men get good care."

When the wounded had been prepared for evacuation, Corporal Poole led his party of bearers back some 3,000 yards in the dark to the Regimental Aid Post. The route was subjected to continuous shellfire. Enemy patrols had infiltrated along both sides, the area was heavily mined, and even the natural hazards were enough to deter any but the very brave. But Corporal Poole led his party with confidence and all the casualties were borne safely to the Regimental Aid Post. Undoubtedly his leadership and the persistence with which he carried out his duties against any odds was vital in saving the lives of one officer and three other ranks and in preventing two of the wounded from falling into the hands of the enemy.

Throughout the day of 3 Oct, all that night and the next day, Corporal Poole continued his task of attending the needs of the wounded. Whenever first aid was required, he was present to administer it. He was utterly tireless in his work. During the operation one thought only dominated his action: that his duty was to tend his wounded comrades. No obstacles, no hazard, no personal danger, was allowed to stand in his way; his selfless devotion to his work was in the highest traditions of military service.

Corporal Poole's conscientious determination to carry out his duties, his complete disregard for his own well being, his exemplary conduct under the most adverse conditions and his outstanding leadership resulted not only in saving the lives of five men and making possible the evacuation and treatment of many others but, even more, inspired his comrades to maintain

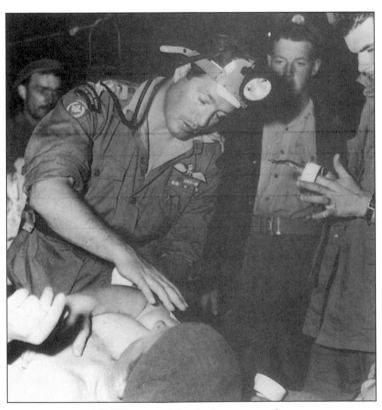

**2RCR casualties being treated at
25 Canadian Field Hospital, 20 May, 1951**

the fight and contributed largely to the successful
attainment of the objective.

The repetition in these four citations is obvious, but each one spells
out the courage and devotion to duty of this corporal. John M.
Rockingham, the brigade commander, supported the Victoria Cross
recommendation and passed this recommendation for a special award
on to Major General Cassels, commander of the Commonwealth
Division. On 23 January 1952 he downgraded the award to a DCM. In
that Ernest Poole's action did not have a direct effect upon the 25
Brigade battle it made the Victoria Cross inappropriate. Lieutenant
General Bridgeford approved the DCM on 9 February 1952.

When the final battle casualty list for COMMANDO was released,
Canadian losses were four killed and twenty-eight wounded.

When I contacted Ernest Poole in June and again in October 1996,
he truly wanted to forget his decoration of forty-four years before. He
said on 20 October 1996, "When I see what is happening in the
Canadian Forces today, I do not want to be associated with it or the
past." A sad ending for a career that had such a wonderful beginning.
After searching for a photo of Ernest Poole, I finally located one. This
picture of Ernest was taken at the RCAMC School in Camp Borden.
My thanks to Gordon Strathy, who located this group photograph.

This quote seems appropriate for this story:

> But the bravest are surely those who have
> the clearest vision of what is before
> them, glory and danger alike, and yet
> notwithstanding go out and meet it.
>
> Thucydides

Ernie Poole, DCM

PART II PEACEKEEPING

Canadian Brigadier H. Angle, first Chief Military Observer in India,
Pakistan. He was killed in a plane crash on 17 July, 1950.

CHAPTER **10**

THE BRIDGE BETWEEN WAR AND PEACEKEEPING

NED AND JEAN AMY

WHEN I BEGAN to write this book it became obvious that stories that had both wartime and peacekeeping events would strengthen my theme that wartime skills could become skills for peacekeeping. One such set of stories is that of Ned and Jean Amy. Ned Amy was my commanding officer in the Royal Canadian Dragoons in Petawawa Camp in the 1950s.

Ned's military career began in the fall of 1936 when he became a recruit at the Royal Military College in Kingston. Ned not being the tallest of people said that when the order came for "the tallest on the right, shortest on the left in one rank size," he knew that he would be on the left. Weighing 114 pounds on enlistment he saw a fourteen-pound gain by Christmas that first year.

The Second World War began in September 1939 and all the fourth- and third-year cadets were commissioned and sent to full-time duty in the Royal Canadian Navy, Canadian Army and Royal Canadian Air Force. Ned tried to enlist in the RCAF but failed the test when he had to rotate on a piano stool and still be able to stand and focus on the face of the civilian doctor. During the army medical the doctor said, "You are too short for the army." Fortunately his assistant intervened and said the

Ned Amy, 1939

rules had changed; and therefore Ned Amy became an officer in the Canadian Armoured Corps. Ned says:

> I ended up in Camp Borden at the Armoured Fighting Vehicle School with fellow classmates Stu Nicol, Dick Caldwell and Spike Hopkins. Our Commanding Officer was Lieutenant Colonel F.F. Worthington MM and Bar, MC and Bar. After a year at the school a group of officers and men were sent to Great Britain to serve with British units. I served with the Royal Gloucester Hussars and the 4th County of London Yeomanry. I returned to Canada in April 1941 and went to Brigade Headquarters as a liaison officer, but soon after I was moved to my first regiment.
>
> The Ontario Regiment, 6 Troop in "B" Squadron was my first command. The tanks were named "Bing," "Bang" and "Boom." In 1943 the Ontarios went to Sicily and in October I was promoted to major and sent to the Calgary Tank Regiment as a squadron commander.

It is here that the official history, *The Canadians in Italy*, by Lieutenant Colonel G.W.L. Nicholson (1957), has a story that explains how Ned won his first decoration—a Military Cross.

> On the climb up to San Leonardo, the leading tank struck a mine and blocked the road. Major E.A.C. Amy, the squadron commander, immediately led his tanks off to one side to continue the attack. . . . Finally at ten o'clock, five tanks—all that were left—broke into San Leonardo . . . when twelve German tanks approached . . . Amy, ordered to hold on, dealt with these in "a determined and gallant manner" . . . knocking out several, and driving off the rest. [Not mentioned in the book is that Ned was wounded in this action.]

The Calgarys began that battle on October 9, 1943 with fifty-one tanks and at day's end only twenty-four remained battleworthy. In 1944 Ned was chosen to leave Italy and return to England to join the Canadian Grenadier Guards, who were getting ready for the invasion of Normandy.

Before leaving Ned's story in Italy, I am reminded of a story he told me in Petawawa when I returned from a Mines and Booby Trap Instructor's Course in 1955. It was an event that had happened to Ned when his light weight saved his life. He was inspecting a Mark 4 Panzer

**Jean–graduation from the
Ottawa Civic Hospital**

tank, knocked out beside a building. Ned walked up a wooden plank, inspected the turret and was about to jump down on the same plank when his Jeep driver yelled, "Don't jump!" The plank was resting on a Teller mine, which the Germans had booby trapped. Ned's slight weight had not set off the trap on the way up to the turret, but had he jumped, the mine would have exploded.

Ned was the commander of Number One Squadron in December 1944 when he was named as second in command of the grenadiers. On February 25, 1945 the commanding officer, Lieutenant Colonel "Snuffy" Smith, was hit in his tank and lost a leg. Ned became the commanding officer. Ned saw the grenadiers through the heavy fighting in Germany, where the regiment lost over fifty percent of its tanks. The war was coming to a close, but the war in the Pacific was still raging. On June 13, 1945, Ned returned to command the tank regiment, which was to go to fight the Japanese. The atom bomb brought the entire war to an end. Ned closes this part of this story by saying, "Curt Greenleaf replaced me as CO, George Hale was a fellow squadron commander, Pat Grieve was the adjutant. All went on to command peacetime armoured regiments."

Jean Amy's account adds another dimension to the story. In 1937 she met Ned at Evangeline Beach in Nova Scotia. They continued to see each other during vacations until September 1939, when Ned joined the active army. Jean says, "I was at Acadia University, but despite my mother's plans for me, I went into nursing at the Ottawa Civic Hospital." After graduation Jean joined the army. She had hoped to serve overseas but that was not to be the case.

Jean's story continues:

> I was stationed at the St. James Military Hospital in Saint John, New Brunswick and was later sent to Sussex Military Hospital. I kept hoping for an overseas posting but the last military hospital unit had gone overseas and

our only hope was to be a reinforcement and that never
happened. Ned and I were still writing frequent letters
and in one memorable letter he proposed marriage. Since
he wrote the letter while lying under his tank. I assumed
that he may have been feeling depressed and might later
regret his proposal; so I decided to ignore the offer. Ned
was very amazed, as he was deadly serious. I later
suggested we wait to be married until he returned from
overseas!

When Ned returned to Nova Scotia he went to visit Jean and they
made the decision to get married. Jean's mother had just five days to
make the arrangements for the wedding. It was to be in the family home
on July 4, 1945. The wedding photo shows Jean and Ned in uniform.
Jean had to leave the army, as Nursing Sisters could not continue to
serve while married.

Jean and Ned, July 4, 1945

The remainder of this chapter is the story of how Cyprus began as
a peacekeeping mission. In the March 14, 1964 *Toronto Globe and Mail*,
there is a front-page story with a photograph of the very first
headquarters staff getting ready to leave Trenton for Cyprus. The photo
is reproduced here.

Ned Amy's letter of November 1, 1999 is reproduced here with no deletions, for it is only right that his memories not be changed.

Army Headquarters Planners under Brigadier Love were working on this in January 1964. I was director of Armour at the time and subsequently the Combat Arms directors were brought into the planning, presumably on the likelihood that one of them would command the contingent if it were decided to send one. Whether "A" for Amy or "A" for Armour, I know not; however, I was selected and was included in many of the planning meetings.

I recall we had difficulty finding maps of Cyprus and had very little intelligence and information on what was

Ned Amy, Vince Cook, Major Crowe, Capt. Murray; *at rear,* **Maj. Gen. Bernatchez;** *at far left,* **F/L Wilson**

happening on the island. Fortunately someone discovered
that Lawrence Durrell had written a book on Cyprus,
Bitter Lemons, and in short order it hit the best sellers' list
in the Ottawa bookstores. In the meantime our
information source was from Arthur Andrew, our high
commissioner in Cyprus, whose wonderfully descriptive
messages to external affairs were forwarded to us by Mr.
Menzies' office. These helped us understand the situation
as it was developing on the island; and their humour
brightened our day.

I believe the original thought for the composition of
the force was to be an infantry battalion with a small
contingent headquarters and support group. With time
and a better appreciation of the geography and the nature
of the conflict it became apparent that a reconnaissance
capability was desirable and eventually an anti-tank
capability as well.

The Royal 22nd was designated as the battalion and
the RCD was to provide the recce squadron. The anti-
tank element was scrubbed but in the fullness of time its
need was recognized and the anti-tank platoon joined the
battalion in Cyprus. It took time to locate some of the
staff officers and specialists for the contingent
headquarters and the support group, since many of the
potential candidates could not be spared from their
current employment. We were fortunate with those
selected and particularly so that Lieutenant Colonel
Vince Cook was available; a more competent, dependable
officer could not have been found to fill the key position
of AA&QMG [senior administrator]. Since
administration was the prime task of the headquarters, he
carried the load for the six months he was in Cyprus.

During this planning period, I had no contact with
either unit. My diary had an entry to visit them in
Quebec on 16 March and then on to Gagetown. On 14
March I arrived in Cyprus with the advance party, so my
first contact with both units was after they arrived on the
island.

Departure Ottawa/Trenton
The Contingent advance party left Ottawa for
Trenton around noon. I received final orders by

telephone from General Walsh, the CGS. I had no idea who it was when I was called to the phone and after a few pleasantries the chief said, "These are your orders." The phone was on a desk with not a scrap of paper or a pencil and I interrupted him in mid-sentence to explain that I had to get them. Every army officer who ever knew him will have a good idea of what he said about this. Fortunately Vince Cook had a pen and with the both of us listening on the same receiver, he wrote some notes on the back of a cigarette package. Apart from the details in the order, this was our mandate: "Canadian Contingent UN Forces Cyprus will use its best efforts to prevent a recurrence of fighting and as necessary contribute to the maintenance and restoration of law and order and a return to normal conditions." He explained that the House was in session and the decision whether to go or not was being debated. The call concluded when he wished us good luck.

G/C Howard Morrison, the AFHQ representative who was tasked to set up air transport arrangements in Cyprus, joined us in Trenton. In the late afternoon A/C Lane, commander, Air Transport Command, explained that if we didn't leave by 1800 hrs he would have to reposition air crew, and would I agree to depart before then. Since this seemed a major problem for them, I agreed after he said he would reverse the flight in mid-ocean if Parliament had not yet approved the operation. When we were several hours out over the Atlantic, we received the message that Parliament had approved.

Departure Marville, France

During a fuel stop in Marville on Saturday 14 March, I tried unsuccessfully to contact the Headquarters in London to get a SITREP on Cyprus. As we neared Cyprus the pilot asked me where we should land in case the Nicosia airport was closed. G/C Morrison and I eliminated both Greece and Turkey and agreed on Beirut. The need didn't arise.

Arrival Nicosia Airport (1900 hrs after dark)

G/C Jim Davies, the military attaché to High Commissioner Arthur Andrews, greeted me on the plane with news that the International Press wanted to interview me. My exit was somewhat undignified because when I went out the door I was blinded by the very bright lights focused on the exit. If Jim hadn't caught me I would have fallen down the ramp. I had vision of a newspaper headline "First UN troops arrive in Cyprus. The Canadian commander appeared to be intoxicated."

When we arrived General Gyani, commander, UNFICYP was in India so we were met by General Paiva Chaves, who was standing in for him, General Michael Carver, commander of the British Division deployed on the island, several Greek Cypriot officials, and the International Press. Nothing on the horizon was competing with the Cyprus crisis so they were there in great numbers and I found myself front and centre in a press interview. This was a new experience, for in 1964 soldiers steered clear of the press and politicians. What they asked and what I told them, I remember only vaguely.

In due course and to my great relief, I was whisked away by the two generals while the remainder of the advance party was led to temporary accommodation. I slept very poorly that night because a reporter pounded a typewriter in the adjoining room until well after 0300.

The Contingent

Initially the contingent comprised a headquarters, a support group and an operational element, made up of the First Battalion Royal 22eme Regiment command by Lieutenant Colonel Andrew Woodcock and the RCD Reconnaissance Squadron commanded by Major John Beament. On 17 April, Brigadier A. James Tedlie arrived with the advance party of his brigade headquarters from Petawawa, followed later by an additional 132 all ranks. This increased the size of the operational element and raised the strength of the contingent to slightly over 1,100.

Contingent headquarters and the support group were not under UNFICYP Command. They freed the operational element of a heavy administrative burden and permitted the contingent to be self-sufficient by providing such support as legal, discipline beyond the powers of the CO, medical, dental, chaplain services, supply and accounting, public relations, secure [restricted] communications to and from Canada, air transport, in-theatre leave arrangements, personnel replacements, soldiers' welfare and visitors from Canada.

Airport Ceremonial

General Chaves was anxious to greet each group on arrival. This necessitated alerting the troops about fifteen minutes before they touched down to be ready for an inspection immediately they left the aircraft. After a long flight, one could imagine their comments; however, the R22eR took this in stride and came storming out as though they had rehearsed this dismount for years. The unilingual English-speaking staff officers lined up as well and it was interesting to see them in front of the troops, reacting to French commands that they didn't understand. I recall a major who seemed to have one eye looking to his right and the other to his left, to see what everybody else was doing. We had many laughs with him about this.

Settling In

On arrival the troops from the battalion were billeted at Camp Troodos until they were deployed to their operational area and on day two we had our first crisis. The troops complained that the peas were the wrong sort for their soup. It pleased me greatly to send an urgent message to Ottawa pointing out this error. The next plane arrived with 500 lbs. of the proper peas with the compliments of the minister.

From the outset Vince Cook and his staff worked miracles and within a week the contingent headquarters was established in rented accommodation in Nicosia with the Canadian and UN flags flying.

During the period when the CO was busy with arrangements to relieve a British battalion in the line, his troops, to the delight of General Chaves, were touring the country in trucks showing the UN Flag. When he was satisfied with the mission assigned to his battalion, I released them to the commander UNFICYP and at 0500 hours on 27 March the regiment took over an operational area in the Nicosia/Kyrenia sector. It came under command of a British brigade that had been policing the sector and that now was also under UN command.

We and the other contingents, which were to follow, were fortunate that General Carver, commander of the British Division, which had been coping with the crisis on the island, remained to be deputy commander and chief of staff UNFICYP. If this had not happened, the early days of the operation would have been very difficult, as national contingents had limited intelligence of the situation in Cyprus and some contingents were not self-sufficient.

The Press

Captain Eric Luxton, our PR officer, was in his element and for the next few weeks kept arranging interviews that he convinced me the press wanted in order to ask about our contingent's role and our plans. In retrospect, I am not sure whether it was they or he who wanted these interviews. In the early days before we were clear on how UNFICYP would evolve, they kept asking me for our terms of reference. Since I considered these were too general to satisfy them and would simply lead to questions on detail for which I had no answers, I told them I couldn't disclose my terms of reference until I had discussed them with the UN military authorities; and to my great relief they accepted this explanation. Interestingly, the question most frequently asked was, "Are you going to disarm the island?"

The Canadian press was understanding, and I have great respect for those who were in Cyprus during those early days. There were many and I remember Charles King, David MacIntosh, Tingley (Ting), and later Ralph Allen. Former Governor General Romeo LeBlanc told me in 1998 that he had been there as well.

There was an amusing story of the press who congregated at the bar in the Ledra Palace Hotel waiting news of the next outbreak. One member couldn't get a place at the overcrowded bar so he left and then returned, shouting, "They are at it again in Kokina!" whereupon the bar emptied and he remained alone with a gin and tonic.

Contingent Commanders Meeting with Archbishop Makarios

Before our troops were deployed, General Carver arranged for the contingent commanders, then in Cyprus, to pay their respects to Archbishop Makarios. We met at the palace and after being formally introduced we went into the garden where some press photographers were waiting. It was a relaxed atmosphere and Makarios had his photo taken with the various contingent commanders. I remember when General Carver and I were standing beside him and a photographer said in a loud voice, "Mr. Carver, would you move over so Mr. Amy can stand next to Mr. Makarios." With some embarrassment and side-stepping around the general, I stood next to the archbishop, who smiled and said, "A Canadian photographer, I believe."

Ned meets Archbishop Makarios

Meeting with Dr. Kuchuk

When I paid my respects to Dr. Kuchuk, the vice-president, I was introduced to Turkish coffee, a drink for which I never developed a taste. I was at his residence on other occasions and he was always courteous and interesting to listen to. As time progressed one attended receptions given quite frequently by both sides in the conflict. The Turkish Cypriot receptions were invariably in the Saray Hotel on the Turkish side of the "Green Line," while those of the Greek Cypriots were in the

Ledra Palace on the other side. It was obvious that both groups were checking out who had failed to turn up.

The Anti-tank Platoon

During the planning phase, we suggested the inclusion of the battalion's anti-tank platoon but General Walsh ruled it out. The Greek Cypriots had a makeshift armoured vehicle converted from a bulldozer and known as "the pig." In time it was considered that it might be a potential threat so in a letter to Ottawa I jokingly mentioned that I had a nightmare of our soldiers being chased by the Pig. It struck a chord and out came the previously vetoed anti-tank platoon.

The Arrival of the Recce Squadron and the *Bonaventure*

We received word on Easter Monday that HMCS *Bonaventure* was due to arrive at Famagusta with the RCD Squadron on board. We had to veto our zealous PR officer's suggestion that we ask Captain Bob Timbrel to delay his arrival until first light for a dawn photo opportunity of the arrival of his ship. Our high commissioner, Arthur Andrews, General Gyani, Mr. Pelegaris and I, along with a host of other officials, went aboard to greet the RCD Squadron and the ship's captain.

Arrival of Brigadier Jim Tedlie's Brigade HQ

The contingent was well established by the time Brigadier Tedlie and his brigade headquarters arrived so they settled in very quickly. His takeover of the operational area from his British counterparts was on the basis of two experienced commanders with their staff's sorting out the details and agreeing on the arrangement and timings.

Visit of the Defence Minister

Understandably, we had many visitors to the contingent, but the most significant one was Defence Minister Hellyer's visit on 15 June as a guest of Arthur Andrews, our high commissioner. An outdoor reception was arranged for him with the R22eR at their location in the hills overlooking Kyrenia. I was seated next to him during lunch and he asked if we had any problems and I said only one: "The troops have been here for three months and have not been told how long they are to stay and obviously they and their families would like to know." I was asked what I recommended and I said, "Six months," to which he agreed and told me to tell them. His next question was, what did I think about the plan for integration and unification? Since I had never heard of either, he explained what he had in mind and with no prior knowledge of possible implications, I said saving money sounded great provided it didn't reduce the fighting capability of the army one iota. He said it wouldn't; he was wrong and it did.

Activities of the Contingent Commander

It turned out that I, as the contingent commander, had a less interesting job than either of the three commanders and the AA&QMG, each of whom had a challenge and were extremely active throughout their tour. I could not say this about my job. While I was free to sit in as an observer on the chief of staff's weekly briefings with his commanders, I was in no way involved with operations. I looked after some of the visitors and I represented the contingent at the many social events, which were frequent and popular throughout the period. My diversions were bridge in the evening in our mess, visits to the high commissioner's office for a chat, and the occasional game of bridge at his residence, and visits with Jim Tedlie.

The contingent was so well served by the AA&QMG and his staff that this minimized any activity with which otherwise I might have been involved. The odd disciplinary case and the occasional need to smooth a few ruffled feathers within the contingent were almost welcome breaks from the monotony. Six months without a meaningful activity was a long time. Eventually this changed and our contingent commanders had an operational responsibility as well.

In September when our time was up and our replacements had arrived, Vince Cook and I went to Kyrenia to await our flight home. As a Maritimer, I slept like a log with the waves pounding the rocks. When we landed in Ottawa the thing that most impressed me, after six months of continuous blue, sunny, cloudless skies, was to see a beautiful cloud!

So ends the story of Jean and Ned Amy with the 1956 photo of the Amy family on their way to a posting with SHAPE in Paris, France.

The Amy family, 1956

Chapter 11

AN EXCEPTIONAL PEACEKEEPER

DON ETHELL

THE SUBJECT of peacekeeping in this book has been restricted by space alone. Don Ethell retired as a colonel in Calgary after a career that spanned thirty-eight years. In those years, from the rank of rifleman to a senior colonel in the infantry, Don had served on fourteen tours as a peacekeeper. In 1989 Don was a guest on *Front Page Challenge*, representing Canadian peacekeepers. This story was the awarding of the 1988 Nobel Peace Prize.

Don Ethell's story was placed first in this section on peacekeeping because of the broad scope of his career. The fact is that so many aspects of "serving for peace" are recounted just by following Don's career. My first meeting with this Queen's Own Rifles soldier was at the Canadian Forces Officer Candidate School in Chilliwack when he arrived as a

Don stumping the panel

candidate on the Commissioned from the Ranks course. He came first
on the course and commanded the graduation parade of 7208. In this
photo he is accompanying Rear Admiral Stephens, commander
Training Command.

Don as parade commander at CFOCS with Rear Admiral Stephens

The first UN mission was the one created by Prime Minister
Lester B. Pearson, but it did not materialize for the First Battalion of
Queen's Own to go to Egypt for United Nations Emergency Force
(UNEF).

Don's description of the Calgary-to-Halifax flight is remarkable,
considering the equipment:

> The RCAF had to lift the 900-man battalion via two-
> engine, fifty-six passenger C119s, un-pressurized "flying
> boxcars," from Calgary to Halifax. I was on one of the
> advance party flights, which had engine trouble;
> therefore we made eight stops en route to Halifax.

When the Queen's Own arrived, they were housed at both
Stadacona Naval Base and Windsor Park, home of the First Battalion
Black Watch. Don's story continues:

> For those of us in "Stad" our mornings were spent on the
> Parade Square "impressing" the navy with our 140 paces
> per minute—Queen's Own Drill! And the afternoons
> were spent either touring Oland's brewery (free),

attending free movies in downtown theatres, or rowing naval whalers throughout the harbour. I don't think the Oland's brewery will ever forget the line of trucks dropping off soldiers in front of their canteen. Neither will the naval coxswains, vainly trying to convince sixteen soldiers to row together.

Since all of our stores and vehicles were loaded on the aircraft carrier HMCS *Magnificent*, we had periodic picquet duty on the ship. In fact, the hangers had bunks seven-high built to accommodate the troops en route to the Suez. Those of us who mounted the picquets were not looking forward to the long trip on the *Maggie*.

As was the army policy at that time, any posting of a year overseas allowed the married soldier to move his family, at government expense, to a selected place of residence anywhere in Canada. Don's explanation follows:

Unfortunately the deployment of the 1st Battalion was cancelled and we returned to Calgary. Although we were in the throes, due to President Nassar's objection to anything referring to the queen, of changing our name to the "1st Canadian Rifles," the decision was made to deploy Canadian logisticians and communicators. The battalion returned to Calgary via two large troop trains, arriving back in Calgary on Christmas Eve. This deployment was a serious lesson for the Canadian Army as most of the families of the married personnel had dispersed to Selected Places of Residence, and many homes and cars had been sold in anticipation of a long absence of the 1st Battalion. Although it did not affect a young single soldier, there were many "ticked-off" married riflemen.

Don Ethell's first peacekeeping mission was to Cyprus in 1965 as the third battalion to serve there. The RCAF was to provide a much more advanced aircraft. Don's account follows:

We deployed to Cyprus via a RCAF Yukon aircraft, a twenty-five-hour flight from Victoria to Nicosia with four fuel stops. Since, at least in the CO's opinion, tensions were still high on the island we arrived in battle order, with ammunition. I was in battalion HQ working as the records sergeant when a very unfortunate accident happened to my buddy Sgt. Bob Halpin. Bob was a recce sergeant working for Lieutenant Lew MacKenzie. Recce platoon headquarters was located across the valley from battalion headquarters (BHQ) in the Kyrenia Pass. On one of his first patrols Bob was returning from patrol in the mountains when a Turkish military vehicle cut him off, which caused his jeep to roll over. Although his driver was not hurt, Bob suffered severe back injuries and was med-evacuated by helicopter to the British military hospital. I was selected to replace Bob in recce platoon, joining Sergeants Len Quinlen, Fred Mueller and Platoon Sergeant Ken Snowden. What a great six months patrolling the mountains and the blistering lizard flats south of the mountains, including places accessed by only recce platoon.

Of course, Lew MacKenzie's idea of indoctrination for a new patrol sergeant was to lead him up the west end of the Kyrenia mountains, deliberately past a Greek military checkpoint, knowing that they would fire over the heads of the two Jeeps when you didn't stop. Another incident comes to mind when I was on a long-range patrol towards Morphou. I absentmindedly drove out of the mountains into "D" Company's HQ location. The then company commander Major (now retired Lieutenant General) Charlie Belzile proceeded to dissect a very trembling recce sgt. for moving into his area without permission.

During our many patrols we were continuously stopped and sometimes detained by the Greeks or the Turks, particularly the Turkish National Army. I had the dubious record of being "detained" eight times in one day. Another incident occurred very near recce platoon HQ when the Turks pinned down (by weapons fire) half of Bravo Company, commanded by Major Bill Crew, when they were moving up to the "Saddle" position. Recce platoon scrambled up and out to various "sneak and peek" positions. The CO, Colonel Kip Kirby, deployed the battalion mortars and 106 guns from Kato, and trained them on the Turk Bn HQ. He personally located himself in his Tac HQ and proceeded to tell the Turkish commander, "Lift your fire and let my troops move up or I will destroy this HQ including you and me!" Shortly thereafter Bravo Company carried on up the hill.

Don as a model for the new salute and new uniform

Major General Lew Mackenzie, in his book *Peacekeeper: The Road to Sarajevo* (1993), recalls an incident in Cyprus. One must remember that in 1965 all of the senior army instructors had served in the Second World War and/or Korea. They taught no-nonsense lessons based upon experience. General Mackenzie 's words to the wise came about on the subject of "sequence of command" if the leader was hit. "If I'm killed, Sergeant Snowden is in charge; if he gets it, Sergeant Ethel is in charge…" A sobering thought.

Right after Cyprus, Don was sent to Ottawa to "model" the new green uniform and new salute. This photo is from a press release of 1976; note that the badges are the ones proposed for all army units. Just the Cyprus ribbon is on Don's uniform.

It was Cyprus again for Don. He was a warrant officer by now and was Lieutenant Colonel Marsaw's Intelligence Section warrant officer. Afterwards there was a change in regimental affiliation and commissioning. In May 1984, after commanding a company in First Battalion PPCLI, Don was appointed second in command and with that came a promotion to lieutenant colonel. With the promotion came a posting to the Middle East. His story is as follows:

> I was posted to the Middle East as the Senior Canadian Military Observer (SCMO) to the United Nations Truce Supervisory Organization (UNTSO). Although an UNTSO officer, I was seconded to the United Nations Disengagement Observer Force (UNDOF) as their deputy chief of staff with specific duties as the senior liaison officer between the UN and the Syrian and Israeli armies. A number of significant events come to mind.
>
> Approximately six weeks following my arrival in Damascus, Syria, the deputy senior Syrian Arab delegate, Major Fawzi Darwich came to my office requesting the UN's assistance in a large prisoner of war (POW)

exchange with the Israelis. The POWs were those who had been captured prior to, during and following the 1978 Israeli invasion of Lebanon. The then chief of staff/deputy force commander, a Finnish colonel, was on leave in Jerusalem and, when briefed on the pending POW mission, refused to return and assume command. It was left to those of us in Damascus to get on with it.

Following frantic trips back and forth across the ceasefire lines on the Golan Heights to negotiate with the Syrians, Israelis and of course the International Committee of the Red Cross (ICRC), arrangements were finally made to exchange six groups of fifty Syrians (i.e., 300) for six Israelis, and to exchange hundreds of bodies. The operation was carried out within thirty-six hours of notification with agreement by both sides—who were still at war—that by necessity a number of various violations of the ceasefire would probably occur. I was able to convince both parties that when these violations occurred during the POW exchange, the UN would not accept "protests." The Israelis moved up armour and mechanized units just short of the ceasefire line, and the Syrians moved armoured military police units up to their side of the line. The exchange of goods and the bodies, ably assisted by Lieutenant Colonel John Guthrie and his troops from the Canadian Logistics unit (CANLOG) was carried off extremely well.

Then we came to the movement of fifty Syrians for each one of the Israelis. The first five groups moved across without significant problems; however the last group, consisting of all the Syrian POW officers including a general and the Israeli fighter pilot shot down over Beirut, almost led to war!

As for my duties as the Senior Canadian UNTSO, I had the opportunity to work with some outstanding officers. Those who served during my two years performed admirably, some under very trying conditions. The Camp Wars in Beirut were raging and the Israeli withdrawal into their self-proclaimed Security Zone in Southern Lebanon caused numerous incidents for our Canadians. Every few weeks I would travel across the mountains to Beirut to see the likes of Major Pat Chartres (RCA) and Lieutenant Commander Bill Koch and Lorne McDonald. When one sees the remains of the US Marine barracks where 364 marines were killed, the terrible conditions in the refugee camps and the devastation of the embassies in West Beirut, it reminds one of the cruelty of man.

In the south the Canadians continued to excel. As an example, Major Alain Couture (RCA) won the Medal of Bravery for rescuing an injured French officer under fire from the Israelis. Another incident involved Captain Red Grossinger (V11 CH) an officer who was held by one of the extremist groups for one hour with a .45 calibre pistol pointed at his head whilst they demanded compensation for an alleged wrong by the UN. Red's cool-headedness and professionalism prevailed as he successfully negotiated his own and his teammate's release.

I recall another incident involving our newly arrived Canadian commander of all Canadians deployed on UN duty in the Middle East, Brigadier General Douglas Yuill. In the summer of 1995 he assumed the duties as deputy commander UNDOF, however his Canadian responsibilities included command of those officers assigned to UNTSO. Being a dedicated soldier and leader, Doug would periodically accompany me on my sorties to Beirut, where he insisted on "running" the Green Line without UNMOs. Fortunately the general survived both Beirut and Southern Lebanon.

It is worthy to record at this stage another incident, which occurred after I departed UNTSO and UNDOF and was appointed as the director of Peacekeeping Operations in NDHQ, Ottawa. In 1988 I accompanied the then Deputy Chief of Defence Staff Vice Admiral Hugh MacNeil, on a staff visit to the Middle East in order that he could visit all of the Canadian contingents. During our visit an incident occurred in Southern Lebanon when one of our officers, Major Giles Cote (R22eR), whilst on patrol hit a mine. His Australian captain teammate was decapitated and Major Cote was seriously wounded. Due to the terrain in which they were patrolling and the hostilities in the area, it took the backup UNTSO patrol over an hour to find the Cote patrol. In the meantime, Giles Cote, with serious head and torso wounds, shattered hands, legs and ribs, was attempting to revive his mate. Giles crawled a kilometre in an effort to seek aid. He was eventually found and med-evac'd to the Ramdam Hospital in Northern Israel where the admiral and I visited him. Major Cote was returned to Canada for further treatment.

As the end of Don's two-year tour with UNTSO drew to a close, the Canadian commander, General Yuill, asked him to transfer to UNDOF and assume command of the Canadian contingent UNDOF. Included in his responsibilities would be command of the 220-man element of the Canadian logistics element on the Golan Heights in Israeli-occupied Syria. Don went on to say, "As this was an unaccompanied posting my wife, Linda, was forced to return to Canada for the year-long duration of my tour." Concurrent with his responsibilities as the Canadian contingent commander, Don was tasked by the Force commander to retain the position of senior liaison officer with the Syrians and Israelis.

Throughout the year, operational requirements were stressed for the Canadians in Camp Zuliani. Their activities included the acquisition of funding to revitalize the existing buildings and build comprehensive bunkers and other protective elements for the contingent. Subsequently, the Canadians who served in the Golan during the Persian Gulf War were appreciative of their efforts.

It was at this time that I met Don Ethell once again. I had been appointed project director of the Peacekeeping Monument and I found the director of Peacekeeping Operations one very busy man. Busy or not, he encouraged me to seek the advice of all of his staff when I wrote *The Canadian Peacekeeper*.

Don's story continues as the peacekeeping mandate continued. He reports that:

> Shortly after my arrival in Ottawa the UN decided to "monitor" the Soviet withdrawal from Afghanistan with a temporary mission named "The United Nations Good Offices Mission Afghanistan/Pakistan (UNGOMAP)." Although most of the contributing countries dispatched officers from existing UN missions, we decided to dispatch five officers directly from Canada. Due to the hostile action in the area and the potential for continuing conflict, we selected primarily those who had "proven themselves under fire" in the Beirut Camp wars and

Southern Lebanon. Led by Lieutenant Colonel Dave Leslie (RCR), Majors Pat Chartres (RCA), Geordie Elms (RCR), Doug Mair (R22eR), and Captain Murray Allen (RCR) headed off for their fascinating mission of observing a modern army implement a textbook withdrawal. Majors Chartres and Elms rode with the Soviets into the USSR and were subsequently returned to Kabul by UN aircraft. In the meantime, Colonel Dave and the others were running the show at the HQ in Kabul and Islamabad. However all was not peaceful in Kabul, as I recall receiving a call from Dave early one morning in which he stated, "Don, we had a minor incident here, which should be reported. While I was on the roof last night trying to sort out which faction was winning a firefight in Kabul, we received some artillery rounds in the courtyard. Nobody was hurt other than I was blown off the roof!"

If all of this were not enough, with Canada's troops stretched beyond comprehension, another part of the world erupted. Don's story continues:

Next came the ceasefire in the Iran-Iraq war, and the need to provide UN observers along the agreed ceasefire line. The provision of observers was relatively easy compared to the difficulties of inserting the signals element. Due to the size of the area and the need for a dedicated UN communications system, UNHQ in New York requested the services of a signals squadron from Canada. After a series of assessments by the operation staffs of Land Forces Command and NDHQ, a variety of options was presented by yours truly to the then UN Under Secretary-General for Special Political Affairs, Mr. Marack Goulding. Mr. Goulding opted for the recommended larger unit (a signals regiment instead of a squadron), which Canada subsequently provided.

USAF C5 aircraft from Trenton to both Baghdad and a NATO base in Turkey lifted our troops and equipment. As the US aircraft would not fly into Iran, ten Canadian C130 aircraft were positioned in Turkey to shuttle the loads from the C5 aircraft into various locations in Iran. Five C130 aircraft were required to lift the cargo of one C5 aircraft! Colonel John Annand

(RCR), whose professionalism, courage and competence were reflected in the Force commander's choice of John as his chief of staff/military assistant, initially led the Canadian contingent. Unfortunately Colonel John—who received the Meritorious Service Cross for his outstanding service in Iran/Iraq—was med-evac'd to Canada and tragically died three months later of cancer.

Don was next to work on the peacekeeping mission in Namibia, which saw the transfer of power from South Africa to the Namibians. This mission was the first time the Royal Canadian Mounted Police were involved. Don explains:

> Colonel Mike Jeffrey led the Canadian contingents of logisticians, signallers and military police. This mission has been and will continue to be referred to as the "ideal" UN mission, in that its mandate, unlike some others, was correct and provided the stability for an emerging country to "stand on its own." The success of UNIMOG is attributed to the successful integration of a UN police element, a large UN electoral unit and various other UN civilian agencies into a large UN military force.

Don's tour as DPKO was to come to an end with yet another UN peacekeeping planning mission. This time it was in Central America. Don says:

> During the period 1987 to 1990, and concurrent with the foregoing missions, Canada mounted a quiet involvement with Central America and the Arias Peace Plan (i.e., President Arias of Costa Rica). At the time it was apparent that the activities of Nicaraguan Contras had run their course and, following the forthcoming US presidential election, would cease to receive continued support from the USA. President Arias' plan for the five Central American countries appeared to provide the Central America Five (Costa Rica, Nicaragua, Honduras, Guatemala and El Salvador) with an opportunity to end the long series of civil wars.
>   Led by the Secretary of State for External Affairs, the Right Honourable Joe Clark, Canada was at the forefront of the negotiations and discussions. Obviously DND was part of the process. After a series of Canadian-sponsored meetings with various regimes in Central

America (Centam) the effort shifted to include the
United Nations. As a consequence I, along with a
colleague from the NDHQ policy branch Colonel Gerry
Thompson (RCR), was tasked to proceed to the various
Centam countries in an attempt to convince the various
militaries of the positive effects of a UN presence in their
respective countries. This activity was followed with a
number of trips to the area with Canadian political
leaders (as their military/peacekeeper advisors) in their
efforts to support the Arias Peace Plan. During one trip
Joe Clark asked me to develop an outline for the
insertion of a UN Observer mission into Central
America. Upon completion of the plan, Mr. Clark tabled
the plan in the House of Commons, and passed it to the
United Nations for consideration. It was accepted by the
UN and subsequently became the outline plan for the
ONUCA mission.

During the development of the UN plan for
ONUCA I was tasked to participate as the chief of
staff/deputy mission commander for the multinational
reconnaissance mission of the five Centam countries. A
well meaning but non-English-speaking Brazilian
general led our multinational group of sixteen countries.
The reconnaissance took four weeks, followed by
another two weeks in New York preparing the report
and presenting it to Under Secretary-General Marrack
Goulding. Regardless of the problems with the Brazilian
general, and with all due respect to the other
nationalities, it was fortunate that the staff included
some extremely competent Canadian officers,
Lieutenant Colonel Don Ferguson and Major Peter
Hornsby (Logistics).

Age fifty-five was approaching for Don Ethell, but it will come as
no surprise that his final posting was to be in the area where he had
excelled. Final postings are supposed to be a time to prepare for the
transition from soldier to civilian. Don's story continues:

After a very busy three years as DPKO, in June of 1990 I
was posted for what was supposed to be my final year of
service in the army. My position was that of chief of
Liaison Systems for the Multinational Force & Observers
(MFO), and as the Canadian contingent commander for

Canada's small contribution to the twelve-nation Force.

As it was an accompanied position, once again Linda joined me in the somewhat isolated existence in the desert. Regardless, due to my duties as the senior liaison officer, we traveled frequently to Tel Aviv and Cairo. Our quiet existence came to a sudden halt with the advent of the Persian Gulf War. The Canadian government ordered the Canadian dependants throughout most of the Middle East including El Gorah, out of the area, therefore once again Linda was sent home to Canada.

Although the MFO were not deployed in the "front line," the war caused considerable problems and restraints to the Force, in addition to its deployment along the Israeli/Egyptian border in the Straits of Tiran, between Egypt and Saudi Arabia. The increase in terrorism in the various refugee camps and the ingress of guerillas along our front on the Gulf also kept our Force hopping.

Although the personnel of the MFO were restricted from travelling to Cairo and Tel Aviv during the war, as senior liaison officer I was frequently in both capitals meeting with the Egyptian and Israeli military staffs. During my weekly visits to Tel Aviv I always took the opportunity to visit the Canadian Forces attaché Colonel Bill Minnis (PPCLI). Bill was the Canadian hero in Tel Aviv in that he, upon the commencement of the war, immediately organized the few remaining key embassy staff into an operational cell manned twenty-four hours a day, seven days a week.

Following the war, my duties changed in that the MFO requested an extension of my service in the Force as the chief of staff/deputy Force commander. The CO's position is usually held by a US officer; however, a bureaucratic issue precluded the arrival of the designated US officer. Therefore I remained in the MFO for an additional five months.

Don finally retired on 1 November 1991, but his retirement was to last less than a month, as he explains:

I received a telephone call from the colonels' career manager, an old Staff College classmate, Naval Captain "Bear" Brown, who quickly changed my status back to active duty. After only four weeks I had failed retirement!

My new posting was to the European community Monitoring Mission (ECMM) in Yugoslavia, a mission assigned to "monitor" the fighting and various ceasefires in the then-Republics of Yugoslavia. At this juncture please note that the United Nations had not yet arrived in Yugoslavia and therefore the ECMM was the only international body available to mediate and attempt to stop the killing.

Along with the twelve European (EC) countries, Sweden, Czechoslovakia, Poland and Canada provided "monitors." Although the other countries dispatched a strange mixture of military officers, diplomats and civil servants, Canada (and Ireland) sent only military officers. As the senior Canadian I was given the lofty title of Canadian head of mission. Due to my experience on Peacekeeping duties the ECMM mission head, a Portuguese diplomat named Ambassador Joao Salqueiro, appointed me the Force operations officer and senior liaison officer.

After transiting through CFB Lahr, Germany, I arrived by air in Graz Austria, and then by night bus to Zagreb, Croatia. Although technically there was a ceasefire in effect someone forgot to tell the belligerents that there was a no-fly zone in effect in Croatia. Furious fighting in the eastern cities of Osijek and Vinkoski, along with periodic explosions in Zagreb, was the norm; this was not peacekeeping! Just prior to my arrival one of our Danish officers was killed on the steps of the old Army HQ in Zagreb. On the 2nd of January the Yugoslavian Air Force shot down one of our Italian-manned helicopters with the loss of five more personnel. The second helicopter escaped and made an emergency landing.

The months of January to March were spent moving throughout the area negotiating and mediating with the various factions, and visiting our Canadian officers who were scattered throughout the six republics.

Don recalls those brave members of ECMM and their deeds, he named them, they know what they did: Captain Gaetan Brosseur R22eR, Captain Dave Holt RCA; Major Pat Paterson PPCLI and finally Major Jacques Servais R22eR. The ECCM head of mission requested Don Ethell's tour be extended but it was not granted. After thirty-eight years and twenty-seven days in uniform this exceptional peacekeeper retired.

Don retires

CHAPTER 12

THE CONGO (ONUC) 1962–63

LLOYD CARR

(Written by Lloyd Carr.)

LLOYD CARR joined the Canadian Army in 1958, and his first few years were spent in Kingston, Ontario as a soldier apprentice, training to become a radio operator in the Royal Canadian Corps of Signals. In late 1961, he was selected to move to Churchill, Manitoba, to work at a special northern communications centre. As he prepared for this northern tour he had special arctic clothing issued to aid in his survival in Canada's north. Just before his departure date, he was told that plans had been changed and that he was now scheduled for a six-month United Nations tour in the Congo (ONUC).

In early March 1962, Lloyd was at the Fredericton, New Brunswick airfield with several other young soldiers, watching a large Comet jet aircraft rolling toward them. Shortly after refuelling, they climbed aboard and within a short period of time were airborne and heading toward the Atlantic Ocean. They made a short stop in Labrador for fuel, then were back in the air with nothing to see below but water from horizon to horizon. Additional fuel stops were in the Azores and Italy, before finally landing at a British air base (Idris) in the northwest part of Africa. Here they would spend two days to become acclimatized to the hot, humid African weather.

Lloyd then switched from flying in a Comet to a North Star aircraft and was on his final leg into hostile central Africa. After a few hours of flying south, across the western edge of Africa, they started to descend. Looking out the window, Lloyd saw countryside covered with lots of green trees and brown-coloured rivers. To his surprise, as Lloyd looked for the expected grass houses and small villages, he saw concrete buildings and both dirt and paved roads. As he descended toward the airport in the Congo capital of Leopoldville, he was amazed to see many multi-level buildings and backyard swimming pools. Lloyd's personal account continues:

A couple of days were consumed, settling into our new residence and learning about the new job I would be doing. I would be a resident on the second floor of the building, which had no interior walls and shared one large area with about twenty-four others, sharing twelve double bunks interspersed along the outer walls of the room. Ample windows existed but no beds were close to them, as there was nothing in the concrete window frames, and when it rained it got rather wet around these open holes. Each of us built small metal frames around our beds to hold our mosquito nets in place. If windows did exist, what little ventilation that we had would have been eliminated; but with no windows, our area was constantly inundated with mosquitoes and other nighttime crawlers—mainly the cute chameleon, a small lizard.

My main job was to work in the main United Nations (UN) message centre. The HQ building was a modern seven-storey structure, a short four-block walk from our residence. Our office was on the top floor, with the tape relay centre on the bottom floor. Any communications from Leopoldville to other locations within the Congo, or back to New York, were done through our office.

A person would write his or her message on a standard form and bring it to our office. We would mark the message identification in a register book, then sit at a Teletype machine and type the message into the machine. Our machine would produce a long tape (ribbon or strip) of paper, with various punched holes indicating letters of the alphabet. Each ribbon would constitute one message and would be one metre to several metres long, depending on the length of the message. Once the tape was created, it would be fed into a tape distributor (TD), which would electronically send it from our office to the tape relay centre on the first floor of the building. In the tape relay centre (TRC), a new tape was punched. Within the TRC, a separate TD existed for each of the other locations in the Congo plus one to Nairobi—which would forward our traffic to New York City (UN headquarters). Our tape would then be placed in the destination TD and sent out. Each of these TD units was connected, via wires, to our main transmitter building, several kilometres from our office. Incoming messages would arrive in the TRC and be punched on a tape. An operator would then take the tape and send it up to our office, where it would be printed on our Teletype machine. We would then take the printed message and deliver it to the mailroom. They would eventually deliver it to the final destination.

As the soldiers were about six km from the downtown area, trips downtown required transportation. There were few vehicles available, so they eventually decided to buy bicycles to get around. Several of them started out early one day and walked to town. They found a bicycle store and picked out six-speed models for themselves.

Moving around the city was now much easier. To comply with local rules, each bicycle had to have a registration plate. The place to purchase these plates was a small building in the downtown area. When Lloyd's group arrived, there was a lineup of about twenty people. Within a few minutes, he was surprised to see a local policeman approach them, at the end of the line, and ask him if he was a member of the UN forces (they wore civilian clothes when off duty). When Lloyd said yes, the policeman immediately motioned for them to move to the front of the line, which they did. This was surprising, but over the weeks to follow, the soldiers found other instances where the UN forces were well received by the local population.

Being located close to the equator, the weather was constantly hot and it rained frequently. Jackets and sweaters were never required in this

Cpl. L. Carr receives a decoration while serving in the Congo

city, with daytime temperatures in the high 90s to 120 degrees, and nights in the 60-to-80 degree range. Dusk and dawn were different from what Lloyd was used to in Canada. Within ten minutes it moved from daylight to darkness. Lloyd's account continues:

> One of our favourite recreation areas was a classy park that used to be a private club for the departed Belgians. We knew it as the Funa Club. The club was developed at the edge of the city and was about fifteen km from our residence. It consisted of a massive swimming pool, restaurant, outdoor bar, six tennis courts and a small zoo with many types of animals. On our days off, this was our normal hangout. The swimming pool had slides, a large rotating cylinder, and diving boards. A normal day would include a good tennis set, swimming, a beer (Primus) at the bar, then back to the tennis.
>
> Life was not always safe and secure in the city. While the area where we lived and worked was safe, several areas around the city were marked as "red areas" on the city map and we were to keep away from these areas. Within these red areas, pockets of rebels were known to exist and would make frequent attacks against the local forces and even the UN forces. Shortly before my arrival in the Congo, a unit of thirteen Irish soldiers had been ambushed and killed. I do not recall any UN forces being killed during the time I was there but some were attacked and robbed.
>
> After serving nine months in Leopoldville, I was moved out to Elisabethville, in Katanga province. This had been one of the war-torn areas. Our detachment of about sixteen was split between two single-storey homes. Our office was on the fourth floor of what used to be a hotel located several miles from our quarters. It was evident that rebels had occupied this building, as it was covered with many bullet holes over the exterior walls plus a few larger holes, which probably were from rocket or tank shells. Interior walls also showed signs of rifle fire. Electricity was disrupted frequently; therefore a large generator, on a trailer, was parked beside the building. When we lost electricity, we could remotely start the generator from our office.
>
> Elisabethville was not as modern as Leopoldville, with fewer multi-storey buildings and many more trees.

Our duties were the same: sending and receiving messages, via radio and Teletype, for the UN staff.

Our only transportation was one of two vehicles within the detachment, one a Land Rover and the other a Jeep. We were allowed to tour around when off shift, but had to be in a group of two or more and we always were in uniform and carried machine guns. Travel at night was restricted to moving between our office and residence only. Weekly visits were made to the local market, to buy souvenirs and fresh fruit. Within the city was a large zoo, which we visited frequently. No swimming pool existed and very little else existed for recreation. We had a movie projector, and watched movies each evening, listened to the short-wave radio, or played cards or other board games. Paperback books were shipped to us weekly. Once read, they would be returned to Leopoldville and be sent out to one of the other six detachments.

Fortunately my tour at Elisabethville was only three months. When it ended, I was sent back to Leopoldville and processed for my return to Canada. Each week the aircraft would arrive from Canada with provisions and new personnel. My replacement finally arrived and it was my turn to board the aircraft and return home. On our return trip, we stopped in Pisa, Italy, for refuelling. When the aircraft (Yukon) attempted to start one engine, it failed. We spent the next four days in a hotel while a new engine was installed. This unplanned stop allowed us to be tourists and visit the Leaning Tower of Pisa, the Basilica and other historic sites.

On landing at Trenton, Ontario, we were not prepared for the weather. After living in a hot country for a year, we became used to the hot weather. When I left the Congo, it was 120 degrees Fahrenheit. Trenton was minus fourteen and snowing. It took several days to get warm.

My first UN tour had been successful and a lot was learned. Throughout the rest of my career I would be on several more UN tours, but my first one seemed the best.

Lloyd went on to serve for thirty-eight years, retiring as a major, after serving his final year in Haiti as part of UNMIH. Lloyd's daughter Susan also served as a communicator for the last six months of his UNMIH tour. Like her father, Susan joined the communication branch, and had previously completed a UN tour in Croatia. Her brother, Robert, had served sixteen years in the communication branch, and had completed an UNFICYP tour, in Cyprus, during the same period that Lloyd was on an UNDOF tour, in Damascus, Syria. Lloyd's desire to join the military was sparked by his father, who had been with the South Saskatchewan Regiment and the Strathconas during The Second World War. Susan continues the tradition. Lloyd is one of the founding members of the Ottawa chapter of the Canadian Association for Veterans of United Nations Peacekeeping (CAVUNP).

Lloyd with his daughter, Susan, in Haiti, February 1996

Chapter 13

CYPRUS 1964

FRED HERMAN

Fʀᴇᴅ Hᴇʀᴍᴀɴ is a founding member of the Ottawa Chapter of the Canadian Association of Veterans in United Nations Peacekeeping. I have known him since I joined the association many years ago. Nine tours as a peacekeeper is a lot of peacekeeping for one person, but there is one tour that Fred will never forget.

On his very first tour in Cyprus in 1964, Fred was with the Canadian Provost Corps detachment serving with the First Battalion, The Canadian Guards. In those days there was no professional military training specific to a UN tour. The battalion was trained in all the "soldier skills" required in the Canadian Army. Teamwork so essential in war, and in situations short of war, became paramount.

In the story that follows, Fred made a most horrific discovery. This tour made him aware that one should never expect things to be normal or anything like what one would expect at home.

> We were responsible for the transferring of the Greek Cypriot and Turkish Cypriot children back to the school buses after their daily schooling. On occasion we had difficulty with both sides, as they in most cases did not understand why people with blue berets were even on their island. After they all got familiar with us being there, things went much smoother. It was just a simple routing for us on a daily basis to leave Nicosia and do a patrol to the Kyrenia area, and the last thing we did was escort the children to their buses.
>
> This particular day was no different than any other. It was hot, humid and uncomfortable in the bush gear we wore. The Jeeps we drove were armed but our weapons were not loaded. And of course we all had the traditional

"puppy pounder," as the dogs, which were everywhere, were starving and would attack just at the smell of food. That particular day, the birds were singing and the place was so peaceful; but this was to change.

We noticed that there was no activity around the small schoolhouse, and that concerned us. Guardsman Chapelle said perhaps we should just leave, as it looked like the children had already left by some other means. I was the lance corporal, so it was my job to make sure the children were safely escorted from the school and back to their areas on either side of the "Green Line," which separated the Greeks from the Turks. I was leery after sitting there for about ten minutes watching for some activity before entering the school, but it was something I had to do. I approached the door and cautiously opened it, and immediately closed it, with tears running down my face. In the short time I viewed the interior, I had noticed children hung up on what I think were meat hooks and the blood was dripping all over the floor. There was an awesome silence, no moans or groans, but I could not stand the smell, let alone the sight; and certainly there were no signs of life.

We waited for about fifteen minutes and then left the scene, as there were no children left alive, nor was their teacher alive; and there was no one to tell us what had happened There was so much killing in 1964 that I suppose what we reported was commonplace.

We made sure that we were not implicated or involved in this incident and left the scene. It was reported as per police rules and to the proper authority; and nothing was ever heard about the incident. This incident

Fred Herman in Cyprus

caused me to lie awake at night; I think of it every time I see children on the street here at home. The memory has never left me. I do not know who was involved in this massacre or why, but I can appreciate more and more why distraught peacekeepers who have been exposed to such events as this come back with problems.

Peacekeeping became a way of life for Fred Herman as he went from mission to mission. He saw service in Cairo in 1973. His story continues:

> Remustering to the administrative trade gave me once again the opportunity to travel and that I did. In 1977, I was off to Egypt again, only this time working in the Vacation Travel Section as the "Sunshine Airlines Clerk." This was rewarding as we also got to travel to the destinations authorized for people to spend their two-week leave period. All over the Middle East I went and was accompanied by my wife Delia on some of the trips, which gave her exposure to the Middle East environment; but she was always glad to get back to Canada. I did another tour of Egypt in 1977 and the final tour came with the closing of the mandate in 1978.

When Fred had twenty years in the Forces he started to think of retiring, but suddenly there was a chance to go to Israel. His story continues:

> I went again in 1982, working in Syria and the Golan Heights under command of a British general. This was more of a relaxing tour than my other UN ones had been, as finally I was in countries where there was a speed limit, pavement and white lines on the roads. The only thing that was crude was the medical treatment, and I will not forget that. I broke my leg and had it wrapped in plaster. When it came time to remove it, the Syrians put me in extremely hot water and melted the plaster and then cut it off. I had a permanent suntan on my left leg for months after that.
>
> I went back to Canada and posted to the CF-18 program in 1983. A chance to go to China Lake, California came up but I was supernumerary for six months and had to be placed somewhere; so I chose once again to go to the Golan Heights and was under the

command of Colonel Bob O'Brien. He was a great soldier and a super commander. I did my six months there and probably was the only individual ever to fly from Tel Aviv to Los Angeles on a house-hunting trip prior to my posting to California. I remained in California for three years, returning to Canada in 1987 for two years at the recruiting centre in St. Catharine's, Ontario.

Fred took his release in 1995 after a combined career of just under thirty-five years. Fred Herman is presently the president of the Ottawa Chapter of the Canadian Association of Veterans in United Nations Peacekeeping.

November 11th parade, 1998

CHAPTER 14

REFLECTIONS ON SERVICE WITH
UNTSO 1966–1977
(THE SIX-DAY WAR)

J.H. SKINNER

(Here is Jack Skinner's story, in his own words.)

DURING THE MONTH of May 1967, I was a member of the United Nations team in the city of Tiberias in Galilee. On June 3rd, I was detailed to proceed to the UN observation post at Tel Don in Northern Galilee (known to us as OPI). This OP was housed in a small shack with an observation tower on the roof, and for special protection there was a dugout equipped with a wireless set that could reach Tiberias. I proceeded as directed on 4 June and settled in for what would probably be a six-to-ten-day tour of duty at OPI.

Before leaving Tiberias we were given a very detailed briefing on the situation between Israel and the Arab states, particularly the Israeli/Syrian situation. War seemed very likely between these historic enemies. *Be smart, keep your eyes open and your head down* was the advice given to all UNMOS.

June 4th passed without trouble; we did see a lot of movement on the Syrian side but no shots fired yet. We reported all quiet on our midnight report to Tiberias . . . and turned in for the night.

First light on June 5th was a shocker . . . Israeli bombers flying very low towards Damascus were followed moments later by Syrian and Iraqi MIGS at treetop level, all heading towards Tel Aviv. On our front, massive Israeli air strikes began on the known Syrian strongpoints. We experienced just a few Syrian heavy mortar rounds in our general area . . . enough for me and my Danish observer to move our gear into the dugout and test our communications with Tiberias with our first full SITREP. The fight for the Golan Heights had begun.

Israeli artillery began a series of heavy concentrations; we saw a lot of smoke and fire indicating excellent target results. The Syrian forces did a lot of moving about, but well out of range of the Israeli anti-tank positions. We, the occupants of OP1, were sniped at from the Syrian side from time to time, but the Israeli gunners silenced this business with armoured-car sorties. Once the Israeli forces dealt with the Arab forces in Egypt and Jordan, the full fury was unleashed against the Syrians on the Golan.

Anticipating heavy fighting, we were ordered to vacate our OP. We had just heard that an UNMO at OP2 had been killed, an

Jack as an UNMO, Palestine

Irish chap. In between occasional Syrian arty and mortar fire, we packed up and withdrew. The decisive battle for the Golan was over in three days! Once the Golan was taken, we were ordered to return to the front to report on the situation and activities via radio at specific times each day. There was very little fighting, but we saw vast fields full of abandoned Syrian vehicles, tanks and other military material, with some of the Soviet equipment still in their packing boxes!

Slowly we moved with Israeli forces on the road to Damascus until the ceasefire came into effect, and the Six-Day War was over—and we all know who won.

Jack Skinner, retired

CHAPTER 15

VIETNAM—MY STORY

JERROLD JOSEPH DONAHUE

(Here is Jerry's story, in his own words.)

Part 1: 4 April 1966 – 4 April 1967

IN LEADING UP TO my first tour in Vietnam, I should go back to the fall of 1965 and cover the events that made this tour inevitable. After graduation from the Canadian Army Staff College in Kingston in the early summer of 1965, where John Gardam and I were classmates for two years, I was posted to Eastern Ontario Area Headquarters (Kingston) as staff captain (administration). In August, I was promoted to major and assumed the position of deputy assistant adjutant general (DAAG). In late October I received a posting to the United Nations India-Pakistan Observer Mission (UNIPOM), effective mid-November, pending UN approval. Later that posting was cancelled. I was informed a week before Christmas that my new posting was a year's tour in Vietnam with the International Commission for Supervision and Control (ICSC).

I departed Kingston on 4 April 1966 and, after a delay in Hong Kong for a few days, I eventually arrived in Saigon. There was considerable unrest in Saigon at the time with demonstrations, terrorist bombings, and monks setting themselves on fire. Therefore, there was a curfew from nine p.m. until dawn. We did not stray from our lodgings, the Catinat Hotel, after dinner.

The commission had been established in 1954 to supervise and control the disengagement of the French and Vietnamese forces and the withdrawal of the French. Canada, Poland and India made up the delegations, with India acting as permanent chairman. There were three commissions in Indochina: Vietnam, Cambodia and Laos. The Vietnam Commission was the largest and consisted of the headquarters in Saigon and team sites at various locations in the South (only during my time). There was a small group in Hanoi with a permanent representative (civilian) and a military team. The delegations were known by the acronyms CANDEL, POLDEL and INDEL.

My first assignment to a team site was in late April 1966; I was posted to Qui Nhon, a coastal city midway up the peninsula. Life at a team site, I was quick to learn, was routine in nature, usually boring, and rather lonely. As Canadians we were lucky in that other Caucasians in the south were of a friendly nature, i.e., Americans, Australians, New Zealanders and, of course, the ever-present media. It was important not to be seen as fraternizing with participants in the war; so a daily stroll was a must to establish an exercise routine, but was varied so as not to establish a pattern.

Team sites varied depending on the location. Our compound in Qui Nhon was a two-storey building with a common room for relaxation or meetings; and rooms to accommodate each delegation, with spare rooms for visitors or the overflow when teams were changed. Being the only Canadian, I had one room on the bottom floor. Individual Canadians established routines that were passed on to replacements, who added or deleted according to their needs. One that I inherited and continued was a daily gathering of children in front of my room for a handout of candies or whatever goodies I had. It was a ritual to which I looked forward, having a wife and four young children

"Jerry's kids"

at home. Little things like this were typical of Canadians, and I'm sure they helped our image in all operations of this type.

With the war going at full tilt you could not wander outside the city and definitely not after dark anywhere. One night, as I lay in bed reading, there was a sudden burst of machine-gun fire seemingly outside my door, after which ensued a short firefight. The villa around the corner had been attacked. It is surprising how fast one can move when that happens. Without thinking, I had rolled out of bed, turned out the light, and lain along a wall out of the line of sight of the door and window.

My tour in Qui Nhon lasted only two weeks, as I was summoned back to Saigon for reassignment. I was informed that I was going to Hanoi to head our team and to also be Canada's permanent representative.

After a week's briefing and the appropriate additions to my wardrobe, I was ready for this new and rather strange undertaking for a military officer. I took the opportunity to make a quick phone call to my wife, at my own expense, to let her know what was happening and that I would be out of touch briefly until I got settled. To digress a bit, my wife and I had established a daily letter routine on Forces letter forms which were numbered in sequence. This made it easier to keep track in case letters went astray or several letters were received at one time.

So I was on my way to a new job. In the South our air transportation was by Air Vietnam, to which we affectionately referred as Air NucMam, but the commission had old DC3s for their own use between Saigon, Phnom Penh in Cambodia, Vientiane in Laos, and Hanoi. They were piloted by retired French military. The head pilot on my trips had glasses as thick as coke bottle bottoms, but he was an excellent pilot.

Life for me in Hanoi was fairly active. As the PERMREP, I made initial courtesy calls on all embassies of countries recognized by Canada and attended many diplomatic functions, as national days were celebrated. The courtesy calls were very formal, lasted a prescribed time (usually three-quarters of an hour), and consisted of introductions, pleasantries and in some cases a discussion of the war.

The commission dealt with a liaison office in Hanoi headed by Colonel Ha Van Lau, who later was to be the number-two man for the North at the Paris Peace talks that eventually led to the 1973 Treaty in which Canada was once again asked to participate. He was a very astute gentleman who was very precise and expressionless in his dialogues with myself, Chester Ronning, Canada's roving ambassador, and the commissioner, Victor Moore, on his visits. I was always prepared to take notes at a meeting and my cue was to watch and see if his assistant, a dour-faced major, opened his note pad. At the meetings with Ambassador Ronning and our commissioner, I regretted not knowing shorthand, but I nevertheless managed quite well.

Hanoi was a beautiful city with wide avenues in the centre and two lakes in park-like settings. "Le Grand Lac" and "Le Petit Lac" were favourite places for the people on nice days. Small rowboats could be rented to paddle around. There was also a fairly large zoo with one old elephant with one tusk. This was a place to take visitors if you wanted to talk freely, as our accommodations were bugged and we were followed everywhere. One of our favourite followers was a middle-aged gentleman who carried a boxlike portable radio, which had, in fact, a camera concealed inside. The only sound made by this so-called radio was "click-click." At times we dutifully posed for him, which left him a little embarrassed.

Movement in Hanoi was restricted to the city and further controlled by checkpoints strategically placed on main thoroughfares. You were not stopped as you went out through these points, but on return you were detained. We were informed of the location of these points and they were marked on a detailed city map in our office.

The routine of the first few weeks was shattered on June 29, 1966, with the first air raid on Hanoi proper. The target was the oil dumps near the airport and the attack was very successful. The billowing clouds of dark smoke could be seen for miles. I took a picture from inside my bedroom (see below). (Picture-taking was not allowed anywhere unless official permission was given, for example, my Canada Day reception.

First bombs hit Hanoi, June 26, 1966

To ensure compliance, my barrack box had been ransacked and two films had been exposed just after my arrival. My camera had been in our safe with extra films.) Since the US air offensive started on August 5, 1964, most of the activity had been around Hanoi. This raid, and the numerous raids to follow, brought about changes including the frantic construction of individual "foxholes" every ten yards or so on the streets. We had a shelter in our back garden that was usually half-full of water, so we gathered on the first floor of the main building away from the windows.

The most frustrating change for us was the timing of our weekly

Our home: note the foxholes in the garden

flight from Saigon, which was our lifeline for mail and supplies so necessary for morale purposes. The flight was now to land after dark and to depart before first light. The aircraft sat in Vientiane, Laos and waited for clearance to fly into Hanoi. Once the clearance was given, we were notified and either the senior NCO or I would leave to meet the aircraft at the appointed arrival time.

One of the routines we established was one of post-raid damage reports. Late afternoons, when we figured the raids were finished for that day, two of us would take our normal bicycle ride around the city to see if there was any damage. We also knew, as did most of the people, that the raids were usually only in daytime over Hanoi, and that the US pilots were targeting only strategic points—so we felt safe in venturing out.

On one raid we witnessed a plane being shot down and the next day the claim was ten. The pilot of that plane was captured and paraded through the downtown streets that night to the cheers of the people. It was the only chance they had to cheer. The pilot was sitting with his head down in the back of the vehicle and although we could not identify him, a shout of "Chin up!" in English did bring his head up.

One positive thing that happened also helped morale. We had looked for some relief in the food regime by asking for a turkey to be sent up with our supplies. The group in Vientiane took pity on us and sent up a goose. The only problem was that it was still alive. They rendered it unconscious for the trip up in the diplomatic bag and as the courier was walking from the plane carrying two bags the bird began to move. Recognizing there was a potential for embarrassment, the staff member meeting the plane quickly walked closely by the courier's side. They reached the office with no problem. The goose became an instant hit with the group and was named Alice. She was not allowed outside except under escort in the back yard and always had a bowl of spirits for Happy Hour. At times she looked like John Wayne circling the wagons. We had thought about asking for a gander to keep her company but never got around to it. She eventually succumbed after my departure, but the exploits of her arrival did make the Paris paper in an article filed by L'Agence Presse.

There were a few memorable events during my tour in Hanoi. The most memorable was the arrival of Chester Ronning. He was a roving ambassador for Canada who had previously visited to try and come up with some areas where meaningful talks could develop between the warring factions; and to attempt to open up a channel of communication for the US prisoners. I was fortunate to be there for his second and last visit.

The diplomatic functions were interesting as they were somewhat foreign to a young army major. The protocol for arrival and being announced was enlightening and it gave me a chance to meet some very interesting people. Of course, the ambassadors and chargés that I had called on were friendly and chatted briefly. The Vietnamese officials would line up on one side and the diplomats would file past to shake hands and say a few words. This was how I met and shook hands with President Ho Chi Minh. He asked how I liked his country and said he had always admired Canada. It was at one of these functions that I met General Giap, at that time the defence minister, and the hero of Dien Bien Phu. He loved to talk about military strategy, but if you turned to politics he would immediately call over an interpreter and switch to Vietnamese from French.

At the end of August, after four months in the North Vietnamese capital, my tour ended and I returned to the South. My arrival at the headquarters in Saigon saw two changes in my life: I was appointed as assistant political advisor to the commissioner, a civilian position; and I was to be quartered with the senior military advisor, Brigadier Chubb, in his villa with three other officers, Majors Peter Downe and Peter Wilson, and the Brigadier's PA, Captain Camille Blais. Peter Downe replaced me in Hanoi and Peter Wilson followed him. Peter Downe had also been on the staff at the Staff College while John Gardam and I were students. This made the rest of my stay in Vietnam quite pleasant.

My job as assistant political advisor consisted mainly in reviewing complaints sent in by both sides; and in preparing Canada's position for each when they were brought to the commission meetings, which took place once a week or as required. The complaints were primarily from the North about the air raids and were plentiful, as you may have ascertained from my accounts of the daily raids on Hanoi.

As the days dragged on it became easier to get out and visit team sites and to even travel in certain sectors with the appropriate escorts. One trip I made with Major Peter Downe was to our northernmost team site at Gio Linh. They were quartered in a long one-storey building with rooms for the members and a dining area. It looked very much like a run-down motel. There were also other buildings, areas for their vehicles, and a good-sized bunker. This was a much-needed requirement, as they seemed to be close to the routes for excursions from the demilitarized zone (DMZ). When a firefight began, team members would head for the shelter of the bunker. Their area was damaged several times by these clashes and particularly from mortars. One Canadian, Captain Hugo Saudino, was running for shelter one night and was literally blown right out of his boots. He hadn't had time to do up the laces in his haste.

We accompanied the team on their daily visit to the bridge across the Ben Hai River separating North and South, and proceeded to meet the North Vietnamese liaison team halfway across. While we were talking, the jungle to the west and several kilometres away seemed to explode. It was a B-52 raid on suspected routes through the DMZ frequented by the VC and NVA. It was a spectacular sight and very noisy, with the bridge trembling with the shock waves.

On our way back to Saigon, we took the opportunity while in Danang to attempt to contact a US Marine Corps colonel, Bob Dominick, who had been on the directing staff (DS) at Staff College the previous year and, we believed, was now with the 3rd Marine Division in the Da Nang area. We were successful and an escort was sent down to the city to pick us up and deliver us to the headquarters. The division commander insisted on hosting us for dinner, where we met our friend and four others from the staff who had either been students or DS at our Staff College at one time. We were escorted back to Da Nang to continue our journey south. We did manage another side trip to an artillery fire base by invitation, which we can safely admit to now.

We were fortunate to have Canadian Forces aircraft pass through on relief flights and to deposit some of the said relief with us, i.e., Canadian cigarettes, beer, and other goodies, including Christmas trees. We tried putting up a tree for

Jerry in 1966

Christmas in our villa but we became so depressed that we put it outside. That period of time, as well as family birthdays, was the most nostalgic and lonesome of the year's tour. One aircraft stopover had a number of passengers on the round-the-world flight. We planned to have the group out to the villa for lunch and, since one of the air force passengers was a classmate from Staff College, then Major Gerry Morrison, I volunteered to escort them into town. As a joke and to see their reaction, I boarded the plane wearing a helmet and a flak jacket and invited them to accompany me. There was some hesitation before I smiled and they realized I was pulling their leg.

The year away from home was finally over. After a good send-off by the delegation, I was escorted to the airport by Brigadier Chubb and the two Peters, and I departed Saigon on April 4, 1967. With stops in Manila and Guam, I arrived in Honolulu to spend a great week with my wife.

Part 2: February 1973 – July 1973

It seems that my overseas assignments always started on a bizarre note. I had just arrived in London, UK, from Brussels in the fall of 1972 and had not been particularly looking forward to a week's layover because of a lack of space on service air. When I checked into the hotel, the clerk gave me a message to call the duty officer at the Canadian Defence Liaison Staff, London, (CDLS[L]), as soon as possible. The duty officer told me that I was booked on the next service flight, priority one (very high). My boss in Ottawa, then Colonel Bob Theriault, had thoughtfully added "for duty purposes" to the recall message to alleviate any fears I might have of family problems.

I surmised that this meant another tour in Vietnam, as the Paris Peace Talks were coming to a successful conclusion and Canada was a prime candidate to participate. Sure enough, on my arrival home, I was informed that I had been selected for this new mission, which was to be called the International Commission for Control and Supervision (ICCS). The medical and administrative details were completed immediately and then, being on short notice to move from December, the waiting began. The eventual deployment was in two stages with the first group arriving in Saigon on January 29, 1973 and the second contingent two weeks later.

As the OC of the second contingent I was fortunate to be in the VIP section and in close contact with the pilot for the long trip to Saigon. As we approached the coast of Vietnam, the pilot, who was aware that this was my second tour, invited me into the cockpit to give the passengers a running commentary as we progressed down the coast. One thing I prepared them for was the blast of hot, humid air that would greet them when the doors were opened upon landing. It did not disappoint anyone and, in fact, it felt worse than I had remembered from my last visit.

We settled into temporary quarters at Tan Son Nhut Military Airbase on February 12 to await deployment to our team sites.

There were 290 Canadians, 250 being military, in our contingent and three other contingents from Hungary, Indonesia and Poland that made up the ICCS. South Vietnam was divided into eight regions and further subdivided into twenty-six sub-regions. Each sub-region called for a two-man team from each country and were established at a team site. There were also two or three-man teams established for exchange of prisoners, points of entry duties or special requirements, and as a reserve.

Late at night a couple of days after our arrival I was summoned by then Colonel Dan Loomis, chief of staff, along with two other region team leaders, to the operations centre. We were to leave immediately for our respective region headquarters to take a look at the accommodations and facilities of the team sites in the region. The full teams were to follow shortly to deploy to the sites as they became livable.

As an aside, as I was packing my gear that night in Saigon, I said farewell to the young captain in the upper bunk. Little did I know at the time that this was the last time I would see Captain Charlie Laviolette, who died along with eight others when their helicopter was shot down during a reconnaissance mission to Lao Bao in Region 1.

As the quarters in Chu Lai, my team site, would not be ready for a few weeks, the team was to be housed with the Tam Ky team. Two weeks after our arrival in Tam Ky my team, consisting of Captains John MacInnis (arty), Pat McManus (inf) and myself, deployed to Chu Lai with the other delegations, which was a relief from the daily travel to and fro. Capt John Carmichael, who accompanied me to Tam Ky, did not deploy to Chu Lai and Capt Malcolm McCabe replaced John MacInnis after two months. We were fortunate to be billeted with the remaining US advisors who were situated in a compound originally built for and by the US Seabees on a peninsula of the sprawling Chu Lai area. Chu Lai was the main base of operations for the 2nd ARVN Infantry Division (Army of the Republic of Vietnam), commanded by Brigadier General Tran Van Nhut. The headquarters and several divisional units were located in this area.

Canada was to hold the chairmanship of this commission until we were fully operational or until the commission decided to rotate the position. It was advantageous for us to be in this position because of our background in operations of this type and our initiative in getting things done. This was very evident in the quickness of the deployment and settling in of the team sites. The reconnaissance and allotment of quarters were left up to me in both Tam Ky and Chu Lai and, except for a few glitches, everyone appeared to be satisfied. One of the glitches was the inability of the Polish and Hungarian teams to make decisions on their own. When the US pullout of our area was complete, the departing officer commanding, LCol Holland, handed over everything, including the communications facility and their quarters, to me as chairman.

Another interesting aside is that in my assignment in 1980 to the Pentagon as the Canadian Liaison Officer to the Department of the Army, I met LCol Holland again. While I was there, the American hostages in Tehran, Iran, were released. He was among them and was assigned to the Pentagon. We got together a few times to talk about Vietnam and Chu Lai in particular.

The area of responsibility for the Chu Lai team was Quang Ngai Province, a relatively rich rice- and vegetable-growing area along the coast. The more mountainous area to the west was under PRG/NVA control. The province was quite large, and consequently most of our travel was by a combination of helicopter, if available, and ground transport. The province chief, Col Loi, and I had something in common, as we were both graduates of the US Army Command and

General Staff College in Fort Leavenworth, Kansas. In fact, he was on the course previous to me. We became very good friends during the tour.

Our team began our operational role a day after our arrival on site with the assignment by the commission of the first investigation of a violation. As James Anderson, a *Toronto Globe and Mail* reporter who accompanied my team that day, reported in an article for papers back home, "The International Commission of Control and Supervision made its first on-the-spot investigation Sunday—a safe and inconclusive three hours in this ruined little fishing village." The NVA/PRG had mounted a major attack just before the truce started in an attempt to gain an outlet to the sea at Sa Huynh, a village with a natural harbour. The fierce battle lasted over a week with the South maintaining control. He further reported, "After visiting the village, Major Jerrold Donahue of Ottawa commented: 'We got a lot of facts but it is difficult to draw conclusions.'" The account was an accurate description of our activities that day. It took four days to write, discuss and rewrite the report before agreement was reached. The task was made more difficult in that I had to write the report by hand with only one scrounged piece of carbon paper. In order to make four copies, I had to do it twice. It was the only unanimous agreement on an investigation in our region for the rest of our tour.

So the routine of investigations and reports was soon back to the same ritual as the old commission. Subsequent observations made during investigations by the Canadian and Indonesian members were denied by the Polish and Hungarian members. One example was the investigation of a mortar attack on the small village of My Lai (famous for a US attack on civilians). The village was made up of clusters of huts over an area and were notated as My Lai 1, My Lai 2 and My Lai 3. One hut left standing had a hole in the roof and a hole in the dirt floor, obviously made by a shell or mortar bomb. Shrapnel and a piece of a tail fin gave further evidence of a mortar bomb. The two delegations refused to acknowledge the hole in the roof simply by not looking up, and ignoring the crater and the fragments. From then on, minority reports were submitted by the Canadians and Indonesians on one hand, and the Poles and Hungarians on the other. On two occasions the Polish colonel of the day came up to my hooch to say goodbye before changing over the next day and, not having the interpreter there, apologized for their attitude stating that, if they could, they would have agreed with us on each investigation.

One investigation was conducted with both sides represented and in areas occupied by both sides. On this occasion, our instructions were to fly by helicopter along a designated road until we saw a PRG flag on a pole. We were then to land facing again a designated direction, to disembark and proceed along this road until we were met. As we were led off the road along a well-worn track, we were suddenly surrounded by a group of PRG soldiers. They literally seemed to come out of the ground, which they did, as the holes were visible if you looked. After some time we arrived at the usual cluster of huts, where we were offered refreshments—a variety of pirated soft drinks and yams. As I recall, I had a warm Orange Crush.

There were numerous shell holes and quite remarkably a complete 155mm shell with US markings and not a scratch on it. Even duds have some kind of marks on them after landing. As an artillery officer, I did a crater analysis on one shell hole to determine the line of flight and found that it had come from their own area rather than the South Vietnamese area. From the fragments in the hole it was obvious that the crater had been made months before the truce. When we returned to the South Vietnamese side, there was an incident as the team interviewed witnesses in an open area. A civilian burst from the usual group of onlookers and hit the PRG member over the head with a bamboo pole. In the ensuing melee the civilian was arrested. The PRG member was in agony, but refused medical attention. It was only a glancing blow but it did dent his pith helmet.

Venturing forth, whether by helicopter or vehicle, was always an adventure with the artillery battles and the snipers. The latter were the most dangerous and several times the team was caught in a precarious position. It was very unnerving for the Hungarians, since they were really civilians in uniform. We were caught by sniper fire at an artillery fire base one day and it took some time for the protective platoon to clear the area. The other danger when on foot was mines. In our investigation at My Lai, we had to walk through the paddy fields for some time. I had the South Vietnamese escort lead and I would step where they stepped and I had my people follow in my footsteps. We lost about ten civilians a week to mines throughout the province. Minefields generally were not marked and would shift with the monsoon rains. Almost every night the artillery carried out a harassing fire program, which disturbed your sleep until you got used to it.

As I left the helicopter one day I invited the crew to come back on the weekend, if they could, to go for a swim and relax. Unfortunately I never saw them again as they were among those killed in Region 1, along with Charlie Laviolette, the next day when their helicopter was shot down. For some time after this incident most of our movements were on the ground and the escorts were doubled. We always had a bit of a breather since we went out on investigations only when the Canadians and Indonesians were chairman. The established order for the chairmanship was alphabetical in accordance with protocol: Canada, Hungary, Indonesia and Poland; hence the acronym CHIP, which I refused to use on our team site.

As the days and weeks dragged on, the rumour mill started on rotation plans and how long Canada would remain now that the primary tasks of POW exchanges and the American withdrawal were completed in accordance with the treaty. Rotation dates finally started to trickle in by mid-May and I was to return to Canada on July 20. The decision for Canada to stay or not to stay was yet to come. It was finally announced on May 30 that Canada would be withdrawing completely by the end of July.

The South Vietnamese were not very happy about this decision, as they knew that we were the only country trying to do something with the commission. Privately, Brigadier General Nhut told me that the main reason they were unhappy was the knowledge of what would happen after we left. He told me that after the truce his division faced about one plus NVA/PRG divisions, but at this time the North had built up their forces on his front to six plus divisions, and he estimated that the South would only last as a country for about a year after we left. He was pretty accurate in his forecast.

The farewells began with Brigadier General Nhut presenting me with a painting of the inner city of Hue by a soldier in his headquarters. I had it reframed after I had been home for some time, and it was not surprising that the original frame was made of wood from ammunition boxes and held together with big nails. It still hangs proudly in our living room. The province chief, Colonel Loi, presented me with albums of pictures commemorating our time and travels in his province. The ARVN Representative for our team, LCol Loc, gave me a beautiful lacquered jewellery box inlaid with mother-of-pearl for my wife. The divisional artillery commander added a brass ashtray made from the base of a 105mm cartridge case (naturally).

I took my last helicopter ride back to Da Nang and proceeded to join the other teams in Saigon. We departed Saigon in two aircraft at the end of July after a farewell ceremony on the tarmac. It was a long flight home with only two stops in Tokyo and Vancouver. The Ottawa airport was jammed with family and friends and, after being greeted by Mitchell Sharpe and General Dextraze, the CDS, we headed home with the family to really Rest and Recuperate.

The ravages of war are not for the faint of heart and, although we were not in the front lines during action to see the actual death and destruction first hand, we did witness the aftermath, which was equally disturbing. For many years after and indeed to this day I wake up in the night with the sight of women and children mutilated beyond recognition or making their way with crippling injuries. The sight and smell of swollen bodies lying where they fell and left there until we investigated two or three days later is something you do not forget for some time.

Two tours were now completed and, when compared, there were many similarities and differences. The major similarity was the initial mandate and operations, in that we oversaw the disengagement of forces (the French and the Americans), the exchange of prisoners and the withdrawal of these troops. Investigations from then on reverted to minority reports based on facts, from our point of view, and the views of the Polish and Hungarian delegations based on their support of the NVA/PRG. In the ICSC, Canada and Poland supposedly represented each side, whilst India was the neutral chairman. In the ICCS, Canada and Indonesia represented the West, and Poland and Hungary represented the East. This was not a formula for success.

The major difference was the makeup of the commissions as a whole. The ICSC was established in 1954 and lasted until 1973. Each delegation looked after most of their own needs and rotation was, after the initial deployment, made on a man-for-man basis. The ICCS was established in 1973 and deployed as an entity over a short period and, in Canada's case, *not* for an indefinite period. Canada was the chairman for the initial set-up and deployment period and each delegation eventually took the chairmanship in turn. The commission was looked after by civilian contractors down to the team site level and the Four Party Joint Military Commission. On my first tour, when on a team site, I looked after myself and, on my second tour, the whole team was looked after.

It is difficult to assess the success of the commissions from an operational point of view without looking at the political ramifications. As I mentioned above, both commissions were successful in their initial mandate ending with the withdrawal of the French and the Americans but, from then on, there were no operational successes to speak of. From our point of view, in the ICSC, Canada did provide a channel of communication between Hanoi and Washington and, in the ICCS, Canada's role in getting the commission organised and functioning in a short period of time was very successful. The fact that we did, when chairman, investigate and report when asked was an indication that we tried to make the commission carry out its mandate to the best of our ability. We may not have been successful in the full context of the mandate but, as Canadians, we carried out our responsibilities to the extent possible and, in that way, we were successful.

There was no way the commissions could control the political and military moves once the initial mandate was completed. For nineteen years the ICSC sat and watched the deterioration of relations between North and South from a fragile truce to full-scale warfare with yet another outside party involved. As Brigadier General Nhut, commander of the 2nd ARVN Division, predicted, the South would last about a year after we left. This year, 2000, is the twenty-fifth anniversary of the fall of Saigon, so he was not off by much. Perhaps this was to be the eventual outcome, but when you read about the state of the economy in Vietnam today you wonder what might have been if the commissions had been more successful. The saga of Vietnam, historically, will no doubt continue.

CHAPTER 16

MEMORIES OF UNEF

JOHN GARDAM

My only tour as a peacekeeper was from February 1960 to February 1961. The Fort Garry Horse Reconnaissance Squadron under the command of David Taylor was unusual in many ways. The unit was raised in Base Petawawa from troops from the Fort Garry Horse, Lord Strathcona's Horse and the VIII Canadian Hussars. All support troops, cooks, signallers and vehicle mechanics were posted in just before we left for Egypt. My position at the beginning was liaison officer, the captain responsible for the training and operational efficiency of the officers and men. There were 107 in all, strangers every one, but after a year, closest of friends. This tiny unit had the distinction of providing four regimental sergeant majors (RSMS) in future years.

As the team gathered in Petawawa, where I was stationed, we got to know each other's names, but little more. There was a lot of administrative work with medical and dental checkups, making wills and doing our first job in the field. "Operation Running Stag" was an exercise to keep deer hunters under control by patrolling all the camp roads with Ferret Scouts cars. It was a time to check on map reading, first aid and weapon skills.

Captain Tony Hawkins, who joined us from Camp Borden, was not with us for long when he left for Egypt with SSGT Al Simpson, who ran our quartermaster stores. Tony was a former Indian Army officer and Al was a wartime Prince Louise Dragoon Guard veteran. These two stalwarts were to be our advance party sent to learn the ropes from the Royal Canadian Dragoon Squadron under the Command of Major Tom Finan. The squadron was not complete when these two left and thus the complete squadron was never "on parade" until it disbanded a year later.

147

Final parade, Petawawa: Fosberry, Gardam, Murdock and Taylor

When we left Petawawa the incomplete squadron paraded for Brigadier General Scott Murdock, commander of the brigade, and Tom Fosberry, camp commander. This photo was taken just prior to Christmas and I had just been promoted to captain.

During the following weeks the men of the squadron left for Trenton by individual troops at weekly intervals. They were to be flown to El Arish, Egypt by North Star aircraft. As each of our Garry troops arrived, their seats on the aircraft were taken over by RCD troops who were ending their year in the desert. I had been designated as the sole member of the rear party. As the time for my departure came closer the base public relations team decided there should be a press release and a photo to assist *The Globe and Mail* in their story. The photo was one of me saying goodbye to my family at night. I got into uniform and got our two oldest sons out of bed. John was three and Bob one-and-a-half. Our third son David was only a few weeks old and did not appear in the picture. The story was printed the day I left for a year. The "Canada" flash on my right shoulder was improperly placed so that it showed up for the previous parade. When we got to Egypt, the UN flash was put on the right side, and the Canada one put on the left.

My first priority after I had visited the outposts in the desert was to improve the living conditions. The CO agreed with this. The tents leaked, the sand vipers got into clothing and hygiene was terrible. I

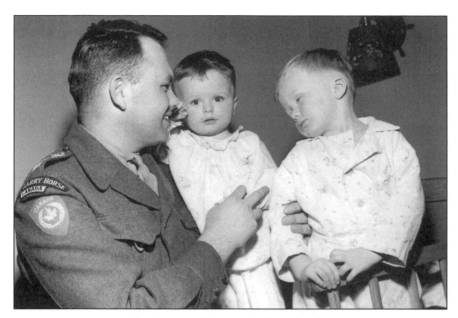

Saying goodbye to Bob and John

convinced the Force engineer, Ron Gourley, that we should be the UN experiment to upgrade from tents to huts. The plan was for a cinder block wall to replace the wooden frame, asbestos roofing to replace the canvas tent, and chicken wire impregnated with plastic to allow light in from these "windows." The newsletter written in June 1960 describes what we did:

> Our building programme had been most successful. The living accommodation—two buildings 16' x 32'—was completed at each outpost by 13 May 60. I was required to submit a report on our building methods on 9 May 60, which, when received at Gaza, drew a certain amount of favourable comment. I was able to pyramid this favour to get more material, and by 11 Jun 60, I hope to have at each outpost, two barrack buildings, one kitchen/mess/recreation building, a troop office (Ops Room) and stores buildings, and a generator hut, complete with generator, for the lighting in the buildings.
>
> The Gardam Construction Co., consisting of Capt Gardam and three Egyptian civilians known (to us) as Hassan, Mohammed and Junior, has done marvels. Hassan is the carpenter, Mohammed is the concrete man

and Junior is, in theory, the helper. The "help" of course, comes from the resident troop and I am most intrigued by the ability of my soldiers to be able to work so hard in the hot sun and still do their patrols.

The civilians, by rule, work only eight hours per day. They live and eat in the outpost while they are working there. My soldiers at the outposts—no union—do about twelve to sixteen hours per day. Maybe it is the psychological urge to conform with the plan, or the idea of making a bit of extra pay, but in any event, while Mohammed and Hassan have been at the outposts, we have acquired wonderful grease racks, POL pits, concrete sand drift walls, and other extras.

One key element was to feed our civilians five times a day. This gave them the energy to work longer hours. We also drove the men home on weekends with extra food for their families. In the camps run by the UN Welfare Relief Agency, food was rationed. Although we called our civilians Egyptians, they were in fact Palestinian refugees. This photo shows the finished product. The RCAF took this picture from an Otter aircraft.

Outpost as seen from an RCAF plane

Tony Hawkins was studying for promotion exams, which were to be written in Canada. The CO decided that I would take over the second-in-command duties and Tony would handle the operational side. When Tony left for Canada it was decided not to have him return for just a few months, so I became the sole captain in the squadron.

Our troop officers were all very young and keen. They all came from different backgrounds. This photo was taken in front of the officers' mess.

Our greatest strength was in the youth of our soldiers, many of whom had less than a year's service, plus some wartime corporals and sergeants. No task was too mundane or tedious. I seldom had to discipline anyone and only two were returned to Canada when remedial action did not work.

FGH Recce Squadron officers. *Back row:* **Fro Renaud, RMC; Burk Barker, lawyer from University of Saskatchewan; Pierre Dionne, COTC, University of Montreal; Don Young, former infantry corporal commissioned as a second lieutenant.** *Front row:* **Tony Hawkins, former Indian army; Dave Taylor, RMC graduate, wartime RCD; myself, former trooper, Strathconas, commissioned as a second lieutenant.**

This final photograph shows how young we were forty years ago. Only the cook, Sergeant Mercier and Corporal McRoberts, the quartermaster storeman are wearing more than just the UNEF ribbon.

As the years have gone by I have used the leadership skills I learned in UNEF on a constant basis. It was a great teaching experience for me and the most valuable lesson was to treat everyone fairly and give our soldiers the benefit of the doubt. So many of our young soldiers went on to great things in the Forces and now are doing well in civilian life. The one constant for me was the fact that my wife wrote an airmail letter to me every day for a year while raising our three young sons.

This story is but a sample of what we actually did while in Egypt. I could have written much more, but felt that this small part of our time with UNEF was important.

Group of Fort Garrys — oh, so very young . . .

Chapter 17

IN DEAD GROUND: UNEF II, 1974

BILL PORTER

(Bill Porter's own words were used in this story.)

BILL PORTER and I served together in Calgary in 1967-68 in the Fort Garry Horse. This story told by Bill came to my attention in 1999. The United Nations Truce Supervision Organization (UNTSO) was assisting United Nations Emergency Force II, which had just been formed and had been inserted between the warring factions, namely Egypt and Israel. Bill Porter's graphic description outlines how a simple matter can become very complex:

> The end of the combat phase of the Yom Kippur War in late October 1973 had left the Egyptian (ARE) Third Army encircled by the Israelis on the West Bank of the Suez Canal around Suez City. The ARE Second Army still held onto its gains in the Sinai farther north, with most of the Israeli Bar-Lev forts along the Suez Canal remaining in their hands. On October 23, 1973, UNEF II was created to monitor and improve upon the initial ceasefire that had been brokered by UNTSO. Long negotiations at Kilometre 101 on the Cairo–Suez City Highway resulted in a detailed and highly orchestrated plan for the redeployment and disengagement of ARE and Israeli (IDF) troops. The end result led to the establishment of a buffer zone in the midst of the Sinai Peninsula with Limited Forces Areas (LFAs) on either side. The disengagement process carried on until January of 1974, when the first UN-occupied buffer zone on the East Bank was established. As part of the negotiation process, agreements had also been reached for the

exchange of prisoners and the search and recovery of missing soldiers.

On a hot midsummer day in 1974, I looked west from a Swedish OP just inside the UN buffer zone in the Sinai Peninsula. The blinding sun floated in a pale blue sky above the gravel and sand of the desert. The horizon was broken here and there by tank silhouettes. Some were complete, others smashed like giant bugs, and all stood motionless. Between the horizon and just off to the south, a narrow asphalt road ran

Bill Porter

through undulating terrain. Not dunes exactly, but arid, gritty sand and gravel, speckled here and there with miscellaneous debris—rows of land mines that had been slowly shifted and exposed by the winds; randomly strewn tank, artillery and mortar rounds; shell casings of all calibres; rusting strands of barbed wire; and, sadly, scattered and tattered clothing, knapsacks, letters, photos and unrecognizable, unnatural pieces of junk.

The dips in the land were just big enough to conceal a tank or an infantry platoon. From my position on a crest, I could see for a mile or more, but anything could be concealed in a dip a hundred yards away. In military parlance, these dips were "dead ground," i.e., hidden from the eye of the observer. Unlike other battlegrounds I had read about, this part of the Sinai held no smells, bodies or useful loot. Nothing bigger than a fly was alive out there; and all the dead soldiers or visible parts thereof, as well as anything that could still move or shoot, had already been picked up by Israeli and Egyptian salvage units. Nothing moved anywhere unless you counted the flies and the small group of UNEF, UNTSO and Arab Republic of Egypt (ARE) troops standing around in the middle of this vast gravel pit and junkyard.

Eight small, crude, wooden coffins lay close to the observation tower in the centre of the compound. A few vehicles were parked nearby, next to the ruins of a small building of indeterminate origin, where the ground was dimpled with eroded slit trenches. The jagged walls had been decorated in graffiti of all colours and languages by IDF infantry before withdrawing several months ago. One line in French expressed the hope that the UN would suffer as much in this hole as they had.

I was there as a representative of HQ UNEF II to observe the passage of those eight coffins to the Adjutant-General's Office of the Israeli Defence Forces (IDF AG), whose representatives were already more than an hour late. I'd had time to think of all this and about the return of the war dead. Many had not yet been recovered from their tombs in the Bar-Lev line and in derelict tanks and armoured personnel carriers (APCs).

At UNEF HQ in Cairo, contingency planning for the move of UNEF troops to the Golan front (later UNDOF), monitoring the activity of both sides, and assisting the Red Cross with humanitarian activities took up most of the operations staff capacity. As senior operations officer, I spent most of my time on paperwork and the supervision of a polyglot lot of duty officers from a dozen different countries. The only other Canadian on the ops staff (Ken Nette) became responsible for Operation Omega, the nickname for the search and recovery of war dead and the exchange of prisoners. He worked closely with the Nepalese troops assigned to assist Israeli rabbis in digging out bodies from the Bar-Lev line and from derelict tanks and APCs. Consequently, Ken saw areas of the battlefield not normally seen by UN troops and sat in on numerous negotiation meetings between both sides, and the UN and Red Cross.

From these meetings, it became apparent that the Israelis placed enormous emphasis on the recovery of their war dead, or at least absolute, incontrovertible proof of their death. This was because Mosaic Law required seven years before a missing soldier could be declared legally dead. Things like execution of wills or remarriage could not take place without such proof. As well, there was a natural desire for the families to have closure. The Egyptians were well aware of this and, being more concerned with the living than the dead (as their representative put it), placed more emphasis on the release of Palestinian prisoners from Israeli custody than the return of their own war dead. Consequently, these sessions soon consisted of bargaining the worth of Israeli war dead against the number of live Palestinians to be released. Negotiations were difficult and touchy with commitments being made and then broken the very next day.

Today was one of the few occasions when I got out of the HQ and into the desert. Normally, Ken would have made the arrangements in conjunction with UNTSO for the transfer of these eight Israeli war dead from the Egyptians to their own troops; but he was away on other duties and I found myself filling in for him. All I had to do was be there as a rep from UNEF HQ, since I was given to understand that UNTSO had already done the coordination necessary for the two sides to meet at this checkpoint.

However, something had gone wrong: no Israelis. There was no movement permitted after dark, and time was fleeting. The UNTSO representative was having problems with his Motorola, but it was finally established that the team from the Israelis had been dispatched to the wrong observation post, some distance north in the Peruvian Battalion zone. There was no way they were going to make it here on time for everyone to get off the desert before dark.

I was bothered that these soldiers would not go home today. Indeed, from what Ken had reported about the increasing acrimony surrounding the Omega negotiations, it was quite likely that they might not go home at all if they remained in Egyptian custody. The answer seemed simple: get the closest IDF elements to come and pick up the bodies. However, since UNEF HQ was in Cairo and the UNTSO communication system had broken down, there seemed to be no way to get in touch with the IDF in time to do any good.

Then, one of the Swedish Officers told me that a M113 APC (nicknamed a "Zelda" by the IDF) usually showed up at this time of day, always positioning itself at the same spot about 500 metres to the northwest. Sure enough, a look in that direction through my binoculars revealed the head and shoulders of someone peering back at us with his own set of binos. A little bit of heat distortion and a very slight engine rumble confirmed that he was indeed perched on a Zelda in dead ground.

The direct route to the APC seemed clear of anything resembling a minefield. The asphalt road led nowhere near it, and the ground was not good going for our wheeled vehicles; nor was it a good idea to walk around in unknown areas of the Sinai. Still, no one else volunteered to go and the minor risk seemed worth it. So, after taking a bearing for prudence' sake, I started walking down the first dip, up to the crest of the next one and then down the slope on the far side. I proceeded across this gully to the next crest, still on the right track for the Zelda, and then looked down again. Damn good thing I did. Just feet away on my intended path were half a dozen grapefruit-sized blue globes with shiny metal plumes on top. Good old unexploded cluster bombs, the type of thing that a child might pick up for a toy.

Avoiding those hateful toys, I went down the dip again and up to the next crest. I saw the Israeli crew commander looking at me quizzically from about thirty metres away. Only one more dip to go.

I greeted the crew commander with a rather nervous "Shalom," exhausting my current knowledge of Hebrew. "Guten Tag," he replied; so we tried out my German and his French before settling for broken English. Once he understood the problem, he took the initiative and made a decision to break radio silence, something that could have gotten him into a lot of trouble. I was impressed by the speed at which he encoded his message and by the response time of less than ten minutes. He advised me that an IDF party would be at the OP within the next twenty minutes. I then said goodbye and returned to the OP to await their arrival.

At the OP, I met up with Lieutenant Magdy, a young commando. He was a typical Egyptian junior officer with a great deal of pride and touchiness. Although the ARE may have lost the tactical battle, they had given the IDF their first taste of defeat, and by regaining terrain in the Sinai, had certainly won the political war. They were thus very conscious of diplomatic slights, real or imagined. I tried to convince him that the IDF's tardiness was not their fault, but I don't think he bought it.

I was very relieved to see a one-ton truck come barreling over a crest on the asphalt road to cross the line of oil drums marking the boundary of the buffer zone. As it turned into the short entry road to the OP, my heart sank and Magdy let out a little growling sound. The IDF soldiers in the back were toting their Galil assault rifles. Worse still, the truck stopped, the cab opened, and out strutted a plump little major carrying a lovingly polished and maintained war souvenir—a former ARE Kalashnikov (AK 47). Magdy started to say something incoherent to the effect that he should have brought the 38.cal snub-nose revolver that he had confiscated from a downed Israeli pilot.

I ran forward and met the IDF major halfway. I advised him that the ceasefire terms dictated that only the UN were allowed to carry arms within the buffer zone, and I pointed to the unarmed ARE squad. Had he been from the IDF AG, he would have known, but these were fighting troops dismounted from their Zeldas, stuffed into the truck, and sent here with very little info. The major argued for a few moments (he was a lawyer from Haifa doing his reserve service) before returning his treasure to the cab and ordering his party to leave their weapons behind and dismount.

Without a word being spoken, the IDF and ARE groups took up positions on either side of the little row of coffins, with Magdy and the major glaring at each other across a six-foot space that seemed miles wide. The pause that followed seemed to go on for hours. Then Magdy looked down at the coffins, quietly brought his troops to attention, and slowly raised his hand in a British-style salute. As he did so, the IDF side stiffened their bodies, but their faces became soft and somewhat bewildered. I believe it was the first time any one of them had really seen an Egyptian outside of combat or a POW cage. The major broke his baleful stare at Magdy, returned the salute, and gave Magdy a nod, as if acknowledging him as one of a certain brotherhood. Magdy smiled a little and the two began to speak quietly together as both ARE and IDF soldiers loaded the coffins into the truck. With no further ceremony, the IDF party then mounted and took off down the road. The rest of us said our goodbyes and I managed to get into Cairo just as darkness fell.

That night I thought about what I had seen pass between Magdy and the major. Next morning in the ops room reality bit me. The ARE lodged a formal protest against UNEF II (i.e., me) for having allowed the IDF to enter the buffer zone armed. Nothing personal, Magdy later said. The IDF had their own stiff complaint about an ARE helicopter flying in the Zone spying upon them, unarmed or not and casualty evacuation be damned. I truly appreciated that one, given the twice-daily overflight violations by IDF Phantoms.

Although I didn't get into much trouble for these things (UN HQ staff rarely do), the whole thing caused a lot of paperwork and firm life reminders to myself that liaison should never be taken for granted and no good deed ever goes unpunished. Yet, once in a while I would again remember the exchange of humanity between Magdy and the major in the dead ground of the Sinai, something I never saw again in my later peacekeeping duties. Even now, despite the cynicism brought on by Canadian UN/NATO peacekeeping in the last decade,

remembering that day brings back a little of that warm
and fuzzy feeling. I hope that what Magdy and the major
shared will one day spread to a wider community than
soldiers, although I have my doubts.

Once again some valuable lessons for future peacekeepers. Bill
Porter has been very active in the CAVUNP; he was the national
president when Kofi Annan visited the Peacekeeping Monument. He is
shown here at the right with Kofi Annan, Lieutenant General Dallaire
and Fred Herman.

Bill Porter meets Kofi Annan

Chapter 18

BOSNIA 1994–1995

WAYNE MacCULLOCH

(Wayne's own words were used in this story.)

WAYNE MacCULLOCH was a cadet at the Royal Military College in Kingston, Ontario, when I first met him. In 1999, after hearing Wayne speak of his experiences in Bosnia I asked him if I could include his story in my book. It all started in the summer of 1994 when Wayne got a posting overseas on very short notice. These words started the saga: "Great, sir. When and where?" "Sarajevo, and right away. We're going to have to recall you from leave."

Wayne soon learned that the job was superb—operations officer for the mission commander, British Lieutenant General Sir Michael Rose. Few jobs could sound better. He was advised not to bring more than he could physically carry, as there was nothing available to help with baggage in Bosnia. Wayne was ready to go the next morning. He says: "The Swissair flight from Mirabel to Zurich and then on to Zagreb was long, but on arrival in Zagreb, there was more paperwork to be done for the Canadian Contingent Headquarters, and then off on the first flight to Sarajevo."

Wayne discovered that life in Bosnia was going to be different:

> I left on a French C-130 Hercules and the first one in
> quite some time, as flights had been suspended after an
> aircraft had been badly shot up. From Sarajevo Airport I
> was whisked down Sniper Alley, the main road into
> Sarajevo—so called because of its proximity to the
> dividing line between the two factions and the small arms
> fire usually experienced by vehicles travelling it.

On arrival at Headquarters Bosnia Herzegovina Command (HQ BHC), handover of responsibilities began in earnest. Detailed explanations of what territory was held by which faction, the political situation, current tensions, and introductions to peers, superiors and subordinates consumed the following week. Wayne's account follows:

Wayne MacCulloch

> As the operations officer for HQ BHC in Sarajevo from July 1994 to January 1995, I had an interesting perspective on the events of the times. At that time BHC was comprised of between 22,500 and 25,000 troops from several countries. Canada had one battalion group, based on the Lord Strathcona's Horse (Royal Canadians) armoured regiment (termed CANBAT TWO), in Visoko, about twenty-five kilometres away as the crow flies. But for the eighteen of us in Sarajevo, it might just as well have been in Zagreb. Travel to CANBAT TWO required a circuitous route, and passing through five checkpoints (three Serb, one Muslim, and one Croat), any one of which could deny passage on a whim. As a result, we were pretty much on our own to form views on the UN operations in theatre. From my vantage point, UN operations fell mainly into one of the following categories: Sarajevo airfield operation; humanitarian aid delivery; anti-sniper agreements; "safe haven" maintenance; exclusion zone enforcement; prisoner exchanges; and humanitarian medical evacuation.
>
> Sarajevo airfield operation was the primary focus of media attention. If anything happened at the airfield, it was certain to result in questions from reporters in short order. The airfield was a short single runway from northwest to southeast. For C-130 Hercules transport aircraft, landings were relatively easy, but not so for the jet-engined Il-76 of similar size and payload. One day the pilot did his best, but there was no way the fully loaded aircraft could stop before the end of the asphalt. Just off

the edge of the runway was an observation post (OP), manned by a seasoned French Marine junior NCO and his conscript assistant. The NCO had apparently seen considerable service, and was so disciplined that he could ignore all distractions from his duty of looking for snipers. Not so the young conscript. This day, the louder-than-normal noise of the landing jet captured his attention, and he turned around to look. Alarmed at what appeared to be looming disaster, he started tapping on the NCO's shoulder. Somewhat irked, the NCO shrugged off the private, growling at him to observe his arc of fire. But the young soldier would not be deterred, and in an act of desperation, grabbed his much-larger compatriot and spun him around. Astonished at the ever-growing size of the approaching nose of the aircraft, the NCO yelled at his partner to abandon the OP. They dove out just as the nose plowed through the rear dirt wall. No one was hurt, fortunately, but the mental image of the incident was humourously relayed throughout the area.

At this point, it is important to understand that the Canadian Forces had provided no course to teach peacekeepers how to negotiate between people who would rather fight than keep the peace. It was in Bosnia that peacemaking replaced the more docile peacekeeping.

Wayne's account continues:

The primary mission of the airfield was the receipt of humanitarian aid. Whenever the tactical situation permitted, aircraft from Canada, the United States, the United Kingdom, France and Germany would bring in supplies from Italy for the residents of Sarajevo. Far too often, someone would take potshots at these aircraft, causing the flights to be suspended. This would result in a flurry of activity as BHC staff would negotiate another agreement for the safety of the flights. These agreements were strong at the outset, but became less reliable with each passing day, until perhaps several weeks or maybe just a few days later another aircraft would be fired upon. Then the cycle would start again with fresh negotiations with the warring factions. And once the aid had reached the airport, it still had to be trucked into the city to distribution points. This ground operation was not an easy one. Several checkpoints had to be passed, at which delays and other incidents regularly occurred. When serious delays occurred, BHC Ops would dispatch troops to resolve the situation. This scenario played itself out seemingly endlessly, and the patience required by both UNPROFOR and humanitarian aid agency personnel to overcome such situations was truly astounding. In comparison, rush-hour traffic jams in Toronto or Montreal are stress-free holidays.

While the effort required to get aid into Sarajevo might have seemed huge, it did succeed. Compared to the dark days of 1992, before the UN became involved, it was obvious that great strides had been made in the relief of suffering in the city.

Another gap in training was handling the press. In Canada soldiers seldom have any opportunity to work with the press. As Wayne explains:

Another favourite press topic was the ongoing effort to maintain the Security Council "safe havens" of Sarajevo, Gorazde, Srebrenica and Zepa free from war. Sadly, the Security Council Resolutions had not established verifiable boundaries for these areas, nor even precisely defined what "safe haven" meant. The press filled in this void with definitions of their own, which were unattainable given the mandate and number of UN troops. But we did the best we could to alleviate conditions, despite often-unwelcome proposals and negotiations. And contrary to media opinion, the United Nations Protection Force in the Former Yugoslavia (UNPROFOR) did not have a mandate to end the war. In fact the original mandate of UNPROFOR had been simply to protect humanitarian aid convoys from being robbed. Having succeeded in that mission well and quickly, the target was set a little higher time and again, each time an objective was achieved. Thus, by the end of my tour, the push was on to mediate a stable ceasefire leading to lasting peace. Sadly, neither consents from the warring parties, nor the resources to ensure such an objective, were ever provided.

When it was time to discuss arrangements for weapons control, the problems were more complex and tricky. Wayne explains some of the details:

> What was a "heavy weapon"? Easy enough for tanks and artillery, but when it came to mortars and machine guns, things became fuzzy. The NATO definition worked for NATO nations, but many nations taking part in UNPROFOR were not associated with NATO, and the warring factions accept NATO definitions. Some of the weaponry in the Zones were derelicts on mountaintops around Sarajevo that nobody was capable of moving. We often wondered just how they had gotten there in the first place, and how long they had been there. But through all this the practise worked fairly well. High-explosive shells had ceased to rain down on the safe havens. Granted, we never did get all of them removed, but like everything else in Bosnia, success was best measured in relative terms.

One story that has always gained coverage in the press has been regarding prisoners of war. Wayne explains the situation in Bosnia.

> One of the more arduous, yet thoroughly rewarding, tasks was the co-ordination of prisoner exchanges. These were not restricted to prisoners of war, but included civilians ranging from children to old women caught in the maelstrom that is civil war. Exchanges were the responsibility of the Red Cross, who did a remarkable job of interviewing all of the candidates and assisting with their reception "back home," but their resources always required augmentation from UNPROFOR. Principally, we provided additional transport for those being exchanged, security at the transfer point, and the C3 (command, control and communications) to make the process as easy as possible. But these things were always frustrating and drawn-out in execution. Numbers of people exchanged from each side had to match exactly, and this was difficult to achieve. In the end, after maybe eighteen hours at the exchange point, forty or so people would be returned to friends and family. The expressions of joy and relief far outweighed the frustrations and fatigue always experienced. In a similar vein,

humanitarian medical evacuations were a routine event. In almost all cases, the people being evacuated were terminally ill, and relief was being sought for them so that they could spend their last days in the best care possible. Remarkably, these evacuations were generally conducted compassionately by all sides.

Wayne's words to the wise are repeated here, for they are so important:

> From my perspective there were a number of professional lessons to be learned that have wide and important applications: time required for battle procedure to take effect [time to execute a military operation]; the constantly changing political scene; the value of delegation/price of centralized control so that decisions could be controlled and adhered to; the accuracy of information; and finally, dealing with the media.
>
> Oftentimes during Canadian military training, time is a scarce commodity. As a result, there is a tendency to overlook the real time that it takes to perform such tasks as planning and co-ordination, in order that the soldiers are not left sitting around doing nothing. But on real operations, reality rules. No matter how much one would like something to occur instantly (if not sooner), time must be allocated and waiting endured if casualties are to be avoided and the mission accomplished.

This comment by Wayne is so true that it has been included in this story to act as a word of warning to those employed in similar jobs in the future. Wayne continues:

> In 1994 Bosnia was the big media story. The daily press conference was never the high point of our day. After all, the media business requires negative press to generate income, while we wished to show the world the lessening of the horrors of conflict through the enormous efforts of not just ourselves in UNPROFOR, but also of all of the other agencies participating in humanitarian assistance. Compounding this is the long-lived feeling of mistrust between the media and the military—the media tells all; the military keeps secrets.

BHC Public Affairs worked very hard to achieve the best relations with the press. A key to this was knowledge of all of the bits of the operational situation, even the really bad ones. They needed the facts distinct from our conjecture, but required the conjecture to stay informed on where the commander was leaning. We were bound only to relate facts in an impartial manner and not to betray any confidence we may have been given by a warring faction. The media were not so constrained, and would speculate freely, often causing problems for us to resolve. While frustrating, the best course was always to be courteous, honest and factual.

Administration in Bosnia took on some frustrating aspects as Canadian-made decisions were used in Bosnia. Wayne explains:

Clothing was an issue. While the Canadian battalions had the latest in cold-weather clothing, the Canadians in Sarajevo had none. As individual augmentees, which meant that we had no Canadian field unit to which we belonged, we had been told that these items would be issued in theatre. But despite having faxed the clothing sizes of all personnel to Zagreb several times, no winter clothing was shipped to us and an embargo had cut off supplies of food and fuel. This meant that Canadians were perfect candidates to become cold casualties, with no fuel to generate building heat, little food to generate body heat, and insufficient clothing to retain heat. Finally, after much haggling and cajoling, the clothing was sent on 23 December, and we enjoyed the warmth it provided.

Every nation has its particular diet, and those items that reminded us of home were important. Arrival of such items in Sarajevo guaranteed that morale for that nationality would skyrocket. Other nations took particular care to ensure that their troops received such comforts, but not Canada. We were told that such "goodies" were the responsibility of the UN, as they provided our rations. But the UN bought from European and local sources, which didn't include delicacies like maple syrup and cheddar cheese. Solving this one was bothersome, but not too hard: I turned to my wife, back in Canada. My care packages were the source of great anticipation and joy: chocolate bars by the case from Hershey's in Smiths Falls; beef jerky from Alberta; maple syrup from Quebec; instant pancake mix, candy—just about everything nonperishable she could lay her hands on. We had all-ranks pancake breakfasts in the officers' mess and other mini-parties as we could, but it remained a disappointment that the CF would not provide anything.

As the care packages came in by mail, so did letters from home to all BHC personnel. But our mail was the laughingstock. Where it took two days for a letter to get from the north of Scotland to Sarajevo, it took nine weeks for ours to arrive in July 1994. And unlike the daily mail delivery to others, ours always came in lumps weeks apart. Through much haggling, and especially due to the extraordinary efforts of the Canadian Postal Clerk, this time was reduced to three weeks, but we were still the worst of the lot. And few things help or hurt morale as much as the quality of mail delivery.

Master Corporal Judi Giesbrecht, the Canadian Postal Clerk running the BHC Post Office, deserved special recognition. She often put delivery of the mail well ahead of her personal safety, and the events of 5 October 1994 were but one example. While returning to Sarajevo with mail, she was stopped at gunpoint several times. Each time she refused to hand over the mail and talked her way out of being held. She then would try a different route. At one checkpoint, she was shot at, but managed to get away and finally make her deliveries in Sarajevo. In the fall of 1999, Judi received the Deputy Chief of the Defence Staff Commendation. While we were all thrilled with the news, I thought it should never have taken so long.

Overall, working in HQ BHC was exciting and rewarding enough to overcome the frustrations and fatigue. Despite the media reports, UNPROFOR personnel realized that they were making things better, and although peace always seemed more or less out of reach, Bosnians welcomed the efforts of the peacekeepers from the various nations. Without their efforts from 1992 through to the passing of the torch to IFOR, it is clear that the suffering would have been much worse.

This story proves that peacekeeping and peacemaking are tough jobs. I was very pleased to be able to have Wayne MacCulloch's story in this book.

Below is a picture of Master Corporal Judi Giesbrecht, who was finally recognized for her work in Bosnia.

Wayne was posted to Banju Luko in Northern Bosnia where he is the divisional chief engineer. Once again he will be looking for mail. Some things never change.

The mailperson in Bosnia

Chapter 19

GULF AND KUWAIT WAR 1990/1991

JOHN STUART

(John Stuart tells us his story in his own words.)

In late June 1988, I was promoted to lieutenant colonel and posted within the Director General Transportation Division at National Defence Headquarters, from my existing position as manager of the replacement program for the Canadian Forces administrative vehicle fleet, into the Directorate of Transport Resources and Plans 2 position. I replaced Lieutenant Colonel Jim Craig, who was posted on exchange with the US Army to their European Command headquarters in Stuttgart, Germany as a movement planner.

Jim and I had attended the last Movements Officers course to be conducted by the Canadian Army in 1968. My new position included management of specialized training programs for transportation members of the CF, and Jim suggested to me that the most important issue I could address was the ongoing resurrection of the Movements Officers course for members of the CF transportation community. It also included preparation of movement plans for deployment and redeployments of CF elements for all operations and training requirements directed by the deputy chief of Defence staff and his director general of Military Plans and Operations staff. The latter part of the job got me to the Gulf and Kuwait War.

Jim had recently completed Ex BRAVE LION, an exercise that moved a mechanized brigade to northern Norway to prove to all concerned that Canada could get the job done. Unfinished business was the completion of an agreement with Belgium that would allow the CF to establish a line of communication from Canada through Belgium to our proposed NATO assembly areas in Germany. He also indicated that I would likely be involved in rewriting many of our operational plans that had to be reviewed as a result of a recent government White Paper that had increased our commitment to NATO. He also said that there were

171

no new UN commitments on the horizon. Little did we know that my staff and I were to become involved in the most intense UN deployment activity since the deployment to Egypt in 1973, and that both Jim and I would become intimately involved in the Gulf and Kuwait War.

The excitement started a few weeks after Jim departed. The director of Peacekeeping Operations, Colonel Don Ethell, asked me to advise him on the requirements to coat vehicles in UN white for a potential new mission. This grew into Operation VAGABOND, a deployment of the Special Service Force HQ and Signals Squadron from Petawawa to support a UN military observer group being inserted on the ceasefire line between Iraqi and Iranian forces when their war (which began in 1980) was to end, on August 20, 1988. My staff and I wrote the deployment move order and later managed its execution from the NDHQ perspective. In the meantime, one of the staff, Maj Dave Stewart, had deployed to Ethiopia as senior logistics officer to support the CF famine relief operations there. The DGMPO staff kept us busy with deployment plans to move peacekeepers and peacemakers to such far-flung places as Kampuchea, Namibia, Nicaragua and Western Sahara.

The Oka crisis consumed the nation for much of the spring and summer of 1990. At NDHQ, the Crisis Action Team met regularly to deal with the situations as they occurred. In late July, my work with the NORAD team to develop the forward basing support plan had concluded and the USAF organized a trip to all proposed deployment airfields in the north. We left Ottawa for Schenectady, NY on July 28 and joined our American colleagues for the trip, which was to be made on a USAF Hercules from the 109th Tactical Air Group. On August 2 when we were flying from Inuvik to Elmendorf AFB in Alaska, the crew advised us that Iraq had invaded Kuwait. That night we were all glued to television sets where we could find them. I got off the aircraft in Edmonton and flew out to Victoria to visit my parents, since I was close by and my father was not feeling well. I called the director from home to inquire about this new crisis and his response was that I should get back to Ottawa as planned on the next scheduled CF Boeing 707 out of Vancouver.

The UN Security Council adopted Resolution 660 on August 2, which demanded that Iraq withdraw from Kuwait. On August 6, Resolution 661 approved economic sanctions against Iraq. In the wake of these significant measures, Prime Minister Brian Mulroney announced on August 10 that Canada would contribute two destroyers and a supply ship to the task of enforcing the sanctions. It was decided that Maritime Command would deploy HMC Ships *Athabaskan, Protecteur* and *Terra*

Nova, under the command of Commodore Ken Summers and designated as Canadian Task Group 302.3.

In my role as J4 Movement Plans, my staff and I were constantly involved in the co-ordination of shipping "things" needed by the Ship Repair Unit (Atlantic) to ready the ships. There was a flurry of activity to make the ships ready that included mounting Phalanx six-barrel 20mm Gatling guns, close-in weapon systems, and new electronic warfare systems; and the fitting of bunks to house the additional medical personnel and army anti-aircraft gunners manning the Blowpipe missiles. We became more and more involved in coordinating the movement of such items, since the senior staff wanted NDHQ to be involved. The ships were ready by August 23 and sailed from Halifax on August 24 amidst much fanfare. The deployment was called Operation FRICTION. The next day, UN Resolution 665 was adopted. It called on participating nations to use such measures as may be necessary to halt all inward and outward maritime shipping to ensure compliance with Resolution 661. The military situation had changed.

Early on, it had been decided that the ships would be supported by a Maritime Command Detachment under Commander David Banks. The location was not decided upon until Commodore Summers and a small reconnaissance group attended a mid-September Naval Coordination Conference hosted by His Highness Emir Isa Ibn Sulman al-Khalifah of Bahrain. At the conclusion of the conference, it was clear that the Canadian operating area should be moved from the Gulf of Oman into the central Persian Gulf, where US naval forces were thinly spread. Prime Minister Mulroney held a news conference on September 14, in which he announced that CTG 302.3 would operate within the Persian Gulf and that a squadron of CF-18 Hornets would also be deployed to the Gulf from our bases in West Germany. The air deployment would become Operation SCIMITAR. The recce team that included Colonel Bill Leach had recommended that the Maritime Command detachment be located at Manama, Bahrain. Commander David Banks had a new location and although I did not know it then, so did I.

Finding a home for the air squadron was a complicated matter. By the middle to the end of September, most of the airfields in the area were already overflowing with combat aircraft. It was not until Colonel Leach and Brigadier General Jean Boyle, commander, 1 Canadian Air Group, completed another recce and set of negotiations that the CF-18 squadron was located at Doha, Quatar. My staff and I were involved in the planning for the move of materiel from Canada to Lahr and then it was up to HQ Canadian Forces Europe to arrange for the onward movement of this materiel plus other equipment from Lahr and Baden to Doha. On September 27, NDHQ established the principle that all CF elements in the area of operations would be placed under the authority of a single Canadian commander.

Commodore Summers was appointed as commander, Canadian Forces Middle East or CANFORME, in military language. Although Brigadier General Boyle had recommended that the HQ be located in Riyadh, Saudi Arabia, Commodore Summers recommended that his HQ be located aboard HMCS *Protecteur* alongside at Manama, Bahrain with a liaison staff located at Riyadh. In the first week of October at NDHQ, Command representatives presented their views, and finally it was agreed on October 7 that the HQ would be located at Manama and be formed upon a signals squadron similar to that attached to an army brigade. This unit would form the core of the HQ with staff coming from Maritime and Air Commands and NDHQ. The communicators would originate from across the CF. Commodore Summers' recommendation to use Manama was accepted but the use of HMCS *Protecteur* was not. In unison with CF practise to name units according to the year they were approved and the core capability, 90 Headquarters and Signals Squadron was formed with an establishment of 160. I was not aware of much of the deliberations except that I knew the unit was to be formed. I had been on a short list to go to the UNDOF operation earlier and had not been selected, but my needles were up to date for the Middle East and I had a new passport. I let Colonel Leach know that I was available and thought that I would be able to at least be deployed to get the new HQ up and running. I had always wanted to be "first in." On the Friday following the meeting, he asked me if I would go to the HQ as deputy chief of Staff Support. A quick check with my wife Linda and I said yes.

I was introduced to Colonel Romeo Lalonde, the chief of staff designate, and Major Simon Arcand, CO designate of 90 HQ & Sigs Sqn as we went into a meeting with the J3 Operations chief of staff, Colonel Mike O'Brien. He briefed us on what had gone on at the meetings, including the information that Commodore Summers was not enamoured with the prospect of going ashore to establish a Joint HQ, against his wishes. I knew there were no standard operating procedures for the establishment and operation of a Joint HQ, so I assumed that the operations staff had slapped together a modest set of operating instructions. I "innocently" asked that I be provided with the written instructions that would guide us; to which Colonel O'Brien replied, "It's simple, find a headquarters and make it work. There are no instructions." Then Colonel Leach notified us that we had to leave on Wednesday to conduct a recce to find a suitable site in Bahrain. We were to return to

Ottawa and Kingston to brief NDHQ and the unit and help it deploy. If I had known that my comrades in naval logistics had formed a pool about how long I would last with Commodore Summers, I might have had serious doubts right then about whether I should go. Our deployment was named Operation ACCORD.

In the few days that I had left, I arranged for a new identification card, drew my kit and signed off everything that I was working on to one of my staff. It was rather strange walking around NDHQ clearing and drawing kit for a new assignment without a message in my hand, but everyone I encountered was more than helpful. I wear size twelve shoes, and since there were none available that would fit, I had to shop for desert shoes. During the weekend, I concluded that if the HQ was to be operational by October 28, then I should not return to Canada. I recommended that information briefs regarding our activities be sent and that Major Arcand should return alone to get his unit sorted out.

Accordingly, on October 12, 1990 we departed Ottawa for Mirabel airport and took a Lufthansa flight to Frankfurt, Germany. During our overnight stay there we got to know each other somewhat better. We shared a small bottle of Scotch that Colonel Lalonde had bought in Mirabel and that he thought would be our last alcoholic drink for a while. The next afternoon we departed for Manama and the unknown. We wondered why other passengers were getting on board with their bottles of duty-free.

The flight to Manama was uneventful. Our route took us south over the Mediterranean Sea to Cairo and then across Saudi Arabia to Manama. After clearing immigration and customs, where we received a seventy-two-hour visa, we were met by Commander Banks, who had been there for some three weeks as commander, Canadian Maritime Command Logistics Detachment (CANMARLOGDET). His introduction to us included the fact that we could not wear uniforms and that we would not be permitted to establish a separate military camp or living area. We would be in the Inter-Continental Regency Hotel until we arranged for more permanent accommodations. We noticed that the duty-free bags were allowed in.

What a shock it was to walk out into the open air. The heat and humidity hit us like we had walked into a wall. Having served in the UNEF during the mid-1960s, I should have remembered the heat. The hotel was much more inviting and there we met the other members of the team. Commodore Summers had come ashore with Commander J.Y. Forcier, deputy chief of staff operations, Commander Bill Manchester, medical officer, Lieutenant Commander John Maguire, legal officer; and the public affairs staff, Lieutenant Commander Ian Thompson and

Warrant Officer Vic Johnson. WO Johnson was a surprise, since I had last seen him in Ottawa, where we usually rode the bus to work together from the community of Blackburn Hamlet.

Commander Banks introduced me to Mr. Rishi Trivedi, who had acted as his agent to locate support services for his detachment. Rishi was a tremendous asset to us and provided invaluable service. He was an employee of Bahrain Maritime & Mercantile International, part of the Grey-McKenzie Group of the UK. I told him that we needed a building to house our HQ and adequate accommodation for about 120 people. He needed a few days to locate buildings that we could look at so Colonel Lalonde and I flew down to Doha to check out the situation there.

My old friend Lieutenant Colonel Garry Furrie commanded the Canadian Support Unit (Qatar). He and his staff from Lahr and Baden were working exceptionally hard at getting the support bases known to Canadians as Canada Dry 1 and 2 organized. Canada Dry 1 was used for the headquarters and infirmary plus the majority of CSU (Q). Canada Dry 2, established on the airfield property, housed the Canadian Air Task Group Middle East, including the pilots and servicing crews and M Company, 3 RCR who were assigned the task of guarding the facility.

We arrived just prior to the judging of the competition for the best-decorated living quarters at Canada Dry 1. The occupants of the prefabricated huts that comprised the living quarters had been provided with paint with which to decorate their huts. It was rewarding to see such enthusiasm and genuine art that went into these decorations. The competition had certainly raised the morale of the occupants. I was also impressed by the positive attitude of the folks working at Canada Dry 1. The atmosphere at Canada Dry 2 was different. There seemed to be an unfortunate split between the pilots who were being treated as "prima donnas," and the rest of the group. One item that I resolved to rectify was the use of rented pick-up trucks to transport the infantry company on their rounds. The officer commanding M Company, Major Blanchard, told me that the decision had been made to task them at the last moment, and since 3RCR had a NATO role, they could not bring their M113 armoured personnel carriers with them.

On return to Manama that night, Commodore Summers tasked me to contact HQ CFE to ask that the infantry be equipped with something that would be more suitable, should the company find themselves in an emergency situation. Another old friend, Colonel Clive Addy, assured me that he would sort the situation out and within a few days Grizzly vehicles were brought from Canada. The other problem of note was the visa requirement and process that we needed to go through to enter Qatar. Colonel Lalonde suggested that it might be better to request that we be provided with a helicopter or aircraft for travel between the locations in the Gulf. Travel by commercial airline was going to be cumbersome. Shortly afterward, a tasking order was issued by NDHQ assigning a CC-114 Challenger from 414 Squadron under operational control to CANFORME as a communications and liaison aircraft. (I was to look after tasking the aircraft but the task was shared with the J3 air staff, since the flights had to be recorded in the daily Air Task Order that was issued for all allied aircraft in the theatre.)

Colonel Lalonde and I agreed that should anyone coming over complain about the facilities that were provided in Manama, we would arrange for a speedy attachment to Doha.

Rishi Trivedi had located several buildings in Manama and on the outskirts of the city. It was beneficial that I had visited Doha before we inspected these buildings. Anything we saw was luxurious compared to the relatively austere conditions at Canada Dry 1 and 2. The buildings on the outskirts of the city were too far away from the HQ locations of the US Navy 5th Fleet HQ and the airport for quick travel. Plus, all accommodations were located in the city. We had seen a vacant apartment building called the Bait al Houra that would be a suitable home for the majority of personnel from 90 HQ & Sigs Sqn. I still needed to find another accommodation building for the senior officers and for visitors. No one had been impressed with the other buildings that we had seen until Rishi took us to an abandoned two-storey building that a tugboat company had used as a headquarters until the Iran-Iraq War (1980-88) had made tugboat operations in the Gulf untenable. The building had not been used since 1985.

The property was accessible by both road and sea, except that when the tide was out the sea option stopped several hundred metres away. The access road led from the industrial area surrounding the port. As a location it was ideal. It was about six kilometres from the downtown area and close to the US Navy HQ area. When Rishi had the caretaker open the doors, I almost walked away. The heat was unbearable and my first thought was that with one spark the whole thing would go up in flames in a matter of seconds. We opened all the doors and as many windows as would open and went for a coffee. An hour later, the heat was not so intense and we were able to walk through. My eyes took an awfully long time to adjust and I could not see much in the upper storey. I thought that the heat had adversely affected me. Then I realized that the walls and ceiling were painted black. The floor was a dark brown linoleum. However, it was big enough and there were several offices and a large room on the second floor that could be used as an operations centre. It was also the least expensive building per square metre that we had seen.

I quickly got Colonel Lalonde to have a look and we agreed that this building would do, albeit some repairs were needed. Commodore Summers agreed with our recommendation and tasked me with the arrangements. I told Rishi that we would take the building and shook hands with him on the deal. I wanted to assure him that we were serious about it and thankfully he took the handshake to heart as a "done deal."

Rishi and John Maguire drafted lease agreements for the HQ and the Bait al Houra that were acceptable to the owners. John had told me that I had exceeded my signing authority with that handshake and could be in serious difficulty. However, my motivation was to secure the buildings as quickly as possible so that we could get the unit on the move to Manama. I was also quite aware that the RAF, USAF and US Navy teams were fast on my heels looking for buildings and were just as anxious as I was to find suitable buildings. I initialled the leases and sent them off for approval at NDHQ by the deputy minister, who we thought had the right level of approval. The leases were faxed back within twenty-four hours.

The next task was to locate repairmen who could hook up the electricity, repair the plumbing and fix the air conditioner. As well, I hired painters to paint the walls and ceiling white. In the meantime, other staff planning went on. Colonel Lalonde and I scoured the city looking for furniture and were able to buy half of the requirement as used furniture. The rest we either leased or bought new. At the end of each day all of us briefed the commander on the progress we were making. I was able to report that we had signed the lease on October 18 and the buildings would be ready for occupancy, except for ongoing painting, on October 23. I had yet to clear a major obstacle, and that was to pay the rent.

When the leases were being drawn up, I contacted NDHQ and asked that the funds be forwarded to the bank account that I had opened in Manama with the British Bank of the Middle East. This was a long-established bank with origins in Hong Kong dating from 1889. My message traffic to NDHQ was to the effect that we needed to pay our first six months' lease in advance, as was the custom throughout the Gulf. The first response was, "Tell them to bill us and we will pay within thirty days."

I knew this would not do. Several phone calls later the message was still not getting through. I could see my arrangements slipping through my hands. The US Navy wanted the building and could pay the money instantly. (We would get our repair costs back.)

My plight was finally brought to the attention of Rear Admiral Peter Martin, who reviewed my request, increased my budget estimate to $2 million (CA$), and directed that the funds be sent to the account.

He also set in motion the process for ministerial authority to designate Commodore Summers the spending authority required for large financial commitments. However, I knew that the money would arrive too late. Rishi had negotiated all the grace that we could get from the vendors and we would be out in the cold unless I could come up with the money by close of business the next day. So I returned to the bank and arranged a line of credit with the bank manager sufficient to pay the 85,000 dinars for the leases. I knew that I could explain this later at my trial and might get a sympathetic hearing. To my amazement, the managers at BMMI produced a cheque for the entire amount made out in my name and insisted that I deposit it in the bank account as a no-interest loan, which I did. Rishi explained that they liked the way we did business and would rather lease the buildings to us than to the Americans, who employ a very complicated process for such arrangements. Our finance officer, who arrived a week later, was so shocked at this irregular procedure that he initially balked at paying the money back. We eventually worked it out after I convinced Doug that it would not be him going to jail.

My next major hurdle was benefits and allowances. I did not have a set of Queens Regulations and Orders and thus did not have any guidance documents to follow. I found that this was new territory and there were no regulations that specified what allowances should be granted. Lieutenant Colonel Mary Romanow from the Directorate of Compensation was very helpful in sorting out living costs for me. I asked that since we were not permitted to wear uniforms, we be given a civilian clothing allowance in addition to our clothing upkeep allowance for military uniforms. I also asked that all ranks receive a per diem rate for food. Even though each apartment in the Bait al Houra had a full kitchen, the ability of the personnel to cook all their meals was in doubt. They were working extremely long hours and since the cooking ability of most of them was questionable, a per diem rate was prudent and fair. Laundry service at the hotel was quite expensive and I asked that we be granted a reasonable allowance for laundry and dry cleaning. This was all approved, including authority to negotiate a laundry contract for the Bait al Houra. We were also advised that we would receive the first level of the Foreign Service Premium, but only to that level.

My staff had increased and I now had Major Peter Forsythe as my J1 Personnel, Captain Bill Rostek as J4 Logistics and Captain Charles Dussault as J4 Movements. Other staff members, such as Captains Doug Suky and Rod Gray, were added to the medical and public affairs staff respectively. They were all a godsend to me and I could see light at the end of the tunnel. Commander Manchester had completed a wide-ranging medical instruction that included a system to track Canadian casualties through the coalition medical services. This was going to be a tricky operation and we had better get it right the first time. With the potential for chemical casualties, there would be no room for error in identifying casualties and their treatments, conditions and locations. He also managed to negotiate the insertion of the extra medical staff assigned to HMCS *Protecteur* into the Manama Hospital where they would be more usefully employed and could assist in the treatment of Canadians.

Lieutenant Colonel Jim Bender arrived on October 27 to take charge of determining a fix for the long-range communications requirements of the HQ. The long-range communications radios that were brought over did not work sufficiently well and it was determined that a satellite system was needed. In short order Jim developed a solution and we were soon in business. The solution entailed use of FLEETSATCOM, INMARSAT and INTELSAT systems. These were to provide Commodore Summers with a very sophisticated communications link to every HQ that he needed to talk to. Unfortunately, when the dishes were being installed on the roof of our building one of our heavier technicians put his boot through the roof and we had to cover the resulting large hole with a canvas to prevent debris coming through. It was a wise precaution, since when it did rain in January the downpours were heavy at times. I knew Jim from NDHQ and the CAT where he was J6 Communications. Luckily he and I are the same size, so I was able to loan him some clothing, including a pair of my precious desert shoes, until he got his own.

HQ CANFORME was officially opened on November 6, 1990. The CDS General John de Chastelain and Deputy Minister Bob Fowler were on hand for the ceremony. A personal tragedy overtook me shortly after when my father passed away in Sidney, BC. I knew that he was not well when I last visited but did not expect this to happen so soon. Due to the ongoing preparations to make the HQ ready for future events, I told my mother that it was unlikely I could be spared for the funeral. Colonel Lalonde knew this and I was soon visited by Commodore Summers, who told me that if I did not go home, I would likely regret it later; and stated that I had done as much as I could to get the HQ in motion. I had a capable staff, so I went home for the funeral.

On return from Sidney, I flew home to Ottawa and visited NDHQ. I did the rounds with the operational staff and was advised about Oplan BROADSWORD. Before I deployed, we were involved in developing the movement plan for 4 Mechanized Brigade from Europe to the Gulf. It could be done but the cost was enormous. There were also other considerations, such as the expectation of high casualties. Colonel Alain

Forand asked me to do a recce of ports to determine the best one to use in the event that the government tasked the CF to deploy the brigade. Oplan BROADSWORD was highly classified and I was forbidden to discuss it with anyone except Commodore Summers upon my return. I decided that I should stop in at 1 Canadian Division HQ, Kingston, to borrow a set of Standard Operations Procedures just in case it really happened. The two books that I borrowed were my only operational guidance documents for such a deployment, and for subsequent support.

After a day at home I departed for Trenton. My wife knew the circumstances of my return but my three sons had seen me travel quite frequently over the past several years and it was just another trip to them. The flight to the Gulf aboard a Boeing 707 from Trenton via Cyprus was uneventful.

One item that I brought with me was a *Calgary Sun* cartoon. It depicted Peacekeeper A as a hippie peacenik complete with a "War is Heck" sign and Peacekeeper B as an armed CF-18. It was captioned, "If your country was being ravaged by Saddam Hussein, which one of the above peacekeepers would you like to see come to your aid?" That cartoon was an instant hit and soon disappeared from my wall to reappear on the back of an Operation DESERT STORM tee-shirt being sold at the market. Kudos to the cartoonist, since that cartoon was a great morale booster, considering the negative comments we were hearing from some members of the public and opposition politicians.

I also found that we had been moved into an apartment block midway between the Bait al Houra and our HQ building. I really felt important, since I had a separate suite on the top floor. Colonel Lalonde, J.Y. Forcier and Jim Bender occupied other suites. Commodore Summers was located in a villa near the one used by the Canadian embassy staff in Riyadh for R&R. He had spare rooms for visits by VIPs, and we were now out of the far more expensive hotels, except for a few volunteer staff members for whom we did not have room. On more than one occasion, those suites were occupied by visitors and their sleeping bags.

The rest of November and December was a busy time. Bill Rostek had been organizing an online connection to the CF Supply System. NDHQ had heard that the Saudis were providing free fuel to Coalition warships and aircraft and wanted to know why we were still buying fuel, especially for HMCS *Protecteur*. I assigned Bill the sorry task of cutting through the clutter of agreements and processes to determine where we could save money on the fuel issue. The chief problem regarding fuel was the location of the operating area for *Protecteur* that was not close to a refuelling point. She had to refuel at the nearest port and that was almost never close to Saudi Arabia. Aircraft fuel costs had also risen to unbelievable heights and I was directed to inquire whether or not we were being charged correctly. The invoices were correct.

Peter Forsythe had really organized the personnel management system so that he knew who was coming into theatre, why and when. We were still seeing new arrivals that had been sent on short notice and some were arriving without complete kit, including their NBCW ensemble. We were becoming overwhelmed with letters from school children and others. Plus there were boxes of goodies from all manner of corporations and individuals. I had to task Peter Forsythe with becoming the HQ Amenities Officer so that we could establish some control over the material that was flowing into the area. He had to ensure that these articles were distributed equitably to all units. It is a tribute to his organizational capability that complaints dropped to nothing within a few days. Jim Bender's unit had let it be known that anyone could grab a pile of mail addressed to any CF member in the Gulf and answer it where a response was deemed appropriate. We all wondered where children got their ideas about war. Some of the drawings included with the letters were quite disturbing.

In New York, the UN adopted Resolution 678, which required Iraq to implement all previous resolutions that required Iraq to withdraw from Kuwait. More importantly, Resolution 678 authorized the states co-operating with Kuwait to use all necessary means to restore international peace and security in the area and called upon Iraq to unconditionally accept the will of the UN by January 15, 1991. Thus the military situation changed again.

The US Navy buildup was swift and awesome. One morning I was scanning the waterfront and to my surprise saw two battleships, USS *Missouri* and *Wisconsin*, at anchor. We were also made aware that six carrier battle groups were to be positioned in the Gulf and Red Sea. Commodore Summers advised me that Oplan BROADSWORD was a dead issue. The tension was building and the US Navy established a defensive barrier in the central Gulf. In our harbour area, the US Navy inserted a reserve unit with armed harbour craft to patrol the water against Iraqi underwater intrusions. It was a period of intense military preparations and there was quite a degree of apprehension. The Iraqis were busy too. They held test firings of SCUD missiles and were preparing numerous obstacles and defensive positions to thwart any attack that the Coalition forces could launch from the south.

Some personnel changes took place during December that saw Colonel Lalonde go to Qatar as commander CATGME, to be replaced by Colonel Dave Bartram. The Challenger crew from 414 Squadron went home and was replaced by a 412 Squadron crew. We were also informed that the HMCS *Protecteur* crew would be rotated and that HMCS *Huron* was coming to replace HMCS *Athabaskan* in May. Bill Manchester was to be replaced by Commander Margaret Cavanaugh.

I celebrated my fifty-first birthday in December, and finally Christmas arrived. We held a "Men's Christmas Dinner" in the best of traditions. We had two bottles of Canadian beer each for the occasion. It was great fun and when the cleanup was being conducted the next day, the Pakistani headwaiter of the hall that we rented stated that we were the best-behaved group of all the military groups that had rented the hall. We also relaxed a bit and held a few other smaller dinners. We had quite a variety of visitors during that period, culminating with the visit of the associate MND, Mary Collins, and Vice Admiral Thomas just after New Year's.

When Lieutenant General Kent Foster visited he asked an important question: "How are you going to manage casualty notification?" The issue had bothered me as well, since the news media were all over. I could visualize a video of a Canadian casualty splashed across Canadian TV screens before we even realized we had a casualty. My response to him was that we would use the fastest means available to notify the commanders and leave it to them to notify next of kin. What else could we do; Commodore Summers did not have full command, he only had operational control.

My major concern was casualties resulting from a chemical attack. The medical system would ensure treatment, but those who were killed became a logistics problem. I discussed the situation with NDHQ and with the US Graves Registration unit from Dover AFB, New Jersey. They would ensure that the remains were positively identified. Contaminated remains would be placed in a double body bag and sealed in a casket. Other remains would be identified and placed in body bags as well, and full mortuary services could be provided. All remains containers would be stored in locally hired freezer trucks and trailers until a full aircraft load was ready for transport to Dover. Canada would be responsible for arranging pick-up of the remains from Dover and delivery to the place of interment.

This period of heightened tension caused us to take some prudent measures. Due to the potential for a pre-emptive Iraqi strike at any time, 90 HQ & Sigs Sqn had initiated an alert system. We practised putting on our NBCW protective gear in a series of exercises designed to ensure that everyone knew what to do. We started a duty system to ensure that we guarded our accommodations, and the military police personnel remained on guard at the main gate. Sandbags were filled and protective bunkers were constructed from rented shipping containers. A duty roster system to guard our accommodations was initiated. Bahrain provided security guards at our accommodations, since we were receiving daily threats of violence by phone calls from some members of the public. These were police troops and while I am sure they would have defended us to the end, they only had three rounds each for their bolt-action rifles.

It became clear to me that my staff and others could not man a guard duty roster and do their jobs at the same time. I recommended to Commodore Summers that we ask for an infantry platoon to be sent for guard duty purposes. He was quite reluctant and I could not understand why. His reluctance stemmed from loyalty to the military police, who had done a commendable job to date, and his built-in resistance to adding more people to the establishment. He finally agreed with the caveat that the platoon would leave their crew-served weapons at home. Again, I called Colonel Clive Addy and he again came to the rescue by quickly arranging for a platoon from 3 RCR to be tasked. I never did tell Commodore Summers that the platoon arrived with their crew-served weapons. These were quickly placed in the 90 HQ & Sigs Sqn stores for safekeeping.

In early December the Canadian Embassy Bahrain Office had issued an "Advice to Canadians" notification that dependants should depart from the area by early January. Towards the end of December, I had produced an evacuation plan for the embassy that included a warning system, household emergency preparations, emergency kit and a warden duty system. The embassy staffs were quite helpful in these preparations. We were also tasked to issue gas masks to Canadian civilians living in Bahrain and Qatar as well as to assist the embassy in Riyadh with issuing masks to Canadians living in Saudi Arabia. Personnel were brought over from Canada to assist us in this matter. Masks were issued from our HQ location to the embassy staff first and then to other Canadians and later to non-Canadian embassy staff. I never did understand the strict adherence to the "Canadians first" policy in initially denying masks to non-Canadian embassy staff members.

I accompanied Lieutenant (Navy) Dwight Houser and Sergeant Gilles Fortin of the R22eR when they were giving a briefing to Canadians about wearing the masks. During the question period, one of the attendees stated that he had heard that if you got only a little bit of nerve gas, you would not be affected too much. One woman asked why we could not fit a mask to her babies. Sgt Fortin was quite diplomatic and I could see that some people were still skeptical, so I jumped into the discussion. I was quite blunt and told them that the sergeant had told them the truth and a "little bit of gas was the same as a whole lot." I further stated that the reason children could not be fitted with masks was due to the fact that children were not intended to be anywhere near a gas attack and since children could not be fitted with a mask, they would certainly die if there were a gas attack. That sure quieted the room. The next day there were a lot fewer Canadian civilians around.

We later issued masks to US embassy employees and to US citizens resident in Bahrain. My evacuation plan was used as a straw man at the US and British embassies. During our discussions we learned that if things went really bad, an option would find us driving our citizens out on the causeway en route to Qatar via the desert road In Saudi Arabia while the British were evacuating their citizens the other way into Bahrain.

The governments of Canada and Great Britain had been engaged in discussions about deployment of a field hospital to augment their medical resources, which were stretched quite thin. On January 8, I was tasked to visit the British HQ in Al Jubail to determine what medical resources were required. Accordingly, Captain Doug Suky and I departed Manama and crossed the causeway into Saudi Arabia on our way to Al Jubail.

A Saudi visa facilitated the first entry into Saudi Arabia. Everything was going well until the border guards discovered our weapons and uniforms in the trunk of the car. No one had told us that military personnel were to go into another line off to the side and go through, but after much hand waving and pointing, we got the idea. It started to rain and by the time we got up to Al Jubail the area was in complete darkness. The hand-drawn maps that I had proved to be inaccurate. We came up to a US Marine checkpoint on the east side of the Al Jubail airfield, where we discovered that we were on the road leading to the Kuwait border. We reversed and stopped at a Holiday Inn that I remembered passing.

The next day we found our way to the airfield, the port area and eventually Brigadier Hardy, who was the commander of British Medical Services. We had quite a good discussion about what was needed and what we could potentially provide. Brigadier Hardy explained that they only needed surgical teams, but since the hospital was completely self-contained and mobile they were eager to accept the complete hospital. He made it clear that the surgical teams should arrive as soon as possible so that they could become acclimatized to the British system and equipment. Upon return to Manama, the results of the discussions were passed to NDHQ. This was to be the first of many trips into Saudi Arabia to make arrangements for the hospital. The deployment of the hospital was called Operation SCALPEL.

The staffs at NDHQ and Mobile Command had also been involved at their end in determining the size of the hospital and in discussions to determine command and control plus support arrangements at higher levels. I also knew that before the hospital arrived we needed a Memorandum of Understanding or similar agreement to obtain support for the hospital from the British Forces. Major Norm Heward at NDHQ developed the first draft, which was reviewed at London and was signed off towards the end of January. He later came over to develop a similar MOU with the Saudis.

A Mobile Command recce team headed by Colonel Chris Wellwood arrived towards the middle of January to formally conduct a recce on behalf of their commander. Once we had met the British commanders and completed the recce in Saudi Arabia, Colonel Wellwood was in a better position to make recommendations as to the establishment of the hospital and the dispatch of the surgical teams that the British most wanted. The team was scheduled to depart by Hercules aircraft, but shortly after the aircraft departed from Doha the air war started. So they were stuck with us for a few days until there was a window of opportunity to have the aircraft come in and collect the team. He had sent his rather large recce report by fax to Command HQ in Montreal.

On January 15, Commodore Summers directed that we contain all personnel in the HQ building and that we remain there until the situation was clearer. Just after midnight on the 17th, he requested that all ranks gather in the HQ so that he could advise us that the war was about to begin and wish us all well. Lieutenant Commander Darren Knight, J2 Intelligence was bunking in my office. On the 18th around 0400 hours we were awakened by the public address system being turned on and the duty officer booming out, "Missile Attack! Missile Attack! Missile Attack! Impact in six minutes." That certainly galvanized the place into activity. Darren was out the office door before I had finished putting my NBCW suit on. As soon as I had it on, I was about to follow when a sudden sadness overcame me. I had never felt so lonely. I did not want to die there. I had too many things yet to do. Then I thought, "Wait a minute, how does he know where the missile is going to hit? The launch crews do not even know where the impact area will be. They can only provide an estimate."

In a few seconds I had regained my composure and walked into the operations room to see if I could offer any help and then went to see Jim Bender. He asked me to accompany him to see the troops and we went down to the bunker. Most were sitting there quietly and some were trying to talk to their buddies, but it was a serene-looking group. Six minutes is a long time, but eventually the duty officer announced that the missiles had impacted in Israel. That caused some concern, since Israel had remained out of the fray until then. SCUDs were launched frequently over the next several weeks until the end of the war. I have pieces of one that created a very large hole in the desert about ten kilometres south of our HQ.

At this period, I was also aware that we needed more help. Colonel Bartram, Jim Bender and I worked on the staffing issue to ensure that we were only asking for essential personnel. Our mini-audit indicated that we were desperately short in all areas. I asked that we combine common functions that CANMARLOGDET and 90 HQ & Sigs Sqn both had to provide for. The situation could still change regarding the move of the brigade and I knew that the current staff could not cope with such a surge requirement. We did our work diligently and finally came up with an increase of over 100 personnel across a wide section of functions. The commodore accepted our plan and I was tasked with selling it to NDHQ. We eventually got most of the people we had asked for.

My request for amalgamation of common functional areas was rejected outright. Later, we were visited by a group that I dubbed the "four wise men" to review the case we had presented. The group was led by Colonel Bill Leach and included Captain (N) Greg Jarvis and Colonels Ron Paddock and Bob O'Brien. They were not entirely negative and I thought that we had made considerable headway. At least they had endured a SCUD attack. Little did we know that the day they departed Commodore Summers was requested to change his operational plan, and we took steps to consolidate CANFORME at once.

My next order of business was to write an operation order to pass operational control of 1 Canadian Field Hospital from Commodore Summers to Brigadier Hardy. (Bob Crane had volunteered to write about 800 words to describe the composition of the hospital communications organization that was rather unique for the period, but there was not enough time to wait for it.) We then had to arrange the reception of 1 Advanced Surgical Group. They were to start arriving by air on January 26 with the movement control staff on the first aircraft. I had arranged as the first order of business that the incoming personnel would be bedded down in quarters, due to the long flight.

The first three aircraft were out of sequence and all timing projections ended as soon as they departed Lahr. At Al Jubail airfield, incoming aircraft were being directed towards an unloading area on a ramp that was extremely congested. The aircraft, with all engines running, were kept moving during the off-loading process, since it was important to get them off-loaded and refuelled and out of the way so that other aircraft could come in. The US Marines provided us with ground guides and miraculously it all worked. The Iraqis even provided a SCUD attack just as we were unloading one aircraft, for added dramatic effect.

Captain Alain Boisvert arrived as my movements officer along with Major Hazen Codner, who had been sent by Commander Air Transport group to be the Air Lift commander on the ground. His arrival was a surprise, but we agreed to work the thing out. Alain developed the arrangements to off-load the ship that would be used to transport the bulk of 1 Canadian Field Hospital over to the Gulf and Hazen took over the remaining aircraft reception and onward movement tasks. We still had 2 ASG and the main body of the hospital personnel to move in. On one visit, I had no sooner left when the Iraqis launched an attack on the village of Khafji about thirty-five kilometres away. Hazen reported that the hundred or so helicopters located on a nearby ramp were very quickly evacuated out of there and the airfield went on full alert.

The MV *Arnold Maersk* arrived on February 19. I had arranged that it be berthed at Al Jubail port about twenty kilometres from the base camp instead of farther south at Dhahran. That port was too congested and we were subject to loss of the berth due to higher priority cargo. The Jubail port had its problems too, since an oil slick caused by the Iraqis was slowly moving along the Saudi coast with the Gulf current. It had also been subject to frequent SCUD attacks and it was the major ammunition port for the US.

Alain had developed a plan to use all available hospital personnel. Those who could drive were assigned tasks to drive vehicles off the ship, and others were employed to guard the main camp and otherwise assist the British Movements Group personnel who provided stevedoring services. We were able to import Captain Jude Maier from 4 CF Movement Control Unit to assist in that effort as well. I knew Jude to be a very experienced movements officer, and the British were worn out at that time, as were the US Marines personnel that were also providing assistance. The ship was unloaded in quick time and the vehicles were driven to the base camp inside of ten hours. It was a tremendous effort by all involved.

The oil slick was a huge problem for Saudi Arabia and Bahrain. Neither nation had enough resources to cope with the problem and had asked for international assistance. Canada provided a team escorted to the area by my old friend Lieutenant Colonel Andre Seguin to assess the situation and report back to Ottawa. Lieutenant Commander Al Cole was appointed as our liaison officer for this operation, which was to be known as Operation SPONGE. Naturally Al Cole became known as the "Sponge Officer." Canada was particularly involved in the air transport of several tons of equipment by Hercules aircraft both from Canada and Germany. Jose Carreiro from the Canadian Wildlife Service, an expert at bird rescue, joined Al Cole.

As planned, the ground attack succeeded quickly and by late February we had begun planning the return of the CF element home. The plan was to become Operation SCABBARD. I had suggested to Commodore Summers that we needed assistance in arranging disposal and retention of equipment and that we needed a supply assistance team to do the job. Lieutenant Colonel Bob Hinse arrived with a team to ensure that the equipment to be retained was properly identified and that all other items were properly disposed of. This was a tremendous help to us since I was determined that we would depart with a clean slate. During this activity, another old friend, Lieutenant Colonel Bob Chamberlain, arrived with a research team to collect Iraqi items from the battlefield. We arranged the storage of this equipment with the US Marines remaining behind in Bahrain at the airfield ammunition compound.

By then the movement organization had grown considerably. Major Steve Tighe was assigned the task of organizing the return of 1 Field Hospital from Al Jubail and Captain Charles Dussault was responsible for all other arrangements in Manama. This took time.

We were gradually thinning out the headquarters as well. The majority of the staff had departed by April 16 when Commodore Summers closed the HQ and returned to Canada on one of the last Boeing 707 flights. I remained to complete all arrangements and to ensure that we had paid all the bills. I also had to stay until Major Bill Legue in Qatar had confirmed that he and his remaining staff were able to depart as scheduled. It all went well and finally on April 23 I turned over our buildings and remaining cars, which Canada was still paying for, to the advance party from HMCS *Huron*. Rishi took us to the airport, where we said our farewells. He had been a good friend to us all. Major Ken Johnson, Captains Doug Day and Charles Dussault and the Chief Clerk, MWO Walsh, were the last out and I ensured that I was the last to get on the KLM aircraft that was to take us home via Abu Dhabi and Amsterdam. I arrived home to be met by the family and our friends Jack and Sue McGuire on April 24, 1991.

I learned from Jim Craig that he had been involved at the outset of the US Army VII Corps out of Germany. He was later tasked with the movement of supplies into northern Iraq where the Kurds were in revolt against Saddam Hussein.

Commodore Summers had presented me with a Commanders Commendation certificate and in March Commodore Summers, Colonel Bartram, David Banks, Jim Bender and myself were all awarded the Order of Bahrain by His Highness Emir Isa Ibn Sulman al-Khalifah. Commodore Summers's certificate was 1st Class and the rest were at the 2nd Class level. An honour, to be sure, but not well received by the bureaucrats in the Government of Canada. It took us two years to gain authority to wear the honour. I was to learn later that I was to be awarded a Mention In Dispatches award by Canada. All Canadian participants were awarded the Gulf and Kuwait War 1990-91 campaign medal and those of us who were there during actual hostilities were also awarded a bar to go on the ribbon. Saudi Arabia also awarded all participants the Kuwait Liberation Medal, but Canadians are not allowed to wear it due to a bureaucratic decision. I find that totally unfair to our participants and unworthy of the Government of Canada.

John gets his medal

CHAPTER 20

NO TWO MISSIONS ARE THE SAME

GEORDIE ELMS

(This story is in Geordie Elms' own words.)

THE ARMY that Geordie Elms joined in 1974 when he was commissioned into the Royal Canadian Regiment and posted to its 3rd Battalion in Petawawa was a "Post War-Cold War" one. For infantry officers at that time an overseas tour for Canadian soldiers meant service with 4 Canadian Mechanized Brigade Group in Germany, and peacekeeping duty meant service in Cyprus. Most Canadian soldiers would see service in one theatre or the other a couple of times during a career. The 3rd Bn, The RCR was Canada's commitment to NATO's Allied Mobile Force (Land) and had been left out of Cyprus rotations since it had returned to the Regular Force Order of Battle in 1970. In 1976 while serving in support of the Olympics, members of the unit were informed that would change in 1976 and that 3 RCR would go to Cyprus in the fall of 1976 as OP SNOWGOOSE 26.

Geordie spent his first wedding anniversary as the senior duty officer in the battalion's Joint Operations Centre ("Joint" because it was also manned by members of the Austrian civilian police contingent) in Nicosia. It was a quiet tour in a mature theatre. Signs of the 1974 fighting remained, but events on both sides of the "Green Line" had returned to normalcy as politicians on both sides hurled rhetoric and their soldiers moved lines of bunkers and barrels forward and backwards within the demilitarized zone. The busiest officer in the battalion was probably the Ops "B" or economics officer, who was actively involved in repatriation of refugees—generally through the checkpoint outside the former Ledra Palace Hotel that housed most of the Canadian battalion. By Christmas there were rumours of a pending Canadian Forces restructure; and that perhaps 3 RCR would be the last Canadian battalion to serve in Cyprus. However, when Geordie left Cyprus in April 1977, Canada's commitment to UNFICYP remained in place and would do so until 1992.

United Nations Truce Supervision Organization in Palestine

By April 1983, Geordie was serving as a staff officer at Force Mobile Command Headquarters in St. Hubert, Quebec. He and his wife, Shirley, were preparing to return to regimental duty with the 1st Bn, The RCR in London, Ontario. One Thursday morning LCol John Boileau asked Geordie to come and see him at 1600 hrs. After eight hours on pins and needles, Geordie went into his boss's office to be told, "There has been a change in your posting." The upshot was that his return to a battalion would be delayed for a year so that he could go to serve as a military observer with UNTSO in the Middle East. Geordie found it hard to hide his enthusiasm for that, because he had requested it on several occasions. Shirley rapidly became excited too when they learned it was an accompanied posting.

Their house sold, Shirley moved in with Geordie's parents in Toronto and Geordie went ahead. Once he got to one of UNTSO's six duty stations and found housing, Shirley would be able to join him. His first duty station was the mission's newest—Observer Group Beirut. In the summer of 1983 the Israeli Defence Forces still occupied most of the southern and eastern parts of the city. On 4 September they left and moved from southern Lebanon, taking up positions on the banks of the Awali River. The American-led Multinational Force (MNF) remained

the only significant international presence in the city, but by the end of August 1983 they were perceived by the non-Christian communites as partisan supporters of the Maronite-led government. Intra-communal fighting broke out and barricades between East and West Beirut became a "Green Line." Rocket attacks, car bombs and kidnappings became hallmarks of service as an unarmed observer in Beirut. During the worst fighting in decades, Observer Group Beirut (OGB) evolved as the international communities' eyes and ears in war-torn Beirut.

Shirley had been unable to join her husband in Beirut because of the fighting. One Canadian wife, Katie Bennett, had arrived before

**Geordie Elms on the
Northwest Frontier**

National Defence Headquarters prohibited the move of dependants to Beirut.

October 23, 1983 is a day Geordie will never forget. Having done a night patrol with a French officer, they had gone on standby and turned in for a couple of hours' sleep in a room in the OGB Headquarters building at Jahrze, which overlooked most of the city. At about 7:00 a.m. they were awakened by a tremendous bang—unlike the normal Khatusha Rocket or D30 round to which they had become accustomed. From the window they were watching a huge, dirty gray mushroom cloud arising from the area of the Beirut Airport, when a second, smaller boom broke and with it a second cloud. Two car bombs had taken the lives of 241 American and fifty-eight French members of the MNF.

By November things in Beirut had stabilized enough to allow Shirley to make the trip into Beirut aboard a Middle East Airlines flight. Four Canadian wives had managed to make it into Beirut before Christmas and the four families lived in the "Holiday Home" Apartment in West Beirut. On 6 February 1984 Shirley and Geordie took off from Beirut for four days' leave in Egypt. A few hours later the civil war broke out again. Geordie returned to Beirut about ten days later, leaving Shirley in Damascus.

Geordie and the other five Canadian officers who served in Beirut from 1983 and 1984 were awarded Chief of Defence Staff Commendations for their work in Beirut. The observers of OGB during that period were commended by the Secretary-General of the UN. However the most memorable came from the outgoing Chief Observer Group Beirut, Lieutenant Colonel Jean-Jacques Fourriere (French Foreign Legion), who left the mission after two years in May 1985. At that time he held a small reception and presented mementos to those who had served with him through those terrible times.

In May Geordie left Beirut to become the UNTSO military information officer at UNTSO HQ in Jerusalem. He was on a tour of Observer Group Lebanon in the fall of 1984 when a decision was taken to remove United States military observers from Southern Lebanon. As a result Geordie remained behind for an extended tour until replacement observers could be posted from other duty stations. The other Canadians of Beirut moved to other stations and home to Canada. Just after arriving in Jerusalem the Elms first met the new senior Canadian military observer, newly appointed to command UNTSO's Observer Group Damascus, Lieutenant Colonel Don Ethell, PPCLI. It was the beginning of a close professional and personal relationship that three years later would take newly promoted Major Geordie Elms into an area of the world he never envisioned seeing—Afghanistan.

"Good Offices, Not Peacekeeping"

Geordie was attending the Canadian Land Force staff course at Kingston in March 1988 when he was called into the deputy commandant's office and asked if he knew any reason why he was being specially selected to go to a new observer mission being formed to oversee the withdrawal of the Soviet Army from Afghanistan. He didn't—but he was pretty sure he knew who did. Sure enough, Don Ethell was involved and on May 3, 1988 he and four other Canadian officers were on their way to Islamabad, Pakistan as Canada's contribution to the first new UN mission created in over a decade.

It was a new concept and the traditional UN Military Observer title had been changed to UN Military Officer. Control of the mission came under a special representative who did not report to the office normally responsible for coordinating peacekeeping operations within the UN headquarters. It was a small mission of sixty officers drawn from twelve nations. The basis of their mandate was the Geneva Accords between the USA, the USSR, Pakistan and Afghanistan. No "Green

OP HAYRATAN. Major Geordie Elms (*second from right*) discusses arrangements for monitoring the final withdrawal of the Soviets from Afghanistan with a Soviet liaison officer while Polish and Ghanian team members look on

Line" and no role for the Mujahedin rebels. The most significant involvement was to be the monitoring of the Soviet withdrawal. From the mission's two headquarters in Islamabad and Kabul, officers manned observation posts on the border between Afghanistan and the Soviet Republics and patrolled the frontier between Pakistan and Afghanistan.

As the final stage of the withdrawal loomed, Geordie was serving in Kabul. He was asked by the Swedish Observer Group commander to draft a plan for the monitoring of the final phase of the withdrawal. That done and approved by the necessary authorities on all sides, he was then given the privilege of commanding the observation post at Hayratan that overlooked the Friendship Bridge, which spanned the River Amou Daria. Across that bridge he and his small detachment watched the main element of the Limited Contingent of Soviet Forces leave Afghanistan.

Geordie stood on the north end of the bridge and watched General Boris Gromov as he crossed the bridge and walked into the arms of his young son—he was the last Soviet soldier to leave Afghanistan. After that, Geordie and the other four members of Team Hayratan were taken by a Soviet aircraft to Tashkent. The next day the special representative arrived with the UNGOMAP mission's aircraft to take them back to Islamabad. UNGOMAP lived for nearly another year before it faded into peacekeeping history. Geordie left the mission in April to return to National Defence Headquarters as a staff officer in

Soviet convoys lined up prepared to cross Friendship Bridge, Hayratan, to return to the Soviet Union

the Department of Peacekeeping Operations (DpkO), working for his old friend Colonel Don Ethell.

OP Cavalier—Bringing Humanitarian Assistance To Bosnia

Geordie's return to regimental duty was delayed by a serious car accident in 1989 in which he suffered, among other injuries, a broken neck. However, by the summer of 1992 he was ready to return to regimental duty as a company commander with 2nd Bn, the RCR in Gagetown. The battalion had just returned in April from duty as Canada's second-to-last Cyprus contingent and was preparing to settle into a period of rebuilding and regeneration.

Geordie had only been in the battalion a week when reports began to appear in the press that Canada was considering a contribution to a newly reorganized Bosnia-Herzegovina Command being formed as part of the United Nations Protection Force in the Former Yugoslavia. Within two weeks, before heading to Zagreb and then into Bosnia, he was participating in a reconnaissance mission that saw him stop off in Lahr to arrange for the battalion to take over equipment that had been destined for Canada as part of the closeout of Canadian forces stationed in Europe. Here again as, the Battle Group's administration company commander, Geordie experienced the frustrations of mounting a new mission.

Political complications delayed the move of CANBATT 2 into Bosnia and 2 RCR moved into temporary camps within 3 PPCLI's area of operations in Croatia. They sat, trained and prepared, for nearly three months before they moved by road, rail and ferry into their new area of responsibility northwest of Sarajevo. The administration company was nearly 240 strong and drew heavily on reinforcements from outside 2 RCR and across the army. Geordie's fourth mission left him with a great sense of pride in the way this mixed group, drawn from every environment and trade, had evolved from a large collection of groups into a team that rapidly built two camps to house the contingent, while providing combat service support to the rifle companies as they carried out their mission of providing humanitarian aid to the Bosnian people.

Geordie Elms later returned to 2nd Battalion, The Royal Canadian Regiment as deputy commanding officer. In August 2000 he was promoted to LCol and appointed commanding officer of the Argyll and Sutherland Highlanders of Canada (Princess Louise's) in Hamilton, Ontario.

CHAPTER 21

MEMORIES OF SOMALIA

MIKE KAMPMAN

(Mike's words evoke a vivid sense of "being there.")

THE OPERATION in Somalia in 1992-1993 was in many ways a startling revelation for Canada's army. The disciplinary hearings and inquiries that followed overshadowed the true nature of the mission. It was not peacekeeping; it was *peacemaking*— something quite different, for the soldiers of the Canadian Airborne Regiment Battle Group were allowed to shoot first and ask questions later. This was, in UN terms, a "Chapter Seven" operation, with the expectation of combat and casualties.

For "A" Squadron, The Royal Canadian Dragoons, it was especially significant. For the first time, we were taking our aged Cougar armoured cars into operations. For the first time, we were deploying by air into a combat situation. And for the first time, we were deploying to the Horn of Africa.

The Americans called it RESTORE HOPE, and we called it DELIVERANCE. And for the most part, that is exactly what happened. While history may remember the torture of a young Somali man or the tragic desecration of the body of a brave American soldier, those of us who spent six months in the heat and choking dust of the Ogaden desert on the border of Ethiopia and Somalia will remember the heroism and selfless commitment to duty of our comrades-in-arms.

The memories are still clear:

The abandoned Somali Air Force base at Baledogle surrounded by skeletons of old aircraft and empty hangars. Trenches and stand-to drills, while a few metres away the American Seebee (construction) battalion hung their laundry in the sun and cranked up their ghetto blasters. The battle group orders group on Christmas morning, with a terrain model of the airstrip at Belet Weyne laid out at the bottom of a hillside covered with staff officers concentrating on the CO's words and the new mission.

The long wait of the crews at Christmas, standing by through the holiday season for the word to board the US Air Force transports to fly with the Cougars across the Atlantic. The word finally came in the last days of 1992, just before New Year. And it was on New Year's Eve itself that the first Cougar crew arrived in Mogadishu, to an empty camp on the end of the runway, with no amenities to help celebrate the passing of one year and the beginning of another. Then the remarkable generosity of the crew of HMCS *Preserver*, who gladly came ashore to construct camp facilities for the growing numbers of soldiers.

Like a scene out of a cheap Vietnam movie, US Marine Super Cobra attack helicopters rising in the morning air above Mogadishu and unleashing destruction on an invisible enemy, to be answered within minutes by heavy mortar fire landing amidst the coalition forces on the airfield. And all the while, soldiers carrying on with morning ablutions, as if such actions were everyday occurrences.

The final planning of the long road reconnaissance to Belet Weyne with the HQ staff, still afloat on HMCS *Preserver*. A long ride in a tiny rubber raft with the Canadian commander through cresting waves in the night, aiming for the welcoming lights of the replenishment ship, unaware of the sharks that infested the waters around us.

The German news crew who jumped at the chance to join us on the long road to the Ethiopian frontier, with nothing more than a sense of adventure and a story in the making. Such a sharp contrast to the Canadian press, who had lost interest and headed for home.

The first contact with hostile forces and the green tracers of AK47 fire lancing across the road in front of us. The calm confidence of superior firepower as the supporting attack helicopters came roaring in to reinforce our intent to achieve the mission.

Canada's flag is raised at Camp Holland, Matabaan, 19 January 1993

The link-up with the Airborne forces in Belet Weyne. The shock of finding no camp preparations, and the generosity of the Engineers in giving us a place to stay for the night. Then the new mission, to shepherd the battle group vehicles back up the same road we had just traversed. Climbing back into the vehicles for another run down the long dusty road to "the Mog."

The enthusiasm of the Sea King pilots as they supported everyone and everywhere, with some kind of superhuman ability to make their aged machines fly yet one more mission over land and sea. Flying "nap of the earth" in the same ancient machines, which were never intended for desert flying.

The orders for the security of the new Canadian sector. And the sudden rush to occupy the isolated village of Matabaan to prevent an attack by Somali National Front (SNF) forces. Crossing our first minefield, and entering Matabaan only to find more mines scattered about the village. The excitement of the village elders, hopeful now that help had arrived.

The decision to move the squadron away from the main Airborne camp at Belet Weyne to our own camp at Matabaan. The negotiations with the local United Somali Congress (USC) forces, led by Colonel "John" Hussein, Mohammed Farah Aideed's best armoured commander, in the civil war still raging beyond the Coalition boundary. The move of the squadron up the long road to the frontier, past the bloated carcasses of dead camels that morbidly welcomed our arrival to our new home.

The shock of being issued blank maps, proof that no detailed survey had been carried out on the "provisional administrative boundary" between Ethiopia and Somalia. The long, drawn-out process of area and route recces to fill in the details, greatly aided by our newly issued Global Positioning Systems.

The first advance to the northern extremity of our sector, to make contact with the SNF forces in the village of Balenbale. Our first mine casualty, the squadron sergeant major's Bison Armoured Personnel Carrier (APC) blowing up on an anti-tank mine and miraculously surviving with only external damage. Then our first mine-clearing operation to clear a way for the recovery team. Walking beside the lead probing team, all the time chatting with the sergeant major, who sat perched on top of his blackened vehicle, obviously glad to be alive.

The reorganization of the squadron into a true reconnaissance organization, and the gathering of detailed information on the route and forces at Balenbale, all in preparation for another push. The arrival of a US Special Forces "A" Team, who were quickly adopted by the

**Admiral Anderson, CDS, with Mike at Matabaan,
speaking with a village elder; March 1993**

Dragoons at Camp Holland. These American elite soldiers rapidly adapted to our ways, and became an integral part of squadron operations, especially enhancing our scouting and intelligence-gathering capability.

The second push to Matabaan, this time with far better preparation and organization. Contact with the local inhabitants and the final brief with the Americans to ensure no one opened fire unless absolutely necessary. The first glimpse of the village, and a wall of women and children running out to greet us. The flash of a 106mm recoilless anti-tank gun, the blast of 120mm mortar fire and 90mm tank fire. The frantic few minutes of our first major firefight, with the Americans calling for support. The relief of the ceasefire, with no casualties except the infamous Somali cow hit by a stray Cougar 76mm round.

The return to Balenbale the following day to establish the ceasefire in the sector. The meeting with the SNF commander, and the satisfaction of creating the first peace in the area in three years. And all of it recorded by a CNN news crew, who broadcast it around the world less than twenty-four hours later.

But the danger never let up . . .

Two days of shocks, as first one Cougar blows up on an anti-tank mine, then the other Cougar in the same patrol goes up trying to rescue the first. The growing sense of invincibility of the vehicle commanders was evident in the cavalier fashion that they treated the whole incident, but the tremendous stresses of facing danger every day began to mount.

Then the worst day. The lead Hummer Jeep of the Special Forces Team struck a mine just south of Balenbale. All four members of the crew were badly injured, but the Team medic took the brunt of the explosion. We worked for over an hour to keep him alive, while the medevac chopper from Belet Weyne made its way across the desert to find us. And all the time a sense of hopelessness mounted, and the medic himself, still conscious despite multiple amputations from the blast, knew that he was not going to make it. Sergeant Bob Deeks died on board the helicopter on the way to the field hospital, and suddenly the

Sgt. Webber, Cpl. Tetz and Tpr. Smith beside their Cougar after hitting a mine, February 1993

vehicle commanders didn't feel invincible anymore. The incidence of stress reaction began to mount.

Another Cougar hit a mine, and one of the Engineer Bisons struck one while conducting a mine-clearing operation. Again a miracle. All of the explosives stored in the back of the Engineer vehicle failed to explode. These two proved to be the last of the six mine casualties in the Squadron area, amounting to twenty percent of the squadron's vehicles. But even more important than the vehicle damage was the invisible damage to men's nerves, which were becoming more frayed with each passing day.

And more incidents with local forces, as major weapon systems were captured and cantonned in the two areas guarded every day and night by Canadian crews. T54/55 tanks, 106mm recoilless rifles and heavy machine guns on Toyota Landcruisers, twin Chinese 30mm anti-aircraft guns, and heavy mortars. And piles of ammunition of every description. Then the news of more insidious weapons beyond Coalition territory that we could not get our hands on—artillery shells carrying mustard gas, anti-aircraft missiles, and more tracked vehicles.

The Canadian commander's mission to negotiate a more robust peace. Three days beyond Coalition territory, without a mandate and without support. Cougar crews protecting forward refuelling points for the helicopters, and the long drive back to our side of the boundary. And no idea of the success or failure of the initiative.

Soldiers finding ways to pass the long, hot days and cold nights. Camel spider and scorpion fights in washtubs, and blowguns carefully constructed under the supervision of the American Special Forces experts. And who will forget the Camp Holland Golf and Country Club, the only eighteen-hole mini-putt in all of Somalia?

The many acts of humanitarian kindness by our soldiers. Rebuilding three schools and two medical clinics. The food convoys, and the impromptu children's health clinics off the back of the armoured ambulances. And the relief in the faces of the local people. And most of all, the smiles on the children's faces on the first day of school in three years.

The last week, and the handover to the Nigerian UN troops. The crash of a Somali truck on the side of the highway, with over forty casualties. Our last act of humanitarian kindness, as over thirty-five people were evacuated to our hospital to be treated for injuries, and the dead were transported to the local elders. And sitting in a tent that night, with hands that refused to stop shaking.

The last goodbyes to our neighbours, and the long road move back to Mogadishu. The vehicle cleanup, and a few hours on a beach that turn into a nightmare. A French nurse, her legs bitten off by a shark, carried to a medevac chopper by Canadian soldiers who were more shaken by the event than by everything they had faced in the months before.

And taking off for the flight home, and realizing that your knuckles are ghostly white, and consciously trying to unclench your hands from the arms of your chair.

> To Sergeant Bob Deeks and the Soldiers of Operational Detachment Alpha 562 of the 5 Special Forces Group . . .

> To the soldiers of 2 Combat Engineer Regiment, 2 Field Ambulance and the others who supported us . . .

> To the sailors and airmen of HMCS *Preserver* . . .

> And most of all, to the soldiers of "A" Squadron, the Royal Canadian Dragoons . . .

> The greatest honour was to serve with you.

CHAPTER 22
UNITED NATIONS PROTECTION FORCE
"A" SQUADRON RCD DEPLOYMENT, SEPTEMBER 1994–MAY 1995

DEAN MILNER

(Another first-hand account–Dean Milner's story.)

IN EARLY 1994 the Royal Canadian Dragoons were tasked to commence preparations to deploy an Armour Battle Group to Bosnia-Herzegovina (B-H) for September 1994. The Battle Group was commanded by LCol W.N. Brough and consisted of a regimental headquarters, one Cougar squadron, two mechanized infantry companies from 1 RCR, one administration squadron, including an advanced surgical centre, one combat support squadron and one field engineer squadron, for a total of 819 all ranks. The Battle Group CANBAT 2 deployed into Sector South-West in Bosnia-Herzegovia command. Sector South-West also included British, Malaysian, Turkish and Spanish battalions. CANBAT 2 was assigned the following tasks: monitor the confrontation line and report all ceasefire violations; man observation posts (OPs) and checkpoints; provide assistance to United Nations High Commission representatives and non-government organizations; demilitarize the Kiseljak Pocket; provide convoy escort; and provide mounted/dismounted patrols in the area of responsibility (AOR) and in the separation zone.

As officer commanding "A" Squadron (Cougar Squadron), I was initially tasked to man OPs along the confrontation line between the Bosnian Serb forces and Bosnian Muslim forces. "A" Squadron consisted of a squadron headquarters, three seven-car troops and an administrative troop. Each of the troops was assigned responsibilities for OPs on a rotational basis. The majority of the OPs were located on the Serbian side of the confrontation line, and this involved crossing through both a Bosnian Muslim and Bosnian Serb checkpoint to carry out our tasks. Our main camp was in the town of Visoko on the Bosnian Muslim side of the confrontation line. The situation on arrival in B-H was tense, as both sides were regularly shelling each other's respective positions, including civilian buildings, and sniper fire between the warring factions was a common daily occurrence. It was clear from the squadron's first few days on the ground that a presence on the confrontation line, and reporting and investigating ceasefire violations, were major priorities.

In addition, the squadron was keen to provide humanitarian assistance. This was not, however, an easy task, as freedom of movement was difficult at times and the Serb Brigade made it problematic to cooperate with civilian agencies. Minor humanitarian accomplishments were made through the Serb Brigade liaison officer, but it was evident that this was not a priority. Daily routine for the squadron was very busy, as ceasefire violations occurred frequently and each violation required a detailed investigation. For the troops the task at hand was sometimes frustrating, as it was difficult to monitor the ceasefire without a robust mandate to deter further ceasefire violations. One of UNPROFOR's major concerns was the number of violations into the Sarajevo exclusion zone. On a number of occasions NATO, through the UN, threatened the Serbs, but to no avail. Finally, late in October 1994, NATO bombed Serb targets within the Sarajevo exclusion zone. This was predicted by LCol Brough and myself, and fifty-five "A" Squadron personnel were detained on the Serbian side of the confrontation line as a result of the bombings. Just prior to the bombings, with the Serb Brigade announcing that their intentions were to detain Canadian soldiers and other UN troops on the Serb side of the confrontation line, I was visiting one of the squadron OPs on the Serbian side with SSM Skelding, just outside of the town of Ilijas. The duration of the detainment for the fifty-five "A" Squadron personnel was sixteen days.

The detainment was a difficult experience for many of the soldiers, because all connections with the battle group were disrupted and the soldiers were unable to contact their families back in Canada. During the detainment, the Bosnian Serbs threatened the Battle Group camp in Visoko by firing approximately eight rockets at the camp, one of which landed inside the camp. Fortunately no was injured, as it was early in the morning and very few soldiers at the camp were up and moving about. The remainder of the detainment was uneventful, but it was an unforgettable experience and a test of leadership to maintain morale and confidence throughout the sixteen-day detainment. It should be noted that I refused to give up squadron personnel weapons; and the OPs maintained their daily routine, in essence keeping the task at hand as the focus for the squadron. For the remainder of the Battle Group, the burden of contingency plans to break us out of detainment added to the stressful situation and an already busy daily schedule.

After the detainment and "A" Squadron's two-month deployment on the Serbian side, all sub-units were rotated and "A" Squadron was tasked with operating in the Visoko area. "A" Squadron's main responsibility was manning OPs and liaison with the many Bosnian brigades manning the numerous trench lines in the area. During this timeframe "A" Squadron also manned checkpoints along one of the heavily traveled routes from the Bosnian-Croat side into Visoko known Route PACMAN. Humanitarian Ops was a main focus during this two-month period, and the squadron did an outstanding job providing humanitarian assistance to numerous schools in the Visoko area that had been affected by the war.

Of the remaining three months of CANBAT 2's tour—three months in actual fact, as the follow-on Battle Group was delayed—the squadron was tasked to conduct reconnaissance tasks throughout the Battle Group's AOR. This was an excellent opportunity for the squadron, with its highly mobile capability, to conduct patrols throughout the AOR. The Cougars were highly manoeuvreable and the squadron interacted with the local people wherever they deployed.

In summary, the tour was an excellent experience for "A" Squadron and the regiment. Regardless of the difficult situation, officers and soldiers of the Battle Group made a sizeable contribution and assisted immensely with the humanitarian effort in the war-torn region. The Battle Group was also instrumental as part of UNPROFOR in providing the stability and deterrence to enable families in the Visoko area to get on with their daily routine and lives.

**Major Dean Milner receives his Bosnia Medal
from his father**

CHAPTER 23

THE COLD WAR WARRIOR:
NATO 1951–1993

To INCLUDE A NATO chapter in this book requires an explanation. I have never served in NATO, but what happened there affected my regular force career in many ways. In January 2000, Paul Manson, former chief of the defence staff, suggested a chapter on this subject would be most appropriate in that NATO was the major part of our Canada's defence policy, along with peacekeeping.

I had been a member of the reserve army since 1947 and joined the

active force in 1951. I was stationed with Lord Strathcona's Horse (Royal Canadians) as a trooper in Calgary when almost overnight "Panda Force" (27 Brigade) came into being. When I joined the Royal Canadian Dragoons in 1952 as a newly commissioned officer, the RCD "C" Squadron was already in Germany.

To set the stage from one person's point of view, here are the words of Paul Manson, from the January 2000 *Friends of the Canadian War Museum Bulletin*:

> So what did I do? Well, I was very much a NATO person. As a fighter pilot, I spent ten years on operational assignments in Germany and France, and most of my work back here in Canada was related in one way or another to NATO. It makes a point that is sometimes forgotten as the Cold War era fades into history. For many years, the confrontation between East and West

dominated the political and military scene, and Canada was a major player. Our 5,000-man infantry brigade in Northern Germany was composed of highly trained and well-equipped soldiers. The Canadian Air Division, based in France, Germany and the United Kingdom, was the best force of its kind in NATO, with as many as 350 fighters on strength at its peak. Our navy was a respected and very effective component of NATO's Atlantic fleet.

I did a rough calculation a few years ago and came up with the startling conclusion that more than a half million Canadians lived and worked in Europe over the years as a result of our NATO commitments. Every one of these young people—and most of us were very young—came home to Canada with a better understanding of the external world; and I would like to think that, in turn, we presented our European friends with a proud image of our own country.

As Cold [War] Warriors, we were not combatants, but that is surely the greatest measure of our success, since our whole purpose was to deter the nuclear war that threatened the globe with such profound devastation. I believe that history will record the peaceful end of the Cold War as NATO's greatest achievement. Canada and Canadians paid a high price for this peaceful victory. I recall that, in the year 1955, the Royal Canadian Air Force lost 110 aircraft in flying accidents, in which ninety-six aircrew were killed, which in that one year alone was almost as many as Canada's total military fatalities over the entire forty-three years of peacekeeping operations.

In the Canadian Army we were always training for war—nuclear war. Our individual, sub-unit and collective training never changed from that scenario. When I was at Staff College in Kingston from 1963–1965, our lectures, exercises and many visits to the USA all were designed to train us to be staff officers at major headquarters overseas. There was little or no training for static headquarters such as National Defence Headquarters in Ottawa.

In 1978 I became the career manager in the other ranks "world," and our primary aim was to keep the NATO Canadian units up to strength. In my case this was the first time I was faced with providing sailors, soldiers and air personnel for NATO. In that it was our first priority it took precedence over all other units. When I retired from the Forces in 1984 we were still sending additional people to Germany because the establishment had been increased.

In 1992, Europe was to become heavily involved in an action they had not anticipated: peacekeeping or peacemaking in Bosnia and Hercegovina. The Army in 4 Brigade was to provide the first troops; UNPROFOR was a reality.

Canada's NATO force would come to an end in August 1993. As written by Sean M. Maloney in *War without Battles 1951-1993* (1997), "It would have been easy to delay the draw-down, to subvert the process bureaucratically . . ." The brigade did not do so, and its professionalism was maintained right to the end.

CHAPTER 24

THE UNKNOWN SOLDIER

"A reminder to all Canadians of the human cost of our country's commitment to the cause of peace and freedom in the past, in the present and in the future."

Don Ives, Senior Advisor for Commemorations,
Veterans' Affairs Canada.

On May 28, 2000 Canada's Unknown Soldier's remains were re-interred in a granite sarcophagus at the base of Canada's National War Memorial. The National War Memorial has been the focus of national Remembrance Day ceremonies since 1939 and is a fitting final resting place for the Unknown Soldier. In 1920 the British Commonwealth's Unknown Warrior was interred in London, England and has represented all members of the British Empire who gave their lives in the First World War of 1914-1918. It wasn't until 1993, when Australia repatriated an Unknown Australian, that the accepted rule of the Commonwealth War Graves Commission for non-repatriation of War Dead was changed for this special event.

The story of Canada's Unknown Soldier is not a new one. When I started work as the assistant secretary-general of the Commonwealth War Graves Commission (CWGC), North American office, in Ottawa in 1984 there was a plan to repatriate an Unknown Soldier. The idea was raised again in 1996 when Jean-Yves Bronze of Kirkland, Quebec put forward a business plan to follow the 1993 Australian example. This plan gained support but was not implemented. In 1997, The Royal Canadian Legion proposed that Canada establish a tomb of the Unknown Soldier for the year 2000. I was a volunteer on this project for the Department of National Defence, in the very active part they would play in this national event. Two of my proposals were accepted early on: to not tour all the provinces and territories with the coffin, and to incorporate into the May 28th burial, soil from the provinces and territories along with that brought back from the original grave near Vimy, France.

The Millennium Bureau of Canada endorsed the Unknown Soldier sponsored by the Royal Canadian Legion. Many departments were involved from the start; to name a few: Gerry Wharton of Public

Works Canada, and Major A. Levesque and CWO D.G. Palmer of the Canadian Forces. In a special edition of *The Canadian Forces Newsletter* 6/2000, these words were written:

The Canadian Forces supports the Tomb of the Unknown Soldier Ceremony.

The Department of National Defence and the Canadian Forces (DND/CF) have visible and demanding roles in repatriating and entombing the remains of the Unknown Soldier at the National War Memorial on May 28, 2000. This singular occasion envisioned by The Royal Canadian Legion as a fitting project to mark the turn of the millennium [ended up] involving over 1,000 DND/CF personnel, both military and civilian, including Canadian Rangers and cadets, plus thousands of hours of dedicated labour.

The difficult task of steering the project for those "thousands of hours of dedicated labour" and all other departments fell to Duane Daly of Dominion Command, The Royal Canadian Legion, who chaired the large committee that planned and produced the actual event.

This photograph of the Vimy Memorial shows where the Unknown Soldier began his journey home early on the morning of May

The Vimy Memorial, France

25, 2000. M. Jean Dussourd, Prefect of the Pas-de-Calais, initiated the ceremony. The vice-chairman of the CWGC, Admiral Sir John Kerr, GCB DL, commenced the official transfer of the Unknown Soldier's remains from their guardianship to that of the Government of Canada. The coffin was passed to the Canadians after a short ceremony and then it was taken to Lille where it was placed on a CF airbus for the flight home to Canada.

On the evening of May 25, some twenty members of the Perley and Rideau Veterans' Health Care Centre came to the Cartier Square Drill Hall to view the Unknown Soldier's coffin as it was placed on top of a twenty-five-pounder field gun before being moved to Parliament Hill. The veterans, most of them from World War Two, found this a very emotional event. There were some twenty members of the Ottawa Chapter, Canadian Association of Veterans in United Nations Peacekeeping to assist the veterans with their wheelchairs and walkers. We left the veterans behind with the health centre staff and rushed to Parliament Hill to welcome the Unknown Soldier. Visitation began in the Hall of Honour.

Next day we were all shocked and saddened by the news that The Royal Canadian Legion Dominion president Chuck Murphy had died in his sleep. Chuck Murphy (a peacetime member of Lord Strathcona's Horse [Royal Canadians]), hailing from Coquitlam, British Columbia, had been elected Dominion president in Winnipeg, Manitoba in June 1998. He was a prime mover for the Two-Minute Wave of Silence of 1999 and in the realization of The Tomb of the Unknown Soldier project.

Sunday May 28 dawned as a cloudy, overcast day and I walked to Parliament Hill to join the pallbearers. I was honoured to have been chosen as an "Honourary" to represent all retired peacekeepers. When the time came to take my position at the front left beside the gun carriage I was filled with pride. The order to slow-march came and I focused on the feet of Brigadier General Michel Maisonneuve, the funeral commander, to stay in step. On arrival at the National War Memorial I could not believe the applause that thundered forth for the veterans on parade. As I was so close to the coffin I had a clear view of every part of the service. Brigadier General Farwell, the chaplain general, did not rush the service and every word he spoke was full of meaning. Our commander-in-chief, Her Excellency Adrienne Clarkson, gave a wonderful eulogy. I have included portions of it here, for in future years Canadians may want to recall what was said on that very special day in May in the year 2000 when our Unknown Soldier came home.

"He is every soldier in all of our wars"

The following is an edited text of the eulogy delivered by Gov. Gen. Adrienne Clarkson (taken from the *Ottawa Citizen*, Monday, May 29, 2000):

Wars are as old as history. Over 2,000 years ago, Herodotus wrote: "In peace, sons bury their fathers; in war, fathers bury their sons." Today, we are gathered together as one to bury someone's son. The only certainty about him is that he was young. If death is a debt we all must pay, he paid before he owed it.

We do not know whose son he was. We do not know his name. We do not know if he was a Macpherson or a Chartrand. He could have been a Kaminski or a Swiftarrow. We do not know if he was a father himself. We do not know if his mother or wife received that telegram with the words "Missing in Action" typed with electrifying clarity on the anonymous piece of paper. We do not know whether he had begun truly to live his life as a truck driver or a scientist, a miner or a teacher, a farmer or a student. We do not know where he came from . . .

Did he have brown eyes? Did he know what it was to love someone and be loved back? Was he a father who had not seen his child? . . .

We will never know the answers to these questions. And we, by this act today, are admitting with terrible finality that we will never know those answers.

We cannot know him. And no honour we do him can give him the future that was destroyed when he was killed. Whatever life he could have led, whatever choices he could have made are all closed off. They are over. We are honouring that unacceptable thing—a life stopped by doing one's duty. The end of a future, the death of dreams.

Yet we give thanks for those who were willing to sacrifice themselves and who gave their youth and their future so that we could live in peace. With their lives they ransomed our future.

We have a wealth of witnesses in Canada to describe to us the unspeakable horror and frightening maelstrom that war brings. What that First World War was like has been described in our poetry, novels and paintings. Some of our greatest artists came out of that conflict, able to create beauty out of the hell that they had seen. The renowned member of the Group of Seven, F.H. Varley, was one of those artists. Writing in April 1918 he said: "You in Canada . . . cannot realize at all what war is like. You must see it and live it. You must see the barren deserts war has made of once fertile country . . . see the turned-up graves, see the dead on the field, freakishly mutilated . . . headless, legless, stomachless, a perfect body and a passive face and a broken empty skull . . . see your own countrymen, unidentified, thrown into a cart, their coats over them, boys digging a grave in a land of yellow slimy mud and green pools of water under a weeping sky. You must have heard the screeching shells and had the shrapnel fall around you, whistling by you—seen the results of it, seen scores of horses, bits of horses lying around in the open—in the street and soldiers marching by these scenes as if they never knew of their presence. Until you've lived this . . . you cannot know."

In honouring this Unknown Soldier today, through this funeral and this burial, we are embracing the fact of the anonymity and saying that because we do not know him and we do not know what he could have become, he has become more than one body, more than one grave. He is an ideal. He is a symbol of all sacrifice. He is every soldier in all our wars.

Our veterans, who are here with us today, know what it is to have been in battle and to have seen their friends cut down in their youth. That is why remembrance is so necessary and yet so difficult. It is necessary because we must not forget and it is difficult because the pain is never forgotten.

Whatever dreams we have, they were shared in some measure by this man who is only unknown by name but who is known in the hearts of all Canadians by all the virtues that we respect—selflessness, honour, courage and commitment.

We are now able to understand what was written in 1916 by the grandson of Louis Joseph Papineau, Maj. Talbot Papineau, who was killed two years later: "Is their

sacrifice to go for nothing or will it not cement a
foundation for a true Canadian nation, a Canadian nation
independent in thought, independent in action, independent even in its political organization—but in spirit
united for high international and humane purposes . . ."

The wars fought by Canadians in the twentieth
century were not fought for the purpose of uniting
Canada, but the country that emerged was forged in the
smithy of sacrifice. We will not forget that.

This unknown soldier was not able to live out his
allotted span of life to contribute to his country. But in
giving himself totally through duty, commitment, love
and honour he has become part of us forever. As we are
part of him.

During the entire process of meetings and decision-making, I was
putting this book together. All the time I kept hoping that maybe one
voice could rekindle interest in our military history. The Unknown
Soldier did that perfectly. This article written by Graham N. Green, a
member of the editorial board, appeared in the *Ottawa Citizen* Tuesday,
May 30, 2000, and says it all.

The unspoken message of the Unknown Soldier
We buried more than just our Unknown Soldier at
Sunday's emotional ceremony at the National War
Memorial. We also buried our indifference to the
sacrifices the men and women of Canada's Armed Forces
have made—and continue to make—on our behalf.

No one planned it that way. It just happened, as
Canadians from all walks of life and all age groups
spontaneously abandoned their normal reserve about
Canada's military history and traditions to pay tribute to
the sacrifices war demands of all of us. In the process, we
sent a powerful message—to the veterans, to those who
continue their legacy on active service with today's
Armed Forces and, most importantly, to our political
leaders—that our military is important, that it is worth
supporting and that it is worth spending what it takes to
do the job . . .

Canada's politicians seem to have convinced
themselves we are uncomfortable with our military past
and see ourselves only as peacekeepers, not warriors. But

the politicians are wrong and the tens of thousands of
people who paid tribute to the Unknown Soldier made
that clearer than perhaps at any time in the past forty
years.

This chapter was supposed to be short and factual, but I found that
impossible to do. I saw the ravages of the Second World War caused by
German bombing first-hand as an English schoolboy. I first put on a
Canadian Army uniform in October 1947, when I joined the reserves
while attending school in British Columbia. The Unknown Soldier was
very important to me as I thought about the young men I had gotten to
know in England who went overseas and never returned. I was project
director of **Canada Remembers,** which took place overseas in 1994
and 1995, but this event in Ottawa truly pulled at my heartstrings.

Here is the photograph taken by Wayne Cuddington of the *Ottawa
Citizen*. It was the only photo of the National War Memorial that
appeared in the *Citizen*, Monday, May 29, 2000.

The Final Resting Place: Ottawa, Ontario, 28 May 2000

CHAPTER 25

THE VETERAN

In THIS, the second last chapter of the book, I wish to pay tribute to the veteran. *The Oxford Concise Dictionary* defines a veteran as "a person who has grown old in or had a long experience of (especially military) service or occupation."

2nd Lt. Bill Gardam

My father is but one of many veterans to whom I pay tribute. He served in the Middle East in the First World War and was badly wounded in the Second Battle of Beersheba on October 28, 1917, having been shot through the lung. While being evacuated by a cavalry soldier, he was further injured, when the horse carrying him was shot. It fell on Dad, pushing a broken rib through his other lung. He was carried by a London Yeomanry soldier and finally made it to Rafah Railway Station in an oxcart. My most endearing memories of my father are of a man who served his country very well, and who suffered from that 1917 wound until the day he died, on December 27, 1981.

My life has been filled with meeting veterans from all over

Bill Gardam, Victoria, BC

the world. In 1998 I met German veterans who had fought against Canadians at Ortona. The spirit of comradeship between veterans is the same the world over and it proves that friendships made when under duress and fear are stronger than any other kind.

I recall the war years in Britain when I was a schoolboy and met the US Army Air Corps crews after they came back from a bombing mission over Germany. I remember the Commonwealth sailors, soldiers and airmen who staged through our English village on the way to be decorated by King George VI for bravery in foreign battlefields. Above all, I will never forget those wonderful men and women who grace the pages of my previous oral history books.

If you walk behind the wheelchair and listen to a veteran's story and perhaps travel through his memorabilia with him you realize that the veteran's worth to society is an immeasurable boundless treasure of service towards the nation. Veterans accept what is provided for them without question. When I wrote my father's First World War story I strained to hear his failing voice as he recounted his epic story of 1917; it made my respect for him and his generation grow beyond bounds.

When I asked Veterans Affairs Canada (VAC) for statistics on veterans, I was amazed to find that "one in four males over the age of sixty-five in Canada is a veteran." The statistics go on to report that "at the end of 1999-2000 [the estimated veteran population] was 383,000." I knew that there was a small percentage of veterans actually drawing benefits from VAC. It is important to note that the postwar population of men and women who have served Canada in the navy, army and air force grows as the number of wartime veterans decreases. It is from peacekeeping and service in Canada that the veteran population grows. The same VAC source states that "some 28,320 eligible members or former members of the Canadian Forces also received benefits and services." This one statement is repeated for it shows how significant veterans are in Canada; "one in four males over sixty-five is a veteran."

When one compares the statistics between wartime veteran clients and Canadian Forces veteran clients, the first group goes from an estimated 112,128 in 1998-99 to an estimated 93,463 in 2001-2002, while the Canadian Forces group from the same time frame goes from 27,402 to 33,064.

These numbers are very important when one considers the current Royal Canadian Legion (RCL) population and the very essential need for former Canadian Forces members to join it. If the very spirit of the Legion is not to pass into the history books due to lack of interest, something has to be done to encourage new membership.

As noted in Edward C. Russell's book *Customs and Traditions of the Canadian Armed Forces* (1980):

> Canadians in the past learned to their sorrow that
> sometimes a people must stand and fight for the
> principles they cherish. Essential characteristics of a
> military force charged with defence of a people are the
> standards of training, the levels of discipline, the quality
> of leadership, which together constitute professional
> competence. The goal, then, is to prepare the sailor,
> soldier and airman to face with confidence and spirit the
> stresses and demands of modern warfare.

When I look back on the years I spent in uniform, full time and part time from 1947 to 1995, I have to wonder if Edward C. Russell's words have gone unheeded with the passage of time. Peacekeeping has produced a different person from the wartime milieu and the "rules of war" followed by previous generations are not easily followed now. The serviceperson of today has a whole new set of problems facing him or her, yet together they are known around the world for their professionalism and dedication to duty. Regimental associations have no trouble attracting former members to join because there is that common bond between friends. I have found this fact to be true not only for the Royal Canadian Legion, but for the Canadian Association of Veterans in United Nations Peacekeeping as well.

The veterans I know from wartime years often speak of today's armed forces and wonder why public support is not as strong as it was in "their time." It will take solid leadership and public concern for tomorrow's veterans to bring more meaning to a service person's life and make "service before self" come back into vogue.

The 250 veterans who are residents at The Perley and Rideau Veterans' Health Center here in Ottawa are living proof of what the veterans of the past have done for our country. There is an epitaph from the Second World War that applies to all veterans, past and present. It goes like this:

> **When you go home,**
> **Tell them of us and say,**
> **For your tomorrow,**
> **We gave our today.**

My sincere thanks go to Janice Summerby of Veterans' Affairs Canada for all of her help with this chapter.

Chapter 26

THE PEACEKEEPING MONUMENT

THE PEACEKEEPING MONUMENT in Ottawa was produced as a joint venture of the Department of National Defence (DND) and the National Capital Commission (NCC). This chapter will explain the reason a monument was built and why it is located on Sussex Drive opposite the Notre Dame Cathedral.

Even before the Nobel Peace Prize was awarded to peacekeepers in 1988, DND had been working on a plan to commemorate peacekeepers. Colonel Andre Gauthier, a well-known military sculptor, had proposed a statue on the lands of 101 Colonel By. Once the Nobel Prize was announced the focus shifted to something larger. Construction began on the site in the fall of 1991 with completion in

The three figures

just one year. I was named as the DND project director.

The NCC ran the competition to select the winning submission. The winner was the design submitted by a B.C. team composed of Jack Harman, sculptor, Richard Henriquez, urban designer and Cornelia Oberlander, landscape architect. Jack Harman had won the Department of Public works contract for the equestrian statue of Queen Elizabeth II the previous year, and Queen Elizabeth unveiled it on 1 July 1992.

In a Masters' thesis submitted in 1998, John Roberts wrote, "The monument would be Canada's answer to the Nobel Peace Prize and would be a visible commitment of Canada to the United Nations."

Jean Pigott was the chairperson of the NCC and was acting on a suggestion made by Brigadier General (retired) Clay Beattie that a peacekeeping monument be built. The land chosen was an open landscaped circle at Sussex and St. Patrick across from the National Art Gallery. This site was on the Mile of History segment of Confederation Boulevard. The cost of the structure was to be shared, with DND providing $2.3 million and the NCC the remaining part of the total of $2.8 million.

The competition guidelines for the winning team were:

> The Peacekeeping Monument is a tribute to the living, not a memorial to the dead. The intent of the monument is to recognize and celebrate through artistic, inspirational and tangible form Canada's past and present peacekeeping role in the world. In that since it will represent a fundamental Canadian value: no missionary zeal to impose our way of life on others but an acceptance of the responsibility to

Jack Harman, Cornelia Oberlander, and Richard Henriquez

assist them in determining their own futures by ensuring a nonviolent climate in which to do so.

The CDS, General de Chastelaine's guidelines to me were simple: it must be easy to identify, it should need no explanation of what it represents, and peacekeepers must accept it. Those instructions I followed with the NCC throughout the planning stage. On 1 July 1992, the NCC opened the monument site to the public to see the work in progress. Public opinion was very strong that the names of deceased service people who died as peacekeepers be engraved on the walls of the monument. In that this is a monument to peacekeepers and NOT a memorial to the dead, DND compromised by having *Their Name Liveth For Evermore* engraved on the walls of the Sacred Grove of twelve oak trees. The grove is slightly removed from the monument and is on the north side of the area. Its walls were made low enough to be used as seats where people could sit quietly and reflect upon the monument.

When the team from CFB Chilliwack arrived with the three large crates, all the way from Gibson, British Columbia, NCC had arranged for a crane to lift the statues into place. The Public Works crew were ready to do the actual placement when Jack Harman requested that the United Nations Observer (UNMO) and the rifle-carrying soldier be switched. As Jack said, "You cannot have a rifle-bearing soldier above the word 'Reconciliation'—it may mean 'or else.'"

The other change that had been made during the sculpting phase was to alter the UNMO to make him not just an army figure, since UNMOs are selected from all three branches of the service. The radio operator was re-sculpted to make her appear more feminine by moving the accoutrements on the belt around her waist.

The debris inside the walls are fashioned from actual photographs of the "Green Line" that Major General Milner provided from Cyprus. With the passage of time the ruins have become more like the actual Green Line. When the vegetation is in bloom it gives the ruins a softness and tranquillity, and the harshness is muted.

When the actual dedication parade took place on 8 October 1992, all Canadian peacekeeping, with the exception of West Irian, was represented. Major General Lew Mackenzie and several peacekeepers who had just returned home represented the most recent mission from the former Yugoslavia. The actual unveiling of the three statues went off without a hitch because Gerry Wharton of Public Works had members of his staff stay out of camera view, with tapes attached to the blue sheets. As the cord was pulled, the cloth vanished out of sight. The only last-minute change was made when Prime Minister Mulroney asked the

CDS if he could assist in the unveiling of the statue of the radio operator. General de Chastelaine obliged, and I told the other two in the photo what was happening. The CDS kneeled in the photo to make room for the prime minister.

The actual parade went very well with each contingent giving the "eyes right" to the Governor General. In his speech, Ramon Hnatyshyn said, "The monument being unveiled today will stand as a lasting tribute for generations of Canadians and visitors alike, calling us to keep working for peace in diversity." One of the contingents, Dominican Republic 1965-1966, had just one Canadian, Paul Mayer, who had won the George Medal for bravery in the Congo when he rescued missionaries from the rebels on 25 January 1964. The largest contingent was Cyprus, led by Brigadier General Clay Beattie. Major Pierre Lamontagne provided on-line TV assistance to Don Newman and identified each mission as they marched past.

US Secretary of State Madelaine K. Albright with MND Art Eggleton, CDS General Baril, and the author, March 10, 1998

In John Roberts's thesis he writes about each new mission that is inscribed on the mission wall; ten new ones were carved in 1999. John says, "The ceremony re-invokes Canada's commitment to peacekeeping . . . it also provides an opportunity to recognize those who have died in all peacekeeping missions."

The Peacekeeping Monument has been a large part of my life for the past several years. When David Collonette was the minister of national defence, I was asked to be the official guide at the Monument. Foreign Affairs use the site for most official visitors to Ottawa. One such visitor was the US secretary of state, Madelaine Albright, shown on the previous page on a cold winter's day. The minister of National Defence and the Chief of the Defence Staff are in this photo: note the snow on the shoulders of the peacekeeper statues.

When a guest of Canada visits the Monument the same programme is used for everyone. The VIP arrives by car on Sussex Street and is met by the official Government of Canada representative. The Foreign Affairs official introduces him or her to the "duty" general

The author with the King of Jordan at the Peacekeeping Monument

representing the CDS and the senior RCMP officer. At that point I take over and begin my guided tour, pausing at the official plaque at the lower end of the "Green Line," which goes from the street level to the upper level. At least two peacekeepers are at the first stop. The walk up the "Green Line" gives me time to describe the monument and the statues. Passing through the entrance to the dais the guest has his or her national anthem played by the Canadian Forces Central Band. Then a peacekeeper comes forward carrying a special bouquet to be placed in the centre mortar. The official guest book is signed and then our national anthem is played.

The guest then views the Mission Wall. The first mission is Korea 1947, the date the initial disengagement team tried to prevent a confrontation (UNTCOK). Special interesting missions to the visitor are pointed out, with reference to their home country. I then present the guest with a 1995 Peacekeeping Dollar and a copy of *The Canadian Peacekeeper*, which I wrote in 1992, and show the medal ribbon chart that has all the medal ribbons from 1951 to 1992. The CWO in command of the peacekeepers then lines up about six peacekeepers in front of the monument and they are introduced to the guest. Time permitting, this is followed by an introduction to the commander of the Central Band. The visiting person then leaves by the stairs and departs. This parade is kept low key and can be rushed, if required, or made to last as long as the Foreign Affairs official deems appropriate.

At the Peacekeeping Monument parade held on 23 October 1999, The Honourable Art Eggleton, minister of national defence, said these words:

> In the decade since the end of the Cold War, the number and the complexity of peace support operations has grown. Between 1948 and 1989 the Canadian Forces were deployed on twenty-five operations. In the years since 1989 the Canadian Forces were deployed on twenty-five operations. In the years since 1989, they have been deployed no fewer than sixty-five times. That commitment to international peace and security is recognized through today's commemoration of ten more missions carved on the wall of the peacekeeping monument.
>
> With this greater number of missions—many of them involving increased risk—comes the need to take care of our people. In return for risking their lives, unlimited liability, they rightly expect and deserve the

best possible care and attention. Recent initiatives as part of our Quality of Life program are helping to address this. I am personally committed to making sure that any Canadian Forces member who deploys healthy and comes back sick is taken care of properly, quickly and with dignity.

To the families of those who serve, the Canadian people owe you their deep and profound appreciation. Family support has always been vital to the success of our missions, and the increased pace and hazards of operations has put more stress on the spouses, children and families of our troops overseas . . .

To the men and women of the Canadian Forces present here today who have served in the cause of peace, thank you. It has been an honour to be with you to pay tribute to the courage and sacrifice of those of your comrades who served and fell in the struggle to create a better world.

I always say that Canada's Peacekeeping Monument is the only one in the world and I have yet to be corrected. It is fitting to close with this quotation from an editorial by John Marteinson in the August 1992 issue of the *Canadian Defence Quarterly*:

Canadians can be justly proud of the enormous contribution to global peace and stability our peacekeepers have made since the end of the Second World War. That pride is reflected in the magnificent Peacekeeping Monument, which will be unveiled by the Governor-General in Ottawa 18 October. It is a fitting and perpetual tribute to dedication and excellence.

In conclusion, the events at the Monument have already begun for the year 2000. Recently, on April 5, the *Globe and Mail* decided to feature the Monument with a story about my experiences in UNEF forty years ago. The photographer, Jim Young, was delighted that he was able to get a photo of the statues with snow on their faces, due to a recent snowstorm.

I hope that my readers will find the story behind the Monument of interest.

A cold day in April 2000.

EPILOGUE

IN THIS, the concluding part of *Canadians in War and Peacekeeping*, it is my privilege to say how well John Gardam has accomplished his aim. I hope his plea in the Introduction is met and that the book "Will be used by schools to educate, by veterans to recall the past and peacekeepers young and old, and that it will rekindle the flame of interest in Canada's military history."

I have known John for many years and will always recall the time at Cassino, Italy, in 1994 when his **Canada Remembers** colour party provided such class to the ceremonies.

This book makes it very clear that veterans hold a very special place in John's heart. His compassion for the 250 veterans at the Perley and Rideau Veterans' Health Centre is well known. His concern is for all veterans of all wars and peacekeeping missions. Not a bad hobby for one who has had an interest in the military for all his adult life. I believe John has accomplished what he set out to do. Well done, John!

> H. Clifford Chadderton
> CEO
> The War Amputations of Canada

Cliff in Holland

THE LAST WORD

THIS IS MY WAY of thanking all those who assisted me in producing this book. It is hard to believe that I started to research Pat Bogert's story as far back as April 1995, over five years ago. Colonel John B. Boileau was the army adviser at the Canadian Defence Liaison Staff in London, England and acted as my go-between. The Lord Strathcona's Horse Association in Victoria, British Columbia assisted with Frank Richmond's story just weeks before Frank passed the 100 mark. Les Peate was the only one who found all the information on Ernest Poole, and I finally found a photo of this brave, silent soldier. CPO Chris Dykeman found Frank Pearson in Victoria, British Columbia. Rene Charron's son Daniel gave me his dad's story about Hong Kong.

When I came to peacekeepers I found that the problem was one of a surplus of excellent stories, and I had no first-hand knowledge of many of the missions. The cover of the book could not have happened without the skill of Corporal Frank Hudec and the help of Alex Campbell of the Perley and Rideau Veterans' Health Centre staff. Sadly, two of the gallant men on the cover did not live long enough to see the finished book.

In March of this year my wife Elaine and I, her sister Shirley, and her husband Holm all went to Portugal for three weeks. My mind was very active, thinking of those Allied service personnel who died in that wonderful country. Brad Hall of the Canadian Agency Commonwealth War Graves Commission produced the following details about the Second World War dead buried in that country. In Lisbon (St. George) British Church there are thirty-nine, including four RCAF, three from the same crew who died on March 6, 1944 and one who died on March 28, 1942. In Oporto (St. James) British Churchyard there are eleven, three of whom are RCAF, two from the same crew who died on 13 July 1941, and one who died on March 6, 1944.

One day my brother-in-law and I went on a large sailing ship, the *Condor de Vilamoura*. Many of the patrons were in wheelchairs. Here I was, thinking of war casualties, and here was a group of "wounded" from another cause, either accident or birth. Just days later we watched the athletes preparing for the International Almond Blossom cross-country run, which was held in Vilamoura. The two ends of the health spectrum were there for everyone to see.

This is the first book we have produced on a computer, and our son John and his son Jonathan were a big help to my wife Elaine. The editor and proofreader was Jane Karchmar. Tim Gordon, Rosemary Kenopic and Elsie Coulas of General Store Publishing House were a big help to me. Derek McEwen produced the layout of the book.

These past two years have seen some medical problems for me and I am indebted to Drs. Hugh McIsaac, Chris Morash, Chris Skinner and Mike Gardam for their help and assistance.

This book would not have been possible if it had not been for the people whose stories appear in the book. The one group who must have grown tired of my phone calls were the serving officers at National Defence Headquarters. I hounded them for stories of the past when they were trying to solve actual day-to-day problems. I owe a debt of gratitude to all of these people. Many thanks to Jim Young of Reuters for providing the photograph I used in "The Peacekeeping Monument," Chapter twenty-six. Special thanks to Throops Photo for all of their help, and to the *Ottawa Citizen* for allowing me to reproduce the photo used in "The Unknown Soldier," Chapter twenty-four.

My sincere thanks go to Vice-Admiral (ret) Larry Murray for writing the Foreword to the book and to Cliff Chadderton for the Epilogue. To have these two distinguished Canadians take time from their busy schedules meant a great deal to me.

Above all else, my thanks go to my wife Elaine who, despite my promise that there would be no more books, gave her utmost in typing *Canadians in War and Peacekeeping*.

Summer 2000

BIBLIOGRAPHY

Clark, Joe. 1994. *A nation too good to lose*. Key Porter Books Limited.

Fraser, W.B. 1976. *Always a Strathcona*. Comprint Pub. Co.

Gardam, John. 1992. *The Canadian peacekeeper*. General Store Publishing House.

Gardam, John. 1993. *Seventy years after*. Canada's Wings, Inc.

Gardam, John. 1994. *Korea volunteer*. General Store Publishing House.

Granatstein, Jack. 1998. *Who killed Canadian history?* Harper Collins Publishers Limited.

Greenhous, B. 1982. *Dragoon*. Campbell Corp.

Greenhous, B., et al. 1944. *The official history of the Royal Canadian Air Force*. Vol. III. University of Toronto Press.

Hadley, Michael. 1985. *U-boats against Canada: German submarines in Canadian waters*. McGill-Queens University Press.

Mackenzie, Lewis. 1993. *Peacekeeper: The road to Sarajevo*. Douglas & McIntyre.

Maloney, Sean. 1997. *War without battles: Canada's NATO brigade in Germany, 1951-1993*. McGraw-Hill Ryerson Limited.

Marteinson, J.K. 1992. *We stand on guard: An illustrated history of the Canadian Army*. Ovale Publications.

Marteinson, J.K. and G.T. Service. 1971. *The gate*. Commercial Printers.

McAndrews, Bill. 1996. *Canadians and the Italian campaign*. (n.p.)

Miller, E. 1995. *The Persian excursion: the Canadian Navy in the Gulf War*. The Canadian Peacekeeping Press.

Nicholson, G.W.L. 1957. *The Canadians in Italy*. The Queen's Printer.

Raddall, Thomas. 1947. *West Novas*. West Novas.

Reid, Max. *DEMS at war*. Private Papers.

Roy, R. 1969. *The Seaforth Highlanders of Canada*. (n.p.)

Russell, E.C. 1980. *Customs and traditions of the Canadian Armed Forces*. Denau & Greenberg.

Schull, Joseph. 1987. *Far distant ships*. Stoddart.

Seely, J.E.B. 1930. *Adventure*. William Heinemann Ltd.

Stacey, C.P. 1955. *Six years of war*. The Queen's Printer.

Stacey, C.P. 1960. *The victory campaign*. The Queen's Printer.

Vincent, Carl. 1981. *No reason why: The Canadian Hong Kong tragedy*. Canada's Wings, Inc.

Windsor, Lee A. 1993. *Canadian military history*. B.A. Thesis.

Wood, H.F. 1966. *Strange battleground*. Queen's Printer.

ABOUT THE AUTHOR

John Gardam was born in England in 1931. He came to Canada in 1951, joining the Reserve Army a year later. After high school he joined the Active Force and served until retirement from the Canadian Forces in 1984. He began writing books in the 1980s after graduating from the University of Manitoba as a part-time student with a B.A. in history.

John has been fortunate since retirement to have worked for the Commonwealth War Graves Commission; has been the DND project officer for the Peacekeeping Monument; and served from 1993 to 1995 with the **Canada Remembers** project.

John and Elaine Gardam live in Nepean, Ontario.